THE
C.O.R.E.
JOURNEY

DIANNA WRIGHT, PH.D.

Bruce—
Thanks for all
you've done. Enjoy
the Journey...
        Dianna

Outskirts Press, Inc.
http://www.outskirtspress.com

ISBN: 978-1-4787-0180-4

Outskirts Press and the "OP" logo are trademarks belonging to Outskirts Press, Inc.

PRINTED IN THE UNITED STATES OF AMERICA

The CORE Journey is dedicated to all those who have the courage and openness to engage mindful living, pursue mastery and live with purpose.

Acknowledgements

The ideas about the CORE Journey that you will encounter in this book have been evolving in my mind and heart for years. They arose through my interactions and connections with others. Some of these associations have been fleeting; others long-standing. Some have been through rich conversations and collaborations, while others have been more one-sided, as I privately mulled over and expanded on the work of scholars.

The scholars that have so deeply influenced my thinking are woven throughout the book. They introduced me to, and expanded and deepened my knowledge and understanding of, the various ideas that permeate the CORE Journey. Although I've only read their scholarly works, sat in their classes, listened to interviews with them, and watched documentaries about them, I feel as if I've had the experience of strolling in the park side-by-side with a friend exploring ideas and tossing around possibilities. Some of these great thinkers include Joseph Campbell, Jack Kornfield, Suzan Salzberg, Mike Csikzentmihalyi, Martin Seligman, Antonio Damasio, Michael Talbot, Amit Goswami, Peter Senge, Joseph Jaworski, Isabel Briggs Myers, Michael Singer, Kenneth Wapnick, Deepak Chopra, Daniel Goleman, the Dalai Lama and Gary Zukav. Although these people span the spectrum from scientists to philosophers to spiritual leaders to psychologists, the theoretical and empirical contributions of each have inspired me to build upon them.

One scholar who has had a far-reaching impact on my thinking is my father, John. Starting early in my life, my dad, a philosopher and a theologian, taught me about the great questions: "Who am I?" "What am I?" "Where did I come from?" "Where am I going?" and "What is my purpose for being here?" He introduced me to the great thinkers in philosophy, theology and metaphysics, whose ideas filtered into our dinner conversation as a family. He also introduced me to my spiritual path, which has had, and continues to have, a profound impact in my daily living. My mom, Laura, was an elementary school teacher who served as a mentor for other teachers. Seeing the positive impact she had on her pupils as well as the way she inspired her fellow teachers was a primary reason I chose to become a teacher. She also taught me a different kind of intelligence. Her unconditional love and kindness has been a foundation throughout my life. Profound thanks to both my mom and dad for their faith and trust in me and for modeling and instilling a love of learning, a commitment to personal growth, and a dedication to making the world a more peaceful experience for their family and the many friends and students who have shared in their life. I am ever grateful for their constant love and support.

My genuine thanks to my sisters, Renee and Michelle, and my brother, Jay, who are shining examples of thriving—of living lives of mastery and purpose. Apart from being inspiring people, I am thankful for our deep friendship, which has stood the test of distance. Through our ongoing dialogues and exploration of beliefs, theories, concepts and life in general, they have been with me on the path toward getting these ideas about transformation, internal power and living your best life from my mind into yours. They have been a steadfast source of encouragement, insight, love and camaraderie.

I want to express heartfelt gratitude to the hundreds of people who have attended my lectures, courses, and workshops who were willing to open themselves to learning and growth; to my clients who have given themselves so generously and shared their intimate lives with me; to my friends and colleagues who have supported me in writing this book by sharing, listening, and encouraging me. Ken Morton, Sr. helped me to believe in my own strengths and move beyond my self-limiting beliefs. Garry Lester encouraged me to expand my vision in the art of possibility. A special note of thanks goes to my colleague, Dee, a valued friend, mentor, and coach who guided me in further clarifying my purpose.

My deep appreciation goes to those who have worked as my support team and believed in this work and in me. Thanks to my editor, Erica Inderlied, for her editorial knowledge, proficiency and devotion to quality. She demonstrated the remarkable ability to make sure the book represented a unified whole. I acknowledge her for her amazing and enthusiastic dedication, her many excellent suggestions that helped to make my writing so much more accessible, and for her inner commitment to the material. Thank you to Stephanie Faiferek, my designer, for her professional expertise and carefulness in the cover design, artwork and layout of the book and the energy she invested to clarify the specifics of publishing and getting the book to print. Her patience and ability to painstakingly weave in all the changes I made in the last hours are greatly appreciated.

Two of my most cherished teachers have been my dog, Cooper, and my cat, Kinsey, who seem to know an awful lot about non-judgmental love and mindfulness. They have offered their loving presence and kind eyes to me for many years and have demonstrated the true essence of courage, openness, and playful energy.

Singularly most inspiring and important of all, Donna, my life partner, has taught me how transformation and love really work. My deepest appreciation and thanks to her for championing my purpose to help people thrive and for her dedicated endorsement of this project throughout its birthing. I remain forever grateful for her perspective and insightful editorial work that has helped to ensure the character and authenticity of this book. Her cheerfulness, patience and enduring inspiration has been central to this book's existence. Her natural gifts for seeing and acting from the heart, together with her courage to grow personally and spiritually, have taught me over the years to fully trust her wisdom and instincts. Similar to our wonderful Sierras, my love for Donna is strong and expands endlessly, reinforcing our lifelong bond.

Contents

I shall be telling this with a sigh

Somewhere ages and ages hence:

Two roads diverged in a wood, and I,

I took the one less traveled by,

And that has made all the difference.

—Robert Frost

Foreword

By Erica Inderlied

The idea of "self-help" sends most people's eyes rolling.

If you'd never heard of Brad Goodman, Tony Robbins or John Bradshaw, you probably couldn't tell me which among the slogans "Put the you in impr-you-vement," "If you can't you must, and if you must you can," and "Grieving is the healing feeling" is just a satire from a cartoon.

And that's because the notion of self-help has largely made a mockery of itself. So why is there still any demand for self-help books, DVDs and seminars?

Self-help materials promise shortcuts to happiness, self-esteem, and wealth. They promise great revelations and permanent transformation, only to reveal methods for placing blame (something that happened to you as a child messed you up pretty much for good) and manipulating others (pretend you're not interested in a woman to make yourself seem intriguing), common sense (others find it flattering when you remember their names and ask questions about them) and truisms devoid of any inherent insight ("What is, is, and what ain't, ain't").

That leaves the average person—smart enough to smell the nonsense and put it down, but hesitant to waste more time looking for authentic, accessible advice—in limbo.

Self-help materials keep selling not necessarily because their promises are fooling anyone, but because the average person has to start somewhere in the search for advice of value (and start over again when it fails). The contradiction is that, if any of the pop-psych self-help techniques really worked, they wouldn't seem so popular because nobody would need to keep buying more books.

Don't get me wrong—there's plenty of respectable, engaging and useful material out there for both physical and metaphysical improvement. But it rarely avails itself if you're stuck gawking at an endless expanse of shelves at a book store or a bottomless list of search results on Amazon.

The CORE Journey doesn't promise to bestow you with peace of mind, confidence, or realization of your dreams. Instead, it delivers tools for the discovery of the paths which lead there. The book acknowledges that there are no shortcuts, and that the trek will require real commitment and stretching beyond our zones of comfort.

The Journey is practical (and merciful) enough to let the past lie, and wise enough to resist common temptation to identify sources of blame. It instead puts the reader to work examining the present in order to hone the tools to create the future, constantly reminding us that we mustn't become bystanders of either one.

Very early in the process of copyediting, before I'd had a chance to dig much deeper than the Introduction, Dianna asked me what my first impressions were, and I said something to the effect of "It doesn't seem to be your average self-help book," to which she said, "I think of it like a travel guide."

The terrain varies between the anecdotal and the heavily-researched, between internal and external examination, and between concerns of the physical body and of emotional and mental capacity.

One exercise of the latter—simply paying enough attention to always be aware of what you're saying, what you're feeling and how you're acting, and whether those things are actually you being the person you want to be—at first appears to be the most easily-grasped of the book's tools. However, its great value is underscored by the unexpected amount of effort required to really re-wire yourself so you can benefit from continual, real-time self-awareness.

If you're like me, you sometimes catch yourself (and too often, just a moment after the fact) having been a little too self-centered, or inconsiderate, or dismissive, or sloppy, when you really meant no harm and were just in a hurry, having a bad day, or not paying attention. You know that, if you had a ten-second rewind button, you (the kind of person you think you really are) could have just as easily done the right thing.

But when we encounter moments where strangers, acquaintances or loved ones are irritable or impatient with us or say something that seems uncharacteristically hurtful, we're all too ready to assume that the stranger is a just mean person, or feel personally insulted by a coworker, or get into an argument with a significant other.

In these situations, you begin to find that the Journey is worthwhile not just on the merits of its tools for self-awareness and direction, but for the extrinsic benefits that germinate in the rigors of self improvement—such as the enhanced capacity for forgiveness and compassion when you find others to be as far from perfection as you are.

Oh, and Brad Goodman's "put the you in impr-you-vement" is the satire—from an episode of The Simpsons called "Bart's Inner Child." Purported to be a send-up of a real psychologist at whom no fingers need to be pointed here, Goodman's character dishes out his advice in low-budget videos and popular seminars. Inspired by Bart Simpson's heretic, free-spirited example, Goodman ultimately encourages the entire Springfield community to solve their probkems by getting in touch with their "inner child" and just doing whatever they want, with expectedly chaotic results. The episode features other gag self-help material including "Get Confident, Stupid" and "Owning Your Okayness," and is a much more rewarding investment of time than other, unintentionally inane self-help options.

Preface

"...to those who have struggled with them, the mountains reveal beauties they will not disclose to those who make little effort. That is the reward the wilderness bestows on those who exert themselves. And, it is because they have so much to give and grant it lavishly, that men [and women] go back again and again to the mountains they love...the mountains reserve their choicest gifts for those who stand upon their lofty summits."

—Sir Francis Younghusband, *Mount Everest: The Reconnaissance*

In one's life, there are certain experiences that are turning points. Sometimes you don't know an event has had such an impact on you until after the fact. And sometimes, even during the experience, you sense something important is taking place that will affect how you see yourself, the world, and your place in it. A couple experiences like that led me to where I am today and had a tremendous impact on the direction of my life. One was my trip to the highest point in Africa, Kilimanjaro. The other was when I made the decision to leave my corporate job in order to pursue my purpose and vision. Both decisions were instrumental in evolving and sustaining value-based actions in every part of my life. Both experiences furthered my ability to engage fully in a life of self-direction, mastery and purpose.

I worked for a Fortune 100 company for 12 years. I began that career in sales and moved on to Training and Management Development. I realized early on that I had to create my own meaning within the job. Winning contests and being the number one sales representative in the region was rewarding, but it wasn't what motivated me. After a while, one realizes those accomplishments are fleeting and not truly fulfilling. Once I realized that the job would be fulfilling when I chose what it meant to *me* and then brought that meaning to the job each day, I actually felt happier in my daily routine and felt that I was contributing something to the people I interacted with. The shift in my attitude must have been apparent because at one of the district meetings, my regional manger said that I seemed happier and lighter. I said, and it always brings a nervous chuckle when I share my response with my classes, that it had registered with me that, in and of itself, the job was meaningless. What has caused the change in my perspective was the realization that I brought the meaning to the job. Meaning begins inside of me, and then I choose to extend it outward in the appropriate way given the job requirements. I created that meaning in building and nurturing trusting relationships with my clients. After many top-level changes in management, the company changed. Many of the people I had worked with were leaving, and it was apparent the company was going in a different direction. It became more and more difficult to do my job based on my values. It wasn't long after those major changes that I was told not to share certain information with my clients, as it might prejudice them against our products. That was a breach of values I could not overlook any longer. A six-figure income, company car, and expense account didn't justify lying and compromising my values and beliefs and I left the company shortly after. It was a very scary decision, but sometimes values trump comfort.

I became an entrepreneur, much to my siblings' excitement. They had been operating their own successful businesses for years and had encouraged me many times to pursue my dreams and aspirations and really do what I love. So, I entered the arena of life and executive coaching. Those of you who have your own business know that every day is an adventure, a roller coaster of emotions with moments of anxiety and exhilaration. But, when you begin doing something that you're passionate about, you really can't imagine not doing it. I am truly following my bliss as it aligns with my purpose—coaching people on how to create a life for themselves that is rich, full, and meaningful. I can't imagine my life any other way and I look forward to being involved in coaching for a long time.

I started my "coaching" career as a volleyball coach. As is still the case in my personal and professional coaching today, one of my primary objectives as a volleyball coach was not only to help my players reach their physical potential, but to open doors to possibilities in their lives that they may not have not considered.

In the South at that time, volleyball was not played at a very high caliber, and there was no volleyball after the high school season was over. I had competed at a very high level at Long Beach State in Southern California, where the women's volleyball team was ranked number one in the country. Volleyball was a year-round sport in California. The only way volleyball players in the South were going to improve their level of play was to have more opportunities to compete. So, in 1978, I started the Junior Olympic Volleyball Program in Knoxville. Like I said, at that time the skill level at which the game was currently played was low. Players and coaches had no idea of the skills, dedication, discipline, and training that went into the game in other regions of the country. For example, in California, players were diving and rolling on defense against tremendous hits from the opposing side. No one in Knoxville knew anything about that level of play.

So, after graduating from Long Beach State, I returned to Knoxville. I announced the first meeting of the Junior National Team. Five people showed up, one coach and four players. The woman who had agreed to help me looked at me with doubt in her eyes and said, "Dee, there are six people on a volleyball team, not four." I said, "You're right. We'll need to go recruit two more people." And we did. One of them was my sister. Thanks, Michelle!

To make a long, but exciting, story short, that year we qualified for the Junior National tournament in Chicago with seven players on our team. We sold Krispy Kreme donuts to raise the money and recruited a parent and a coach to drive the team to the Windy City.

My team didn't win a match. In fact, we didn't score more than six points in any game. But, the players got to see what the game looked like at a very high caliber of competition. To add to their overall experience, I took them to see live theatre, a one-woman play with Cloris Leachman, which was a first for every single person on the trip, including the parents! I also took them to a very nice eating establishment. At the restaurant, I noticed some commotion at the far end of the table. I went over to check it out and came to find that one of the players didn't know what to make of the "cloth" next to her plate. She had never seen cloth napkins!

Those six young women came home with a wider horizon of possibilities in many aspects of their lives, not just volleyball. The next year, there was an obvious difference between their level of play and that of any other players in the city. When I ran tryouts for the team that year, so many people showed up that I had to have two teams!

One of the players that came out for the team that second year was a young woman who had no interest in college. After high school, she didn't have any plans. She didn't think she was college material. We again qualified for the Junior Olympic Volleyball Nationals, which were taking place in Davis, California. I convinced the parents to let the players go early so we could take in San Francisco and the state capitol, Sacramento. What an experience. Most of these kids had never been out of Knoxville!

Some of the players from those two teams ended up with scholarships to colleges that were nowhere on their radar prior to the Junior National Team. Many of the young women hadn't even considered college for one reason or another. Someone told them they weren't smart enough, they couldn't afford it, or no one else in their families had ever gone any further than high school. Before the players' experience with travel, cultural outings, and seeing volleyball played at such a high caliber, they had a limited perception of the potential benefits volleyball could offer. They had no idea scholarships were an option. Afterward, some went to local colleges and universities. Several went out of state, receiving scholarships to Duke, the University of North Carolina, Clemson, and the University of Virginia. The young person I spoke of earlier chose to play for me for four years at a Division II school in Northern California, but that's not the end of the story. Not only did she finish school, she went on to receive her Doctorate in Cell Biology from Vanderbilt!

From cloth napkins to a Ph.D., those young people realized possibilities they had no idea even existed! I could go on with similar stories from my personal and professional business coaching. The point is that, by expanding the opportunities and vision for their future and seeing themselves as part of the creative process in their lives, players and clients gain an enhanced awareness of what is possible for them to create in their lives. I provide openings, and they choose to engage the discipline and develop the skills necessary to create realities. That was my purpose then, and it continues to be my purpose today—to help people expand the self-awareness of their inherent capacity to create a life that is meaningful and fulfilling.

I have always felt that sense of purpose. I want to provide a safe space for people to learn how to reconnect with their inherent capacity for creativity—to fully engage in designing a life of their choosing. That's why I chose to start my own coaching business—to help people realize their potential and fully engage in the process of their lives.

I have always valued personal growth in my own life. I was raised in a family that appreciated and worked at growing and developing as people. Our dinner conversations were often about self-awareness, growing in relationships, and how to be the best we could be no matter what we chose to do. To this day, we all hold personal growth as a priority at home and at work. My parents and siblings are shining examples for me of what is possible when you combine effort, discipline, inspiration, and "a little fairy dust."

My philosophy as a coach has two basic tenets. The first is to create a safe environment in which the client can grow personally and professionally; the second is to continue to learn and evolve myself. In my experience, one of the best ways to learn and progress is through non-judgmental awareness. I practice non-judgmental awareness to learn to notice what is happening in the moment. It allows me to move beyond fear-based behavior, such as defensiveness, and toward value-based action, such as non-judgmental listening. Through non-judgmental awareness, I can clue in to self-limiting beliefs, which are thoughts that create barriers to full engagement, and the assumptions I bring to situations, all of which I might take as the truth, but may easily have nothing to do with reality.

By exercising non-judgmental awareness, I can move beyond self-deceptions and judgments that interfere with my ability to fully engage in life. By becoming more self aware, I also know and understand my values, strengths and purpose. I know my vision, and I follow a plan to make that vision a reality. Moment to moment, I want to be aware that I have choices in my life. I can engage my values and purpose through my actions, and I can shed self-defeating behaviors so I can be successful on my own CORE Journey. Yes, I am an active participant just like you, and I am making my way up the mountain as well. The experience of one's journey cannot be shared directly, but the vision can. Your journey will be unique to you. So, I communicate my vision that everyone is engaged in creating a fulfilling life. Your vision and the path your pilgrimage takes will be unique to you.

Awareness is corrective and connective. Awareness offers us choices. When we engage mindfully in our day, we can choose our behaviors and our focus, and make sure they align with our values and purpose. Choices offer us clarity about our desired outcomes and keep us moving toward our goals and aspirations. When we feel like we have choices, we have a sense of freedom, of self-determination. We experience an enhanced initiative. Through this personal involvement and participation, there is a diminished resistance to change.

The power to choose your life belongs to you. A coach does not control, but they do offer direction, leaving it up to you to succeed. I will provide openings, but you must be ready and willing to service your values and purpose despite the circumstances. Conviction comes from accomplishment. Engaging your values and purpose regardless of external forces, strengthens conviction in your ability. The ability is your potential to create, achieving fulfillment in your life is its expression, and participating in the unfolding of your vision becomes a natural progression.

As your vision unfolds and your conviction becomes more powerful, you will begin to develop trust in your ability to engage your values and purpose even in the face of challenging circumstances. Non-judgmental awareness supports this trust. Non-judgmental awareness is more than noticing what is going on around us; it is also about noticing what is going on inside of us. We expand our awareness of both our extrinsic and intrinsic environments. Through this awareness, our thoughts, emotions, and sensations become available to us in real time, as they are happening. Non-judgmental awareness allows us to see without labeling our experience as good or bad, or right or wrong, which enables us to respond more authentically.

Non-judgmental awareness affords us the space to observe what is happening in the moment as it *is*, not as it "should" be. Then we can choose not only our response, but our learning experience. We can operate out of freedom to choose our responses and actions no matter what the situation. We become the final authority as to what we can and will learn, and the learning is our responsibility. We learn to tap into our inner genius and resources. We learn we can bring value-based actions to any circumstance. Trust in our ability to enact our values advances an experience of peace.

Non-judgmental awareness, choice, and trust are fundamental tenets of my coaching and the CORE Journey. They lead to truth, freedom, and peace. Truth comes from becoming aware of our true nature as one with an inherent capacity for curiosity and creativity. We all have an innate desire to engage our self-determination to design our lives, and when we reconnect to our true nature, we realize that capacity more and more.

Freedom develops from choice. When we move beyond mechanical responses and emotional reactions, we have the freedom to choose our behavior. When we choose action associated with our values and purpose, we participate in peace of mind. Peace blossoms within trust. Trust extends from your conviction to direct your own life even in difficult situations. Trust extends through the realizations of your conviction. As trust evolves, you will participate in more and more moments of peace. Through awareness, choice, and trust emerge truth, freedom, and peace. The CORE Journey is a process of learning and advancing in these areas so you can fashion a life that is satisfying and joyful.

My own experience in these concepts was solidified when I traveled to Africa and made the trek to the summit of Mount Kilimanjaro at 19,340 feet. I have attempted many times to put words to my journey, but they always fall short of my experience. What I know for sure is that, when I returned from that trip, I saw myself in a different light. I knew I stood at a choice-point for my own life. We all have defining moments, choice-points, in our lives that offer us several different paths that we could travel and the one we choose will tremendously impact our lives. My experience on the mountain transformed me and brought an expanded sense of clarity. More than ever, I knew I wanted to be an opening for people to realize that they hold the key to their own wellbeing and success.

For me, the memory of that trip is palpable today. Not a day passes that I don't remember aspects of that climb—the feelings, thoughts, sensations, hardships, struggles, people, and the mountain. The experience is ineffable. And, it expanded my self-awareness and freedom tenfold. That's why I use the mountain and Cairns, stacks of rocks, as metaphors for the CORE Journey. Cairns are used to mark the way along a path that is not necessarily clear. For example, when you are hiking across granite boulders, or scree where it is difficult to identify visible tracks, Cairns are placed as landmarks. I felt the metaphor of an unclear path was appropriate because sometimes when we set out on a pilgrimage to create our lives, the path is not always clearly laid out before us. We need guideposts to follow. Cairns serve the purpose of guideposts. Mountains afford the opportunity to experience spaciousness, challenge limiting self-perceptions, overcome fears, and participate in extraordinary accomplishments. The mountain is your vision and Cairns are your touchstones. You don't have to climb mountains to have these experiences—all that you need is inside of you right now. The CORE Journey will offer openings and practices to help you realize and experience a sense of clarity and awareness.

What a mountain might demand is that you move outside of your comfort zone. The CORE Journey offers the same challenge; the journey will ask for Courage, Openness, Reflection, and Energy—CORE. To use a popular comparison from physical training, it is like core body training. The Journey will call on your CORE and your CORE will become stronger, more flexible, closer to balance, and more efficient through the process.

The CORE Journey is not about changing who we are. It is about seeing ourselves in a different light. Buddha said, "Be a lamp unto yourself." The CORE Journey will help you reconnect to your inner radiance. The Journey is a process of cultivating two aspects of awareness—our mental/emotional processes and our physical sensations—with clarity. It is a process to experience what we are thinking, feeling, and wanting in the moment. This gives us an opportunity to look at our beliefs, our values, our behaviors, and our strategies for keeping ourselves safe and comfortable. By clarifying those things, by making a space inside of us in which to experience those aspects of ourselves, we ignite a transformation from external motivation to a more genuine, intrinsic inspiration.

Transformation is defined as undergoing a thorough and dramatic shift in form and/or appearance. Our form of interacting and the way we "show up" in the world may change, but the content of who we are, our inherent capacity to create, does not change. We don't need to change anything about the content of our true nature. Our true nature is perfection, wholeness incarnate. The Journey is a metamorphosis of waking and becoming more aware of our true nature, which facilitates a spaciousness in which we can hold all that we are and connect with all that is.

We engage the process of experiencing and awareness, of mindfulness, to transform our perception so we are better equipped to look at our thoughts, beliefs, and judgments and then connect with what really is happening right now. When we engage in the process of mindful living, what happens? Transformation. We begin to see that we are much more than our thoughts and emotions, which really are narrow concepts of "I-as-me." We begin to experience the spaciousness of our open minds and hearts. We begin to "know" our power to create our life from a much bigger space than the narrow view of ourselves that we may have previously held.

The CORE Journey is a process of awareness, choice, and trust. It is about reconnecting, remembering our true nature. Our true nature embodies an open mind and an open heart. Our openness provides spaciousness for envisioning possibilities and creating realities that resonate with our values, purpose, and vision. So it doesn't matter what circumstances you are in. You don't have to change them. You don't have to leave your job or change relationships, even though, through the process, you may realize that might be just what you choose to do. But that's the point. You choose. It is an inward journey to design your life from your own intrinsic power, not an outward focus on how your life "should" be.

And, it takes practice. Like I said, I may coach you along your CORE Journey by offering you practices, tools, and skills, but these things are not what is working. You are what works. You are the best and most effective tool there is. Your innate desire to be the architect of a meaningful life is what works. The journey is a practice and a process, but the joy and learning you experience along the way will be invaluable.

And, like hiking to the summit of a mountain, the Journey is not a straight line. The journey is composed of effort and integration, obscurity and clarity, of disappointment and inspiration, of learning and experiencing. As we walk the path to whatever summit you have chosen, there will be ups and downs. There will be rain and wind, and there will be vistas that astound. There will be "white-outs" and there will be bright, sunny days. There will be scary mountain passes and there will be valleys abundant with flowers. If you are willing to take the challenge, the mountain will offer you gifts you never imagined. All that is needed is a little perseverance, curiosity, and compassion.

I invite you to participate in the CORE Journey—to name your mountain, your summit, and your aspirations. I invite you to have the courage and openness to look inside, and recognize and engage your innate capacity to create the life you want. I invite you to expand your ability to reflect in the moment and make sure your actions are parallel with your values. I invite you to draw on your energy to live a self-determined life. I invite you to know your potential and power to engage in mindful living.

The CORE Journey will afford you openings to do those things and more. The Journey will help you develop your inherent spaciousness for truth, freedom, and peace. What you have to do is step to the edge and trust yourself. I look forward to walking with you on your journey. You are on the edge of something great! I salute you.

Introduction

———

"On the edge of the world of man, standing upon the summit which has been the focus of his dreams, the young mountaineer lifted up his body, his heart, his soul and his secret longings. As far as the eye could see a realm of snow and rock lay stretched out before him, wrapped in the silence and mystery of the infinite. It was like being in another world; the mountains seemed less a part of this planet than an entirely independent kingdom, unique and mysterious, where, to venture forth, all that was needed was the will and the love."

—Gaston Rebuffat, *On Snow and Rock*

Human beings have an inherent capacity for wonder and creativity. When we were children, our hearts and our minds were open to the experiences all around us. We held a spaciousness within from which we could participate in the world without judgment or fear. We were curious and we were open to learning, which we actually considered fun. We would reflect on what happened, and if it wasn't working, or wasn't enjoyable, we would choose something else to play with, or a different game or a different way to interact. We had an optimistic energy to engage in the possibilities that we might encounter during our day and what we might learn from those encounters. We were connected to our true nature—open, free, and loving.

Somewhere along the line, that sense of spaciousness began to narrow. We became disconnected from our true nature. Our sense of curiosity and creativity began to diminish. We slowly constructed a view of the world that said comfort and safety were more important than growth and enrichment. We began to shy away from change and take the path of least resistance in order to maintain the status quo. Our sense of self consisted of judgments and assumptions, which we began to accept as the truth. We began to accept "shoulds" and "oughts" as the way life is. We lost touch with our organic desire and capacity to create—to design and build a life that was appealing and meaningful to us. Not everyone is acquainted with this, but in my experience, it happens more often than not.

The CORE Journey is an excursion to rediscover and reconnect with the fundamental aspects of our humanness—to self-govern our lives, to self-actualize our highest potential: to create a fulfilled and meaningful life. These three aspects have been found to be fundamental motivational forces intrinsic to human beings—autonomy, mastery and purpose. The CORE Journey is a process of recovering the vitality from those three innately human drives. Foundational to the Journey are four CORE concepts: Courage, Openness, Reflection, and Energy. Let's look at the nature of these essential components of the CORE Journey.

Courage underlies the experience throughout the CORE Journey. Because we are used to following the path of least resistance in order to maintain comfort and safety, stepping outside our normal routine takes courage. To actually begin is to look at our life and ask questions like, "What do I really want to create?" "What do I really care about?" "Is there more than this daily routine I am in?" "Is there a different, more satisfying way to experience the fullness life can offer?" "Am I capable of creating what I want and actually getting the results I've chosen?"

All of these questions begin to stir an inner sense of discontent and it is uncomfortable. It feels like leaving a safe place and venturing out into unknown territory. Not only is asking the question scary, it is most often accompanied by the doubt of whether or not you can actually accomplish anything different. It takes much less energy to take the path of least resistance and stay safe. But is that really comfortable? Do you sometimes feel a sense of unrest and can't name what it is, or tell where it's coming from? I believe this subterranean itch is our innate ambition to create, to wonder, and to be curious about new horizons. To look at what is possible and embark on the CORE Journey takes courage.

Another aspect of courage is recognizing that you have the sole responsibility for deciding what you want and creating that result. Whether you choose to stay the path of least resistance or choose a path of your own, it is your choice. This requires an inward journey to look at self-doubts, limiting judgments about ourselves, and unrealistic views of others and our world. It requires you to search your soul for what it is you really want, name it, choose it, and take the steps to bring it to fruition; to realize a sense of mastery.

There is nothing wrong or bad about being scared or afraid to step out of our comfort zone. I came across this passage while reading George R. R. Martin's *A Game of Thrones*: "Bran thought about it. 'Can a man still be brave if he's afraid?' 'That is the only time a man can be brave,' his father told him."

The CORE Journey is nothing to be afraid of, but you probably will encounter moments of fear, anxiety, worry and disquiet. That's a normal response when you begin to travel away from your comfort and safety and into an uncharted territory. Whenever you embark on the challenge of reaching the summit of a new mountain, there will be doubts, questions, and unknowns. We all have fears and doubts and self-limiting thoughts. Sometimes they keep us safe and sometimes they limit us. It's up to us to recognize which is which. But, if we didn't have anxiety or disappointments, it wouldn't take courage to choose to create the life you want to live—to actually say a resounding "Yes" to an extraordinary experience of living. If courage weren't part of the Journey, more people would be living exceptional lives of their own, choosing their own direction rather than feeling limited and lacking a sense of freedom and fulfillment in their lives.

Embarking on the CORE Journey takes courage and it will grow and become stronger within the process. You will learn various ways to recognize and understand fear, and to be with fear without being afraid. You'll accept that the fear you may be feeling is not who you are. It doesn't identify you. With experience, your conviction to choose your direction will grow stronger and you'll develop more and more trust in your ability to create and realize the results you desire.

And, you will encounter obstacles. Whether it is a fallen tree across the path, thunder and lightning, or a high stream crossing, difficulties are part of any journey. The courageous question you will need to ask yourself is, "Can I welcome these obstacles as part of my Journey?" The courage you engage and develop will provide you with the perseverance and discipline necessary to move beyond those barriers. The exciting thing about it all is exactly what draws people to the backcountry experience: it offers an experience of their ability to be self-reliant and self-determining.

The next component of the CORE Journey is cultivating openness to the experiences of life. It is about reconnecting to an innate willingness of an open heart and an open mind before the interference of life began to narrow our inclination to be open to looking and seeing with a beginner's eyes. Instead of viewing a situation, person, or ourselves as the way it, they, or we should be, we are open to seeing things as they are. This gives us freedom to choose and develops trust that we can not only cope, but thrive, in both simple and complex times.

Openness is about learning to say "Yes" to whatever we are experiencing at that moment and all of the accompanying opportunities for engaging and learning. This isn't a compliant resignation that everything is okay and as it should be. It means being open and intrigued about what life is offering us as we experience it. It means not resisting our uncomfortable emotions or thoughts by trying to push them away or avoid them. That just intensifies them, and even if we are successful in avoiding them at that particular time, they are always waiting in the shadows to re-emerge when we are confronted with similar circumstances. Openness is creating spaciousness inside of our being that can hold our discomfort, and hold it with compassion, for ourselves, others, and the situation we are experiencing. In this way we lessen the uneasiness and its grip on us, and despite what we're feeling and thinking, we gain the freedom to choose how we will respond.

Openness is about allowing a space inside of us for both uncomfortable and desirable emotions and thoughts to reside. In this way, we can become more aware of what it is that we are thinking, feeling, and wanting in the moment. Through that awareness, we arrive at a choice-point. From there, we gain the freedom to choose a positive, effective response to whatever situation we find ourselves in. In this way, we can be assured that our actions will be aligned with our values. The concept of aligning actions with values and purpose will be a practice that we will allude to and engage throughout the CORE Journey.

Openness diffuses judgment, both of others and ourselves. Through this openness, we gain a more in-depth awareness and understanding of our true nature. Our true nature is open, compassionate, and loving. Our heart began its journey through this life with passion and zeal that made us feel capable of anything. We were loving and compassionate because we hadn't yet learned how to be judgmental or measure things in terms of "the way it should be." Over time, the judgments became blinders. They engendered thoughts and emotions that were fearful and restricting. They were like holding our hands in front of our eyes, so that we were no longer capable to see what was in front of us. Openness allows us to lay our judgments down so we can gain some clarity around them. Openness lets us set aside our emotions and thoughts and discover the beliefs underlying them. In this way we can begin to see things differently. We begin to see possibilities rather than restrictions. We begin to see openings rather than closing ourselves off from experience. We begin to live with hearts and minds that are unbridled and free to create a life that we find fulfilling and meaningful.

This brings us to the third component of the CORE Journey, Reflection. Reflection is two-pronged. The first prong is the practice of sitting quietly at the close of the day and evaluating whether our actions were aligned with our values. Ultimately, what we are all looking for is an experience of peace—an inner quiet and calm. If we could consistently experience that sense of peace, we could fully engage more often in loving and positive ways with our loved ones, our peers, our friends, and our circumstances.

This world is dynamic. It is in constant flux. We are bombarded with information of all kinds from phone calls, text messages, computers, instant messages, and media. We are expected to multi-task, multi-do, multi-listen, and multi-try. We aren't fully engaged, or being, with any one thing because we are trying to do everything. We have lost the ability to focus our minds on one thing and do it well. That's why the CORE Journey is an invitation to engage in mindful living, rather than mindless busyness. By cultivating the skill of mindfulness, we are able to assure that our responses and actions are aligned with our values and purpose. Mindfulness is a prerequisite to peace of mind, and it is a competency you will learn and expand on the CORE Journey.

Peace of mind comes when, at the end of the day, we are able to reflect on our day and ask, "Were my actions and responses aligned with my values?" If they were—good. If they weren't, what did I learn? How would I approach the situation differently? We don't have to change us, our innate content. Our true nature is open, free, and loving. What we have to transform is how we see things—how we perceive the form and appearance of that which is external to us. When we can see things differently, we can begin to remove the interference that got in the way in the first place of the kind and loving actions that work with and for a value-based life. We learn to live more and more in the moment and from our true nature. We are able to engage the ineffable energy that an open heart and mind afford.

The second prong of reflection is looking inward and seeing that our outward perception is a reflection of an internal condition. Whatever we are thinking, feeling, and wanting will lead to specific ways of viewing others, the world, and ourselves. If we are angry, anxious, or fearful, we will perceive the world and others from that viewpoint. If we feel calm, confident, and positive, we will respond in that manner. When we develop a non-judgmental awareness of our internal experience, we can choose our perception and therefore choose our response. The more we can live out of non-judgmental awareness, the more choice and freedom we have in our actions. Waking up to the freedom we have to choose can kindle peace of mind. When we realize that perception is a mirror, not a fact, then we can choose to shift our way of seeing. If what I said before is true, that an intrinsic drive for human beings is autonomy, some sense of independence in directing our life, then when we actually make a concerted effort to choose, we catch a wider vision that peace of mind is more than just possible. It can be a self-generated experience. Peace of mind can be a phenomenon we mindfully create on a daily basis.

We expand our non-judgmental awareness through mindfulness. We learn to be mindful of our external and internal environments. We typically sleepwalk through our days, responding in mechanical, habitual ways without any thought except afterward (and sometimes not even then). That's why we do and say things we wish we hadn't. By cultivating mindfulness, we are better equipped to respond in effective and positive ways. We are able to respond from an open heart and mind. We are capable of living from our true nature with compassion and love.

Let's talk a moment about this true nature I keep referring to. I am not advocating any particular spiritual path, or by any means indicating the CORE Journey is a spiritual path. If you have a spiritual path, these words may resonate with you. If you do not have a spiritual bent, a different way of looking at our true nature is from a scientific perspective.

The science of sciences, quantum physics, has evidenced that our bodies generate energy, and that energy extends from us to others and our environment. Even though most of us can't see the energy, we recognize it as dispositions, moods and attitudes. We have all experienced situations when things are going well until someone enters the room having a "bad hair day." They are emitting an energy that is palpable and it is evident without them saying a word, that they are not happy. Their attitude fills the room. Their mood affects everyone and the situation. Researchers have been able to measure the energy that emanates from our bodies, sometimes traveling as far out as eight to ten feet. That energy interacts with the energy extending from other people and things.

Sometimes we are aware of how our mood may be affecting people, and sometimes we haven't a clue. What energy will you extend? Do you want to be able to choose the type of energy or have it chosen for you? Our energy isn't good or bad, but we can use it to create positivity in our lives or let it become negative energy. The choice and your openness to exercising your options depend on your internal environment, which includes your thoughts, emotions, sensations, perceptions, and beliefs.

Over our lifetime, our ability to choose to act from within our true nature—unlimited and free—has been inhibited. Some of our experiences have actually interfered with our ability to recognize what thoughts, emotions, and beliefs are driving our behavior. Some of us get interference buildup sooner than others, but in one way or another all of us will experience interference with our true nature.

Some might say that aspects of our true nature include being perfect learners, or perfect leaders, or perfect teachers. Think of all the things you learned to do before the age of five, which might include the ability to tie shoes, run, skip, jump, throw a ball, write, read, and on and on. We ate it up. We were learning sponges. Then we went to school and got frowny faces. Some of us had to sign the "Bad Book" before we went home because we didn't act like someone expected us to act.

From there we went to high school and got Bs or Cs and were told those grades weren't good enough to get into college or become the leader of a company. Then, if we did go to college, we were told girls don't take this major or boys shouldn't pursue this career. All of this is the interference I am talking about. We learn early on that we are not how we should be. And we forget how to see things as they are. We only look at the "shoulds" and begin to see them as the truth. This intrusion on the understanding of who we really are or what we actually want from life can lead to feelings of unworthiness, feelings of lack, not being enough, or just plain not feeling like we are okay.

The CORE Journey is about chipping away at the interference so you can reconnect to your innate curiosity and creativity—in a sense, your beginners mind—open, curious, and willing to learn and grow. Part of the

Journey is developing compassion for yourself as you remember who you really are. It doesn't happen overnight. It takes willingness, practice and patience. There will be setbacks and obstacles. Learning to be compassionate with yourself as you learn and evolve allows you to see possibilities as if you had a panoramic view, an outlook that is much more spacious and open. It provides an increased awareness because you are not inhibiting yourself through self-judgments and limiting self-delusions.

Spacious awareness provides available options for us to play and experiment with. We choose actions and responses that fit our values and check them out, and if they are not taking us closer to our vision, we can choose again. This is part of the practice of mindfulness—we are the cause, not the effect. We will encounter obstacles, which, as we have said, are part of any trek. What we now have, however, is the choice of how we will respond to our situation. We have an intrinsic compass that points to True North and targets our actions to be aligned with our purpose and values. Again, the more awake we become to our true nature, the more we will experience the freedom and creativity that are inherently ours. Thereby, we can create a life of our own choosing that unfolds with meaning and fulfillment.

So, those with a spiritual bent may connect with the concept of true nature. Those without can think of true nature as energy circulating in and through you and extending into the world. My own belief is that we are inherently loving, kind, and open. When we are aware of the interference and our choices, we operate more and more out of kindness, compassion, and love for others, the world, and ourselves. The CORE Journey is a function of truth, freedom, and peace: the truth about who you are and what you are capable of creating, the freedom to choose a life that is fulfilling and satisfying, and the peace of mind that follows from actions that are aligned with core values. Whatever you believe your true nature to be, when you reconnect with it you will live more consistently from that truth, freedom, and peace.

The last component of the CORE Journey is Energy. We will talk about the energy in all four domains of the human experience—physical, mental, emotional, and spiritual. You will learn how to manage and renew your energy systems so that you will be able to consistently work and play at your best.

Energy also refers to the type of energy you choose to bring to your day—positive or negative. Research in the fields psychology, the sport sciences, and quantum physics, to mention just a few, indicates that our moods create energy fields that have an effect on our external and internal environments. They create external environments that limit information by causing fear and anxiety and shutting down dialog. Negative moods also create an internal environment that is not healthy. Prolonged functioning out of negativity creates discomfort and illness. Expanding the ability to engage in positive energy can foster a healthier life and generate a sense of overall wellbeing.

The CORE Journey will give you practices to create positive energy and the skills to utilize it effectively when necessary. You will learn how to manage your energy in all four areas so you can be fully engaged and productive throughout your day, and how to renew your energy stores so you can consistently function at your best no matter what you are involved in, from parenting to teaching to managing to selling, or whatever your performance arena might be.

The CORE Journey is an integration of best practices from performance psychology, organizational development, and personal enrichment. I have consolidated research and practical applications used by companies that have grown from good to great. For example, I use literature from the Harvard Business School that shows how the best companies engage in successful change efforts. I merge these ideas with evidence-based theory and applications from positive psychology, performance psychology, and personal growth to provide concrete evidence and experiential practices so you can assimilate them into who you are, where you are and what you want to accomplish.

Although some may feel the notions of true nature, creativity, and mindfulness are somewhat airy or insubstantial, my organization and presentation of the ideas within the CORE Journey is based on rigorous research that has expanded our knowledge base and our understanding of how the human mind functions and how significant change is initiated, consolidated and sustained. The ideas and concepts offered throughout the Journey are evidence-based and the practices are presented in a methodical, organized, and realistic manner. My addition to the research findings is an examination of their applicability to everyday existence, including the ways in which I have used them in my own life. I'm still learning and growing, but using the practices offered here has broadened my sense of freedom and independence, expanded my sense of mastery, and solidified my trust in the power of purpose.

The CORE Journey concerns itself with how to open yourself to your innate capacity to create. It offers a series of concepts, skills, and practices as a framework to design and build a life you find enriching and fulfilling. The journey is presented as twelve Cairns that guide you along a path toward the summit you have chosen. I dedicate Cairns as guideposts and milestones that guide you on your journey.

The Cairns are divided into three phases. The first phase is looking inward to explore, discover, and name your purpose, values, and vision for the life you want to create. The second phase enters into the process of designing your Mindful Action Plan (MAP). This plan is your way of charting a clear path and being able to measure your progress. This phase also includes becoming aware of any self-limiting or restricting thoughts, emotions, and beliefs. The third phase focuses on learning how to mange and renew the four domains of energy so you can proceed along your journey fully engaged and alive. This phase is also about enfolding all you have learned into the culture of your character. It ensures you have the necessary skills and practices to coach yourself with integrity and authenticity long after you've completed the book.

The Cairns and phases are linear in form, but nonlinear in process. They are dynamic and interrelated. Each step along the way unfolds into the next and enfolds all that has gone before. The Journey is a process. As you evolve, truth, freedom, and peace become more an aspect of your awareness. But don't be fooled: there is never a simple path to freedom and peace. The journey calls for a willingness to notice your inner condition on a moment-to-moment basis. It will necessitate Courage, Openness, Reflection, and Energy.

You've made a conscious choice, so how do you get started and follow through? From my experience as a teacher, coach and someone who has undergone this process, simply wanting it isn't enough. Many of my clients have realized what they want and have chosen to change their life, and even engaged in exercises and practices to help them, but have found that it didn't stick. A framework is needed for organizing the process. The CORE Journey offers such a structure. The structure invites you to live fully and deeply from your intentions and realize your potential by offering you a foundation to help you make sense of your options.

Although there is a structure, the framework allows for flexibility. It is not a program you follow uncritically or without a sense of humor. It's meant to be engaging, agreeable and, yes, fun. It's not something you put off until you are enlightened or in a better place. It is a process that gives you a set of tools that you can personalize to design a path that is unique to you and works for you in your current situation.

The CORE Journey is inclusive in the sense that it provides a conceptual map of human development for all four human domains: physical, mental, emotional, and spiritual. It incorporates core understandings and truths from diverse disciplines and theories. It is a map that assembles insights and evidence from many thinkers, teachers and researchers from philosophy, psychology, spiritual traditions, modern science and many other areas, into a consistent whole, offering a territory for exploration into our own awareness and growth. In order to navigate this map, you don't need previous experience or special equipment. All you need is a little willingness and openness to broaden your awareness of your life.

I often tell my clients it's like learning a new language. At first it will seem difficult and cumbersome as you attempt to express yourself with a new vocabulary. Over time and with practice, it will become second nature. The challenge will be relating your new understanding and awareness to others. As your new language becomes part of your way of being, people will sense a shift. You'll be able to communicate to people in fresh and simple terms because the vocabulary will become second nature.

The practices throughout the CORE Journey are not difficult to grasp. They are designed to be exercised in your life now, as high-leverage tools so you can realize the impact in a short amount of time. We live in a fast-paced environment and none of us has time to waste. The practices are scalable and customizable, meaning you can personalize them to fit with your life circumstances and your schedule. You bring your own passions, strengths, purpose and values, as this is your Journey.

The CORE Journey offers a framework for initiating a path of mastery—ongoing learning and transformation. It is about waking up to our inherent motivation and capacity to be self-governing and creating a life of purpose and meaning. This book is not meant to be uses and, once completed, set aside. It is offered as a process to incorporate mindfulness into daily living and expand our awareness of the continued evolution of our own internal power. It is offered as the beginning of a conversation about an expanded horizon for human potential.

As the ancient proverb goes, the journey of a thousand miles begins with a single step. While we all must embark on our own journeys, this book attempts to clarify a process that you can embody for your success. In my experience as a learner and a coach, the Cairns provide fundamental components for a successful summit. Once you stand at the top of your summit, you can look out and see the vast territory of human potential. The CORE Journey offers you the tools to design your MAP for continued transformation and recognition of your unlimited potential as the creator of your life—a life of autonomy, mastery and purpose. It is my sincere intent that this book will serve as a guide along your path of awakening to who you truly are.

The CORE Journey

Phase 1
An Inward Journey

"If you want to teach people a new way of thinking, don't bother trying to teach them. Instead, give them a tool the use of which will gradually lead them to think differently."

— Buckminster Fuller, attributed

Y ou are preparing to embark on a journey. The CORE Journey is a model for those who are interested in and excited about being the creative force in their lives—self-determined and self-generating. It is designed for those who want to be fully engaged—attuned and awake to the happenings, people, and experiences with which they are involved. It is a process of reconnecting to our inherent capacity for wonder and creativity, independence and mastery.

The Journey begins with knowing yourself. It has been said that the longest distance traveled is from the head to the heart. Phase I includes practices to clarify what's important, satisfying, and meaningful to you. It is the practice of elucidating the essence of you being you—your true nature. This phase affords the opportunity to identify what you care about, which will be your reason, your compelling energy, to be true to your highest values, aspirations, and ideals.

The practices in which you will engage in this initial phase will help you articulate the essence of your life's purpose. They will provide the foundation for your MAP (Mindful Action Plan) and everything you do on your CORE Journey.

You will clarify and articulate your purpose, your foundational values, your individual strengths and gifts, and your vision. Purpose is the foundation from which your destination will evolve. It is what lights us up and gives us the energy, determination, and discipline to pursue our highest goals.

Your values will guide your actions. Together with your purpose, your core values will be a touchstone when challenges and obstacles present themselves. Your values are what you hold most dear. When your actions are aligned with your values, it creates a source of wellbeing. It offers you peace of mind.

Your strengths will help you in achieving the outcomes you want. This travel guide will help you distinguish your strengths and identify ways in which you can engage them in the pursuit of your vision. We will look at ways to expand and engage your strengths and unique gifts.

A compelling vision is your picture of what you see as a fulfilling, satisfying and meaningful life. Your vision is your story of who you want to be, what you want to create, and how you will live your best life. Creating this vision takes reflection, introspection, and energy. It will be a destination as well as a catalyst.

In order to move forward on your CORE Journey, it is necessary to create a compelling energy to make the journey. Your initial reason for embarking on the Journey may be as simple as just wanting something different, even if you are not clear yet what that something is. Or, you may be quite clear about what you want to create in your life, but don't know how to go about making it happen. And, still others engage in the Journey because they know what they want, and have tried to make the shift before, but can't seem to make the change stick. No matter your reason for choosing the CORE Journey, crafting a compelling reason for making the change, the transformation, will provide commitment, perseverance, and resilience. Phase I is about distinguishing your compelling energy and building the foundation necessary for a successful and journey.

Cairn 1

Identify a Compelling Power:
A Choice for Transformation

" ...Choice is the declaration by self that a certain ideal of self shall be realized."

—John Dewey, Psychologist

The first step to making a significant shift in your life is building a case for the desired transition. Change doesn't come easily for individuals or businesses. John P. Kotter, world-renowned expert on leadership at the Harvard Business School, is the author of the international bestseller *Leading Change*. In his award-winning book, Kotter demonstrated that the first step to making a change, for both organizations and individuals, is to establish a sense of urgency—a compelling reason for doing something in a different way. What is the motivation for the transformation? Is there a specific catalyst? Simply wanting something different often is not enough. You must internalize the need for change. You must make a commitment to the change and the realization that it is a process, a journey.

At Cairn I, the Journey begins with harnessing a compelling energy that establishes a resolution on your part to undergo a transformation. It involves garnering an awareness of the change you want to create and then designing a blueprint for your metamorphosis. It starts with the realization that there must be a better way, and evolves into a strong intention to make a change for the enrichment of your life. This will deepen your motivation and the energy you bring to the journey. This is also the step where it is important to recognize the fear and complacency that may have built up around the idea of change, possibly causing unproductive emotions, thoughts, and behaviors.

As mentioned above, Kotter distinguishes creating a sense of urgency as the first step necessary for a successful change effort. Companies who established a compelling force, or urgency, around the change successfully maneuvered through the barriers and setbacks they encountered during the change process. Without a perceived necessity, the change was either slow to unfold or never actually got off the ground. The stories about companies who did not establish a sense of urgency are usually focused around two things: they either were unaware of why the change was needed and/or they failed to address the fear behind the change. This put the change effort in jeopardy before it even started. Do not make this mistake. Proceeding without a compelling force is like trying to fly a plane without any fuel. Clarifying why a change will benefit you will help to assure commitment, perseverance and resilience.

Urgency may seem like a strong word to some. In this context, it means establishing a high priority or a compelling reason to embark on a journey over time for the purpose of expanded self-direction and mastery in your life. It could be as simple as creating more time for yourself, or more time to enjoy your living space, take a language course, interact with a loved one, or take guitar lessons. It could be making a career change, entering into a lifelong relationship, or transitioning into retirement. Whatever the desired result is, whatever you are choosing to create, feeling that it is a compelling reason establishes the willingness for the transition and makes the transformation a priority in your life. Establishing urgency around why you want to create something new and different begins to forge a strong energy that will be capable of fueling your journey.

Some people who seek coaching don't have a specific change in mind. They recognize that something in their life isn't working for them, but can't pinpoint what that something is. Life isn't giving them a sense of fulfillment or purpose. Sometimes it's as simple as life just not feeling right. They just have a sense that something needs to change. They want something different but they are not quite clear about what it is. For some the change may not be external, but rather a shift in their internal processes. That means it could be a change in their thoughts, perceptions, emotions, or the self-talk of judgment versus learning.

Many of my clients come to me thinking they need to change something in their life that is outside themselves. After reflection, exploration, and questioning, they have a growing appreciation that it is their internal environment that needs to shift. Their compelling force is gaining more control of their lives through better ways of managing their thoughts and feelings. Their change is making a transition from judgmental thoughts, which are limiting, to thoughts centered around learning, which generate options, expanding the prospects for their life. They begin to see a distinct difference between imposing past experiences on their present situation and living a life that embraces self-direction.

Through this process, the awareness that people gain is that they are responsible for their lives. We may not be able to take control of what is happening in our environment, but we are in full command of our reaction and our response to the situation, person, or environment that is challenging us. This seems like common sense and a simple realization. But, under stressful conditions, this awareness is difficult to maintain. Once we have developed the skill of actively choosing our reactions, we are extremely empowered and develop more and more trust in our ability to enact that awareness and choice even in the most challenging circumstances.

Developing an understanding of how your thoughts and feelings are affecting your perceptions is an example of a powerful internal change a client might pursue. Their compelling force could range from wanting more control of their lives to a desire for more peace of mind on a daily basis. To realize and accept that the experience of an external environment is an expression of what is going on internally is a major shift for many. With that insight, you have begun to develop a powerful self-determining mastery that will be effective in your personal and professional life.

No matter what it is that someone might desire in their life that is different, looking at the "why" provides a solid foundation from which to set off on an inward journey. Whenever we make a conscious choice to expand our internal power through self-direction, mastery and living "on purpose," we need to be honest with ourselves in terms of the energy and commitment that type of journey requires. A compelling impetus becomes an essential ingredient for success.

What is your compelling force? Your burning desire? What is the foundation for your change? Once you have named that, then you internalize the desire to be proactive about the change, thereby internalizing your power to make it happen. Once the willingness to change becomes part of you, it takes on a momentum that continues to grow. You begin to build on each step that takes you through the transition. You realize that the change is possible and you can make it happen. Now you can tap into your CORE for the energy necessary to continue the movement through the change.

On the following page, you will get started building your case for the change you want to bring about in your life. Even if you think you already understand the need for the change, work through this practice. One of the primary reasons for the failure of change efforts in business, or everyday personal life, is the failure to establish a compelling motivation for change, to give the desired creation or transformation a priority. It is up to you to determine what will make for a commanding force during your journey. Once you understand what is really behind your desire to create, you are well on your way to successfully engaging in your journey.

Even if the change doesn't seem "urgent" at first, you are establishing the underlying reasons for and benefits of making the transition. The more clear you are about this, the more positive energy you will have for the steps necessary to make and sustain the change. All of us need that clarity and momentum even when we know the change will be for the better, even when the change is for ourselves and is something we want. Work the practice and gain clarity on your case for being the creative force in your life!

APPROACH

Three important steps are necessary to generate a compelling energy around the desired change:

- Clearly identify the gap between what you are doing now, or who you are now, and what you want to create or what results you want as an outcome of your journey.
- Pinpoint sources of complacency or fear.
- Identify the strengths and values upon which you will draw in order to implement the change.

PRACTICE

1. Is there any place in your life where you are experiencing limited self-direction, purpose, fulfillment, or mastery? Describe.

2. Are you satisfied with your life? Why? Why not? Do you feel a compelling force to change something about the way things currently are?

To shed light on these questions, let's complete the CORE Journey Compass. On the following pages, you will find eight compasses identified by various themes that permeate our lives. The purpose of this activity is to determine how satisfied you are within each domain on a scale of 1 to 10.

In the main body of each compass, write a few key words or phrases about what is important or meaningful to you in this domain of your life. What do you want to do within this domain? What kind of person do you want to be? What strengths and attributes do you want to refine? What do you want to stand for? If a particular compass seems immaterial to your life, that's okay: leave it blank or add a compass that is relevant, but not named. Some compasses might have similar words. That's okay, too. This points out where similar values permeate various domains of your life.

An Example:

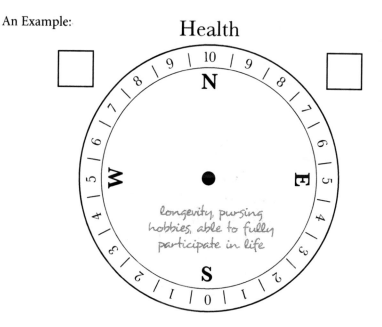

Health

longevity, pursing hobbies, able to fully participate in life

Personal Growth

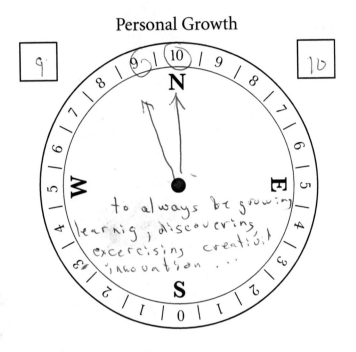

9   10

to always be growing
learning, discovering
excercising creativit
innovation . . .

Finances

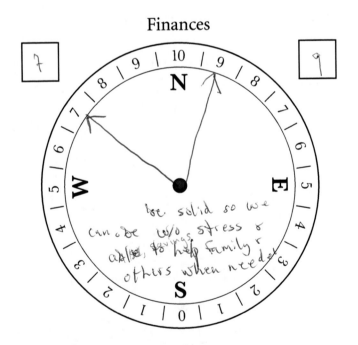

7   9

be solid so we
can be w/o stress &
able to help family &
others when needed

Leisure

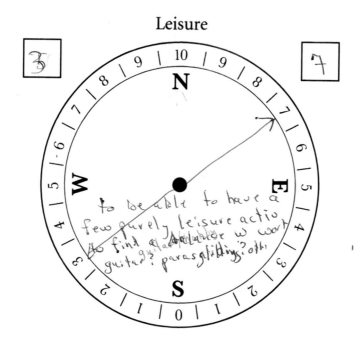

to be able to have a few purely leisure action to find a balance w work guitar? parasgliding? oth

Health

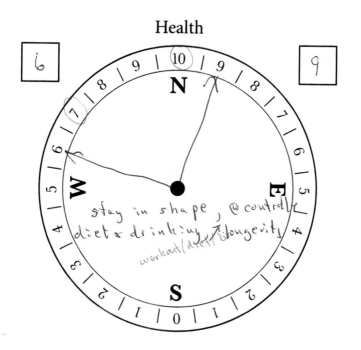

stay in shape, @ control diet & drinking longevity
workout/diet

Career

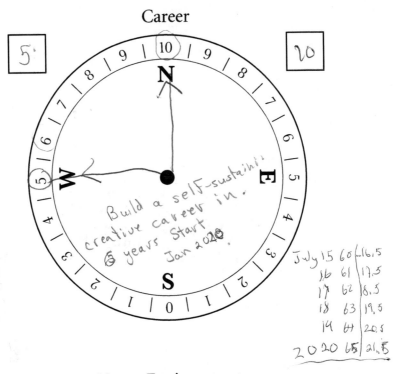

5.

20

Build a self-sustaining creative career in 5 years. Start Jan 2020.

July 15 60 16.5
16 61 17.5
17 62 18.5
18 63 19.5
19 64 20.5
2020 65 21.5

Home Environment

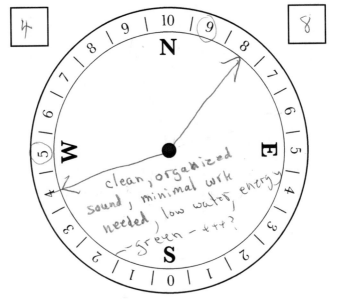

4

8

clean, organized sound, minimal work needed, low water, energy -green - etc?

Community & Environment

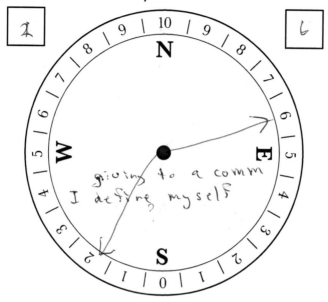

Family Relationships

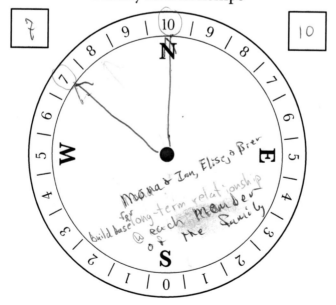

Intimate Relationships

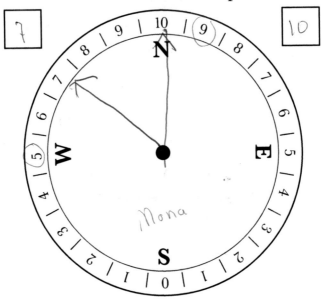

Social Relationships

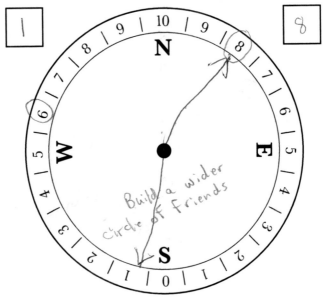

Each compass has an outer ring with numbers from 0 to 10. Now that you have filled in each compass, revisit them one by one and using the numbers on the right side, or "East" side of each compass, on a scale of 1–10, circle the number that indicates how important these words, values, or phrases are to you: 0=no importance, 10=extremely important. Write that ranking in the box at the upper right corner of the compass. Several compasses may have the same rating.

Now, using the numbers on the "West" side of each compass, on a scale of 1–10, circle the number that represents how effectively you are currently engaging the items in your life. Write that number in the box at the upper left corner of each compass. 0=not at all and 10=fully engaged. As before, it's okay if several compasses have the same score.

Lastly take a look at what you have written in each compass and the rating for each one. Based on what you've written: 1) What's important to you in your life at this moment in time? 2) In what areas of your life are you remiss in living your values and the type of life you want to experience?

Now draw an arrow from the center of the compass to the number you circled on each side. Do this for each ranking. You will have 2 arrows per compass. The further the arrow is pointing away from north, the more off the path you may be that leads to your summit. The objective will be to have each arrow within each compass point to true north. This would be a marker that you are on the right path leading to your summit.

An Example:

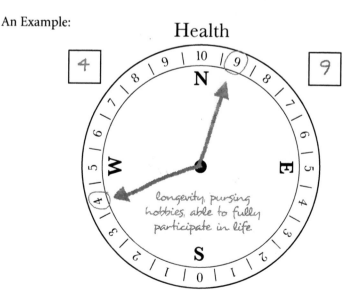

Health

At a later Cairn, you'll have an opportunity to write about what would be necessary to have the arrow for each compass point to north. You'll also be able to prioritize the domains according to which you would like to work on first in order to realize your goal and reach your summit in a timely fashion.

Continue answering the questions below to help solidify your intention for change and to clarify possible roadblocks to the full realization of your aspirations.

3. Do you feel primed to undertake the process of creating something new or different in your life? If not, do you need to revisit, or clarify, your compelling force for your transformation?

4. What would motivate, or is motivating, you to be the creative force in your life?

5. What are some driving forces that would sustain your commitment to making this transformation?

6. How would this change improve or enhance your life?

7. What risks do you see in being the creative force in your life?

8. What would interfere with your desire/ability to change? What barriers/resistance do you foresee in making this shift?

9. Write out your compelling energy for a transformation toward being the creative force in your life.

10. What strengths will you draw on that are critical for the success of this way of living?

Establishing your urgency, or compelling energy will generate focus, commitment, energy, and trust that you are capable of achieving your desired results. As your Journey progresses, your compelling energy can be used as a waypoint to confirm and reenergize your resolve for the discipline and effort necessary for accomplishing your aspirations and vision. The force that your urgency spawns is key to introducing a new dynamic, one of seeing and feeling the enthusiasm for change. Your compelling energy will be the fuel for action because it has demonstrated potent reasons for change that sparks your purposefulness.

REFLECT AND ENGAGE

- What are your CORE learnings from this Cairn?
- How will you apply these things in your life?
- What have you learned about yourself at this Cairn?
- Based on the practices at this Cairn, what will you do to expand your ability to be the creative force in your life?
- How will you acknowledge yourself for completing this step along your Journey?

Cairn II

Purpose
The Foundation of Choice

"People say that what we're all seeking is the meaning for life. I don't think that's what we're really seeking. I think that what we're seeking is an experience of being alive, so that our life experiences on the purely physical plane will have resonances within our own innermost being and reality, so that we actually feel the rapture of being alive."

—Joseph Campbell

It's interesting that the dictionary defines *purpose* as a noun when the root word came from Old French *porpos*, a verb. Webster defines purpose as "the reason for which something is done or created or for which something exists." Deci and Ryan, pioneers in the research field of motivation, found an individual's purpose to be a powerful source of energy, especially when internally motivated. Deci and Ryan's research indicated that when people clarified their own sense of purpose, which they identified as *self-authored* or *self-determined,* they had greater perseverance, creativity, interest, excitement, and confidence. Your Journey's purpose will serve you in a similar fashion. You may realize that your purpose has been a driving force behind your decisions and actions throughout your life without you knowing it. The process of composing your purpose and writing it down provides clarity and direction for future choices and actions. Not only do you become

41

more aware of how your purpose has been an underlying motivation, but you acquire the ability to evoke your purpose at will. It becomes more a part of your daily thought process, thereby enabling you to ensure actions that align with your purpose. Clarity around your purpose empowers you to use it as a bearing to guide you in the appropriate direction. Using your purpose as a bearing, or compass, ensures that your life becomes more self-authored and autonomous. Knowing that your purpose is intrinsic to you enhances your perseverance, confidence, creativity, and excitement in creating a life of your own determination.

Mihaly Csikszentmihalyi (pronounced chick-sent-me-HIGH-ee), one of the pioneers of the positive psychology movement, originated the concept of psychological *flow*. He found that people who were absorbed in an activity recorded a homogeneous constellation of experience, which included a sense of "suspension of time": loss of awareness of self, effortlessness, creativity and joy. In his groundbreaking research on flow, Csikszentmihalyi identified purpose as a source of activating energy. In his work, he found that when people had a sense of purpose, it propelled them forward in a positive manner, creating more fulfillment, joy and happiness in their endeavors, whether it was at work or in leisure. Flow provided feelings of mastery and self-determination as well as an absence of anxiety about losing control of the situation. When people engaged their purpose, they were more likely to experience psychological flow, and this level of involvement facilitated more robust feelings of happiness and meaning.

Joseph Campbell was a mythologist, lecturer, and writer best known for his work in comparative mythology and religion. His work is vast, but two of his more popular books include *The Power of Myth* and *The Hero With A Thousand Faces*. This statement best summarizes his philosophy: "Follow your bliss." In his writing, he describes how the search for meaning and purpose has been going on throughout history and across cultures. He called this search "The Hero's Journey," which begins when something inside of us reaches the point of thinking, "there has to be a better way." At that point, the challenging journey of self-transformation begins. People start to look for something of meaning beyond themselves. They begin an inward journey to discover what their life is really about. As the Buddha said, the journey goes inward and we learn "to be a lamp unto ourselves."

I read an interesting story about a group of people who were offered a large sum of money to attempt to cross over a plank that stretched from one tall building to another. The plank was 175 feet above ground and 12 inches wide. If the plank was laid on the ground, it would be quite passable, but that high in the air it wasn't a risk most people were willing to take. Even when the amount of money was increased to the millions, only a handful raised their hands. When a very different question was posed, the response was quite different. What if their families were in trouble and the only way to save them was to cross the plank? How many would be willing to risk the crossing? Every single person in the audience raised their hand.

I don't know what these people's purpose was, but I know that it gave them courage. No matter who was on the other end of that plank, crossing it took courage. Purpose is part of being human. It gives us courage to persevere and do what matters. We all have a sense that our lives are meant for something. We want to make a contribution in our own unique way. Purpose illuminates our contribution.

Purpose is more than just values. You can lead your life by a set of values. For example, some people live by a code of humanitarian values that champion caring for others, integrity, service and so on. A life in the service of those values would be significant. Purpose goes beyond values and actually gives the values priority, direction and meaning. With direction and meaning, purpose simplifies our lives. It governs decision-making, problem solving, and goal setting. Purpose crystallizes our intention so what we say we believe in is actually mirrored in our actions and words. It allows us to be authentic in our value system.

Purpose is not about money, your job, or your role. All of those things can, and do, change. Purpose, once clarified, doesn't change. It is our reason for being who we are and, therefore, is uniquely our own. It allows us to bring our strengths, gifts and passions into play.

Purpose is a primary source of energy, motivation, and direction. Purpose creates our destination. It is our call to the adventure—our call to embark on a journey up the mountain we want to summit. It is our reason for getting up in the morning. It is what inspires us and draws us into living fully. It can galvanize our spirit in such a manner that we are kept awake at night thinking of possibilities and opportunities to engage our purpose. Purpose is our intention in life. Ultimately, purpose is fundamental to setting our long-term goals and establishing what we want to make of our lives. It is a guide for organizing our life. Purpose is the sails on our boat. It is our GPS system for navigating the mountain and reaching the summit we choose.

Purpose is a powerful and foundational part of your CORE Journey. It is where we will begin and where we will circle back to again and again. As you define and articulate your purpose, you will be creating something that you can draw on for direction.

Richard Leider is the founder and Chairman of The Inventure Group. Leider has worked for over three decades writing, speaking, researching, coaching and facilitating workshops to help people to discover their purpose and the power that figuring out their purpose brings to their lives to be self-authored and self-determined. In his book *The Power of Purpose*, Leider describes purpose as "…that deepest dimension within us—our central core or essence—where we have a profound sense of who we are, where we came from, and where we are going." Leider taught that purpose is the catalyst for organizing life. It can serve as a daily guide and help us use all of our resources in the most effective means possible to realize our potential. It gives us the ability to "feel the rapture of being alive" and experience the summit of happiness, fulfillment and productivity. Abraham Maslow, a psychologist best known for his book *A Theory of Human Motivation* and the development of his Hierarchy of Needs, also believed that to be self-actualized, we must live our purpose. To truly live a life that is "on" purpose is to reach our potential, to become all we are capable of becoming, to become ultimate self-authors and creators of a fulfilling life.

What does purpose mean to you? Have you given it any thought? If you have a purpose, is it yours and yours alone, rather than something imposed from someone else? It will take some searching, questioning, and more looking inside to discover what drives you to do what you do, what matters to you, what moves you to be the best you can be. Once you have clearly defined purpose for yourself, everything else will fall into place.

What is your purpose? Is it to raise healthy children? To be a successful business owner? To climb all the mountains in Colorado that are 14,000 feet tall? To make your parents and family proud of you? To contribute in a positive way to the world? To leave the environment better for the next generation? To follow a spiritual path? If it inspires you and motivates you, you will know it is yours. Once clarified and defined, it will serve as your template for your life's works.

When you have named your purpose, it will enable you to focus your efforts and engage your talents and skills to that end. It will enable you to center your resources and reach your potential. Purpose is key to personal and professional effectiveness.

Once you have established your purpose, it doesn't mean you will never falter or go off course. I've worked with many athletes who were quite clear about their purpose, yet there were times when they had lapses. For example, Peyton Manning, the quarterback for the Indianapolis Colts and four-time MVP of the National Football League, has a clear focus. In the opening half of the first 2007 playoff game, it was clear he was not on his game. He lacked the customary concentration we are so familiar with from Peyton. He was not playing to his potential. At halftime, he said he reconnected with his purpose, his love of the game beyond simply winning and losing, and the desire to lead his team to be the best they could be. Peyton was a different player in the second half. He was on target and had regained his normal confidence and clarity of focus.

Once you have your purpose, you might waver, but the difference is that you will notice it more quickly and be able to adjust and get back on track. When people do not have a purpose in mind, they stray off course without noticing. In those situations there's no telling where one might end up. It is like a ship without a sail. External circumstance will blow you off your path. Knowing your purpose helps you regain focus and get back on your chosen path.

Unfortunately, most people don't invest the time or energy to discover their purpose. Exploring and naming one's purpose is not for the faint of heart. It takes work and, like I said, courage. It takes a lot of thought, reflection and discernment. Clarifying your purpose and then living authentically from your purpose contributes to naming you the hero of your own life. The CORE Journey is your hero's journey and a gift you have given yourself. The initial strategy is to explore, discover, and engage your purpose. Your purpose will be instrumental in determining your summit. Once you are aware of your purpose, it will be the foundation for your actions and the energy to realize your vision. Your purpose underlies what you want to create in your life. It gives you a base from which to view what matters to you.

APPROACH

Here we want to clarify that something that fills you with passion, drive, and direction, that makes you feel like your life really matters, like you are making a difference. This is not some grandiose idea that only a gifted, and lucky, few possess. Purpose is something we all have. We simply need to rediscover it and bring it to a conscious level.

Fundamental constructs at this Cairn are:

- Your purpose.

- Your reason for being.

- Your reason for jumping out of bed in the morning.

Whether it is spiritual, physical, work-related, relationship-oriented, or a combination, the conclusion is clear: to be happy, fulfilled, and able to perform consistently at peak levels, you must discover your purpose and live it!

PRACTICE

- Who am I?

- What am I meant to be?

- How do I want to design and direct my life?

- When I am fully engaged, highly energized, and acting consistently with my deepest values, what am I doing, thinking, feeling?

creating / sharing / enabling / giving / reading

In the process of answering these questions, here are some things to think about to help clarify your purpose.

2 ASTD sis / Br Sci / MORE / wh. Paper

- When you look back on your life, when were you truly inspired? What were you doing when you were actively engaged in the process, when time seemed to stand still, when things seemed to come easily? Why was the activity so absorbing? Why were you fully engaged in that activity?

- Was there a time when you couldn't wait to get up and get going in your day? What was your motivating force? *Creating*

- Is there something that keeps you up at night that is inspiring or motivating? What is it? What makes it so exciting that you can't wait to get back to it? Why does it motivate or inspire you to action?

- A final question that might help to clarify your purpose is to ask, What do I want to pass along to generations to follow? What are the three most important things I have learned over my lifetime? What is my legacy to my work, my family, my partner or significant other, my community, the world?

Want to set them up to "succeed"
listen, ask Qs, learn, humble, givers

- Write with no judgment. Keep asking, "For the sake of what?" Keep drilling until you can go no further. Then, you have your purose.

[handwritten: - Self-support in dep - to create cours progr
→ Support Mona/Me or ___ that's
→ Be creative M of wanted/needed btd/ fth
supports & provides
obtain stimulate r
growth & source f.
help me while Invl,]

PRACTICE

Ideal Self

A clear understanding of our ideal self can serve as a compass so that we can be assured that we are on the road to living our intentions and ideals every day. When we spend time clarifying the self that we strive to become, it shows a willingness to care enough to study ourselves and use that knowledge to manage ourselves and our relationships with others so that we truly live out our intentions, enhance our trust and influence, and engage our values and purpose.

As we develop a crisp vision of our ideal self, our capacity to discover, reconnect and express our greatness expands. Why? Because to be our ideal self demands a complete disclosure of our strengths. As a result, we can begin to fully understand our ideal selves and compare this ideal with how we behave each day. Our ideal self is the self that emerges when we are unencumbered by the burden of irrational thoughts and emotional upsets that can sometimes distract us from our intentions and our values. It's that effectiveness of doing and saying the right thing at the right time in the right way. It's that self that is grounded and poised. It's that self that acts from intrinsic motivation without the need for other people's approval or a need to compete at the expense of others. It doesn't fear making mistakes. It doesn't lash out in anger or spend time fretting or fearing things that it cannot control. It's that self that is self-possessed in both our personal and work lives that produces satisfaction and balance. It's that self that inspires others. It's that self that gives us peace of mind from knowing we lived on purpose today.

Please take this opportunity to write about your ideal self. This is not a time to be modest. This is a time to describe the best self you can be.

[handwritten: Giving, productive, independent from an agency/business, with ample resources to support children... & able to be creative inquisitive but all the time what I do can be of some small service to others...]

REFLECT AND ENGAGE

- What are your CORE learnings from this Cairn?
- How will you apply these things in your life?
- What have you learned about yourself at this Cairn?
- Based on the practices at this Cairn, what will you do to expand your ability to be the creative force in your life?
- How will you acknowledge yourself for completing this step along your Journey?

Cairn III

Articulate and Define Your Values
Essential Elements for Action

"Just as your car runs more smoothly and requires less energy to go faster and farther when the wheels are in perfect alignment, you perform better when your thoughts, feelings, goals, and values are in balance."

—Brian Tracy, motivational speaker

You have your own set of unique values. They form a constellation of what is intrinsically important to you. They emerge from your background, experience and environment, and are part of your character. As you mature and become independent, your values may change to fit a more self-directed lifestyle. With time and experience, specific values become fundamental and are integrated into the essence of your being. These are the values that form your core; they are at the foundation of who you are for yourself, others, and the world. Values are tenets for living that you hold most dear and what you would be willing to strive or even fight for if need be.

Values are not to be confused with morals and ethics. Morals are what are right and wrong for an individual. Ethics are what are right or wrong for a culture. Values are a person's principles or standards of behavior, one's judgment of what is important in life.

49

Your values are bearings that you accept as true for you and they serve as guideposts for choices and actions. As was stated earlier, the mindful awareness of being able to align actions with both your values and purpose is fundamental for peace of mind. You are able to live what you believe when you can engage your values throughout your day at home and at work. In order to act consistently with your values, to be authentic, you must be aware of those driving principles so that you can consciously and mindfully engage them throughout your day.

APPROACH

To clarify and define your core values.

PRACTICE

Here are CORE questions that can help you clarify your values.

My CORE Values
- What are my CORE guiding principles?
- What moves me to action?
- What defines my integrity?
- What are my moral touchstones?
- What brings me peace of mind about myself?

Following is a list of some commonly held values. I have left some lines blank so you can add any values you have that are not listed. Put a check next to the ten values you feel are most important to you.

CORE VALUES

A person's principles or standards of behavior; one's judgment of what is important in life.

☒ Achievement/Success ④	☐ Happiness	☐ Patience
☐ Advancement	☐ Harmony	☐ Quality
☐ Adventure	☒ Health	☐ Recognition
☒ Autonomy ⑩	☐ Honesty	☐ Respect
☐ Beauty	☐ Hope	☐ Risk-taking
☐ Caring	☐ Humor	☐ Security
☐ Challenge	☒ Independence	☐ Service
☐ Communication	☒ Innovation ③	☐ Simplicity
☐ Competition	☐ Integrity	☐ Spirituality
☐ Courage	☐ Involvement	☐ Strength
☒ Creativity ③	☐ Influence	☐ Status
☒ Collaboration	☐ Intelligence	☐ Teamwork
☒ Curiosity ⑨	☐ Justice	☐ Trust
☐ Decisiveness	☐ Love/Affection	☐ Trustworthiness
☐ Dependability	☐ Learning	☐ Truth
☐ Diversity	☐ Loyalty	☐ Uniqueness
☐ Empathy	☐ Open-mindedness	☐ Winning
☐ Equality	☐ Power	☐ Wisdom
☒ Family ①	☒ Productivity ④	⊘ Optimism/Positiveness
☐ Friendship	☐ Prosperity/Wealth	⊘ Engagement
☒ Growth ⑥	☐ Relationships	_____

To help clarify your values even more, list the ten values you chose and assign each one of them a numerical value, 1 being the most important and 10 being the least important. This is an important part of the value clarification process because there will be times when your values come into conflict with each other. For example, honesty and integrity may be two of your chosen values. Another value you have may be human relationships. We all know that, in our most dear relationships, honesty must be tempered with empathy in order for trust to grow. Honesty without empathy can be cruel and uncaring. Clarifying which of those two values ranks higher in your priority list will help determine your actions when the situation calls for empathic honesty. When you can be both honest and empathic, the relationship will continue to be enriched and meaningful.

The next step in the process is to list each value and define it for your self. Words hold various meanings for every individual. For complete understanding, it's a good exercise to clearly define what each value means to you. You can make a list of words for each value, write a sentence, or define it in paragraph or story form. Whatever way works for you, write it down. Don't just think about it—write your definition down so you can actually see it and hear it.

Prioritizing your values also helps clarify those values that are at your core. To further the significance of being able to name your values, I ask my clients to choose 3–5 of their top 10 values that are central to their perception of themselves when they are living on purpose. These 3–5 core values probably will not change over time. They are ways of being that you cherish and have grown to accept as part and parcel of who you are and they are essential to the core of your being. They are how and who you want to be—the person you are being when you are self-directed, pursuing mastery and engaging your purpose. They are your guiding principles within any challenging environment. Choose your top 3–5 values here. List them and describe how and why they are a central code of behavior for you. Describe how you engage each value in your personal and professional life.

There is one more step you can take to make sure you know your core values. For each of the 3–5 top values, ask yourself "What for?" and "Why do I hold this value as a guiding principle?" Keep drilling. With each answer ask again, "For the purpose of what?" When you feel like you have reached the bottom and have no more answers or the answers are becoming circular, you have probably named the core value.

This step is helpful because sometimes there are a number of words that share the same meaning. And there are words that lead to another word. Drilling down in this manner unveils the primary word underpinning the reason you hold it as a core way of being. You get the feeling that there's no other word that engulfs the meaning more explicitly or has greater significance.

Drill down as far as you can go to find the fundamental value. After doing this for each of the 3–5 core values you've chosen, make a list of you final core values. These values form the foundation for your actions. They bring clarity to the decision-making process. Aligning your behavior with your core values will engender a consistency and can offer a sense of peace as it accompanies the feeling that you did the best you could because you stayed with your values. At the end of the day, it's a helpful practice to take a few minutes to reflect on whether or not your actions were aligned with your values. If they were, you'll find that you probably experienced a sense of solace and tranquility. If not, you may experience discomfort.

That being said, acting on your values may also present a challenge at times. There will be times when your choice is not the popular one. Others may not hold your values and push instead for alternate solutions. If you know your purpose and your values, it will make standing your ground much more doable, though it may not actually be easy. And, you'll find that when you do stand your ground in those circumstances, even if things didn't go your way, you feel much better about yourself than if you had given in to pressure.

Sometimes collaboration calls for a joint decision that you may not agree with, but still understand. In my experience, most people's purpose and core values many times transcend themselves personally. Their values support the ideal of wanting the best for everyone and creating an environment where people can flourish. So, even compromise, if it helps people thrive, can still support your values. It's when a choice conflicts outright with a value that you may have to stand apart. If that's the case, and it happens too often, the decision may go as far as it did for me when I made the choice to leave my corporate job. What I was being asked to do on a consistent basis was in direct conflict with my major values. Finally, I couldn't do it anymore. I literally was feeling sick. As I said, it was not an easy choice, but if I was to act with integrity and walk my talk, I had to choose to leave. And even though it was difficult, I did have a greater feeling of reassurance and composure than I had when I went to work and acted inconsistently with my values. And, it worked out for the best because now my values are congruent with what I do and who I am.

Being certain and clear about your values is indispensable for self-directed behavior, mastery and purpose. Knowing your values will offer you clarity and confidence in the things you do and the choices you make. They also offer guideposts for establishing your vision and designing your MAP.

PRACTICE

Internal Power: Autonomy, Mastery, Purpose

The purpose of this exercise is to help you consider your own sense of internal power and how, once recognized, translates into consistently being able to engage your values. Also, this practice is just the beginning of a quest to further develop your power. As we consider how we can be more effective every day, we must question our concept of power. Those who are the most influential and successful know that power is not something to brandish over others. People who are the most impactful know that becoming more powerful happens when you give and/or share your sense of power. They know the importance of creating ways in which others feel empowered, confident, efficacious, and self-determined. They send a clear and consistent message: feeling powerful, literally feeling "able," comes from a deep sense of being effective with your own life. Internal power is a mindful activity that emanates from within and displays itself to others as strength of belief and inner confidence. Research consistently shows that true power emanates from a clear sense of autonomy, mastery and purpose.

How strong is your sense of internal power? Place a mark on the continuum to indicate your level of internal power.

0 _____ 5 ___(6)_____ 10

How would you define internal power?
Positive movement forward daily → goal...
How does internal power contribute to and expand our sense of purpose and our "Noble Goal"?

REFLECT AND ENGAGE

- What are your CORE learnings from this Cairn?

- How will you apply these things in your life?

- What have you learned about yourself at this Cairn?

- Based on the practices at this Cairn, what will you do to expand your ability to be the creative force in your life?

- How will you celebrate the completion of this Cairn?

Ask Diana, what research shows
thap Power emenates from
MAP

AMP from Drive

Cairn IV

What Do You Want to Create?
Conceive and Conceptualize

" 'Who are *you?*' said the Caterpillar. [...]

Alice replied, rather shyly, 'I—I hardly know, sir, just at present—at least I

know who I *was* when I got up this morning, but I think I must have been

changed several times since then.' "

—Lewis Carroll, *Alice's Adventures in Wonderland*

My sister is a mechanical and nuclear engineer. She worked for a Fortune 100 company for many years and did outstanding work. On occasion we would do consulting work together for business teams that wanted to communicate more effectively in order to accomplish more timely results on projects. We used several personality inventories as tools to improve the teams' effectiveness, and one of our primary resources was the Myers-Briggs Type Indicator.

The Myers-Briggs Type Indicator is a self-report assessment tool designed to make Swiss psychiatrist Carl Jung's theory of psychological types understandable and applicable in everyday living. The authors of the MBTI, Katherine Briggs and her daughter Isabel Myers, studied and elaborated Jung's ideas and applied them to understanding people. They constructed the inventory as a way for people to understand and engage the unique gifts they bring to the world and the people around them. The MBTI is founded on more than 50 years of research and development and is currently the most widely used instrument for understanding normal personality differences in the world. The MBTI indicates preferences in four areas: 1) energy for living and engaging, 2) perceiving and taking in information, 3) making decisions based on that information, and 4) how one prefers to organize their life.

It is a robust tool to help people acknowledge and celebrate strengths and appreciate differences, their own as well as other people's. Once the individuals on the team had an appreciation of the strengths and differences of each member, we would engage them in exercises to target the ways in which the unique, individual preferences of the team members would contribute to the project.

Once each team member's strengths and contributions to the team were recognized, we would put them in groups with others who had similar preferences. Their assignment was to compose a story about how that team, with their particular preferences, would organize, implement, and bring the project to a timely and successful completion. This exercise would stump some of the members because they did not consider themselves to be creative enough to tell a story. We would explain that they didn't have to be creative in their storytelling; they simply had to create a story.

My sister would always empathize with that particular group because she never felt like her type was creative either. She thoroughly understood and acknowledged the strengths and contributions of her type, but creative just was not a word that resonated with her. And, therefore, she felt she was unable to create. I don't need to get into the details of her type. Suffice it to say that all types are creative; they will simply create in distinct ways from the other types.

For example, my sister eventually left her corporate job because she felt stifled and unfulfilled. She was unable to engage in what she felt passionate about, which was dance. I use this story as an example because I am sure some of you are having the same reaction that many of my students do when I tell them this tale. What was my sister doing in mechanical and nuclear engineering if her passion was dance? Well, that's another story. For our purposes here, my sister left the company she was working for and created her own dance company. It evolved into the largest and most successful dance company of its kind in Colorado!

Enough said. She created her own company and took it to a level unsurpassed by any other company in the state. Creative? I would have to say yes. Did she create her life around a passion? I would again have to say a resounding yes! So what is it about the word create or creative that confounds people? Why do we sometimes think we cannot create unless we feel ourselves to be creative, like an artist? In the strictest sense of the word, most of us are not artists. I am going to step out on a limb and say that you don't have to be an artist to create, and that to create is in itself an art. We can choose to be the artist of our lives and create our lives to be fulfilling and meaningful. Let's explore this word, to create.

Webster's unabridged dictionary defines creativity as "creative ability; artistic or intellectual inventiveness." Creative is defined in a similar way: "the ability, or capacity, to create original ideas through imagination, esp., in the production of an artistic work." Let's think about this. Merely having the capacity to have a baby does not make us have a baby. Having the capacity to be a father does not make us a father. In a similar vein, having the capacity to create does not make us creative, nor does it make us a creator.

Webster defines create as "to originate, to bring into existence, to cause as a result of one's actions." Create comes from the Latin verb *creare,* to "produce," "to form out of nothing." Webster further defines create as "causing something to exist that did not previously exist, to bring into being from nothing." This definition doesn't talk about the creating being original, imaginative, or inventive. It does not refer to capacity or ability. It simply speaks of bringing a result into existence that did not previously exist. This is what I mean by create: bringing something into being that was not there before.

Is creativity involved in the creative process? Sometimes. And there are many times when it is not. It is possible to create without being creative per se. Conversely, there are many times when creativity is present, yet nothing results. We all know people who have great imaginations who fail to bring anything into existence. They fail to translate their ideas into reality.

This Cairn is about you creating. Your work here is about what you want to create in your life. Do you have to be creative? No. Does creativity have to be involved in this process? No. Can you create your life the way you want to, and create the results in your life that you want? Yes. The strategy is to explore and name the results you want in your life.

APPROACH

Become aware of what you want to create.
Choose what you want to bring into existence.
Trust that you have the capacity to shape your future.

PRACTICE

Conceive and conceptualize what you want to create for a full, rich and meaningful life.

1. Ask the question.

   Ask yourself, "What do I want? What results do I want in my life? What do I want my story to be?"

   Knowing what you want enables you to focus your attention on the results you want. Don't confuse this practice with knowing the process required to create what you want. We'll get to that. For right now, clarify what you want.

2. Write it down.

   At the end of this Cairn there is a space for you to start writing. It's journaling with a prompt. The prompt is written at the top of the page: "What do I want to create in my life?" At the end this Cairn there are additional questions that you can write on your journaling page to get your creative juices flowing. But you don't have to just write about what you want to bring into your life. Draw a picture of it. Create a collage of the things you want to create in your life. Write it in a story. Put it down in a "bucket list." Whatever approach speaks to you, do it.

   Knowing what you want has several other advantages. When you name what you want to create, you eliminate the confusion and wasted energy of being pulled in different directions. When we haven't clearly named what we want to create, it can seem like events and circumstances are pushing us to adhere. There seems to be a lack of focus, attention and intention. Once you clarify and name what you want to create, not only does it give you clarity in your attention and focus, it also gives you a sense of power and illuminates your choices and intention. Choosing what you want to create is actively engaging the practice of autonomy. You are steering your life in the direction that you envision.

What you want is separate from knowing the process to achieve it. The process is independent of the results at this point. Robert Fritz, author, artist, and consultant, contributed his knowledge to the art of bringing something new into existence through his book *Creating*. There, Fritz discusses the fact that creating is bringing something into existence. He says that, if you attempt to choose results that you want based on process, it's almost like putting a ceiling on what you can create. If you make what you want dependent on a process you know, you will be restricting your ability to bring something new into being that has not existed before. Your past will be influencing your future in a limiting fashion. We want to be in the place where we name what you want to create now.

Sometimes the creating process is exploring new paths and discovering things you didn't know you wanted. In some ways, you are making it up. Instead of thinking something is not possible, you are creating the possibility.

Try not to get hung up on what you think is possible. What you want should be a separate consideration from apparent possibilities. Basing what you want on what you think is possible places constraints on your vision. There are numerous stories of people creating things in their life that were not even heard of before. For example, the Fosbury Flop. Up until the early 1960s, the straddle method was the dominant technique used by athletes in the high jump. Dick Fosbury is the track and field athlete who revolutionized the high jump event, using a back-first technique which became known as the Fosbury Flop. Before Dick Fosbury changed everything, it was thought that in order to clear the bar, the jumper must approach and go over belly down. Fosbury went over the bar with his back toward the bar! At the 1968 Olympics, Fosbury took the gold medal and set an Olympic record at 2.24 meters (7 feet, 4.25 inches). Four years later, at the Munich Games, 28 out of 40 high jumpers used Fosbury's technique. From 1972 through 2000, 34 of the 36 Olympic high jump medalists used his method. Today it is the most popular high jumping technique at all levels of competition from high school to the Olympics. Dick Fosbury brought something into existence that didn't exist before and nobody thought that it was possible to high jump any other way than what was currently being done. Do not limit yourself by questions of possibility.

3. Choose.

For each idea or aspiration you have written down, say, "I choose..." If you can say a conclusive and resounding yes, circle the choice. If a voice in your head says no, or you have a hesitation or doubt, cross it off your list. You can revisit the things you've marked off the list at a later time, but for now it helps to clarify exactly what you want to create at this time in your life. Circle your active choices.

Once you have named what you want to create, you move to the next step in the creative process. You choose. Actively choosing what you want to create makes a powerful statement. You are mindfully saying yes to your wishes. When you intentionally make a choice, you unleash energy and resources that might otherwise go untapped. By expanding your awareness of what you want to create, you expand your capacity to choose. Choosing generates clarity. To do your work well and make sure the choices are yours and yours alone takes reflection, self-awareness, time and practice. Mindfully choosing what you want to bring into existence is a skill. The more you do it, the better you will become at choosing.

Making choices is not something we are taught. It is, however, an important part of this process. The power of choosing for yourself brings into play your values, priorities, and experiences. We have all made choices that have not led us to our desired destination. Sometimes a lack of clarity presents too many choices. The goal of this Cairn is that you expand your awareness of what it is you truly want. You actively choose to bring that particular desire into existence. And over time, you will begin to trust that what you can imagine, you can bring into being.

Some questions to help clarify what you want to create:

1. What fills me with joy?

2. Is there something I keep gravitating toward? What is it?

3. What did I used to like to do that I am not doing right now?

4. What do I do now that makes me happy? Inspires me?

5. What do I wonder is really possible for my life and me?

As you conceive the result you want to create in your life, allow yourself to play a bit. Experiment with ideas. Check it out. Live with the concept for a while. Be aware of what the idea feels like to you. And, what do you feel like when you think of having it in your life?

REFLECT AND ENGAGE

- What are your CORE learnings from this Cairn?
- How will you apply these things in your life?
- What have you learned about yourself at this Cairn?
- Based on the practices at this Cairn, what will you do to expand your capacity and ability to be the creative force in your life?
- How will you celebrate the completion of this Cairn?

What do I want to
create in my life?

(1) More creation

(+) writing to support below

(2) Business @ traing, programs or events

(3) Bus ideas

(+) speaking to support above

(4) Reading / combining

(5) Healthy body @ perf wells

(6) Great relationship w Mono
Better? Stronger? More supportive?

Cairn V

Strengths and Individual Success
Reflect and Identify

"It is true that we shall not be able to reach perfection, but in our struggle toward it we shall strengthen our characters and give stability to our ideas, so that, whilst ever advancing calmly in the same direction, we shall be rendered capable of applying the faculties with which we have been gifted to the best possible account."

—Confucius

Now that you have a solid awareness and understanding of your core values, the next important part of the story of who you are is to identify your strengths and passions. At this Cairn, you clarify and acknowledge what you believe to be your strengths, passions, and the various commitments you have in your life. This step affords you the opportunity to reconnect with the passions and strengths that make you the unique individual that you are. It also allows you to look at how and where you are currently engaging your strengths and passions, as well as where you might draw on them more often to enhance your potential and life satisfaction.

Okay, let's stop for a moment and define the word passion. One of the definitions from the dictionary is "an intense desire or enthusiasm for something." More times than not, the word passion brings a look of confusion and bemusement from my students and clients. Sometimes I feel like

I shouldn't even mention the word because I get such odd looks. I bet if I asked you to go back in time to when you were about eight or ten years of age, you could rattle off a host of passions you had. They probably would range from chasing butterflies, catching grasshoppers, playing with your dog, and Friends Friday when you got to invite your favorite friend over for a play date, to that quiet bedtime ritual of reading that you did with your parents. Somewhere along the line in between "stop acting like a child" and "act like a grownup," our passions begin to fade from our awareness and, for many, from our memory. At some point our goals and aspirations become all about being what our peers, parents, or society deems successful. Well, at this Cairn I'm extending an invitation for you to resurrect and reconnect with your passions. You probably are a different person now, so maybe the better approach is to ask yourself, "What am I passionate about now?"

You still may feel a bit uneasy with calling them passions. To some, passion seems to denote a drive, a desire to do or be something, a heightened motivation to accomplish that which you are passionate about. That takes energy, and with work and family obligations, there doesn't seem to be any room for passions. Passions, for many, are relegated to the weekend at best and to retirement at worst. The bemusement comes from the thought that "I can't have passions, I'm busy and have a lot of things to do and a lot of responsibility." So passions are put on the back burner or forgotten altogether. That's the purpose of this Cairn: to reconnect, to raise your awareness and to clarify things that motivate you, things that raise your energy, things that amplify meaning in your life. When you show up to a job, an activity, or a relationship that you are passionate about, have a gift for, or possess strength in, you are greatly increasing your chances of living in the flow. Life has a renewed, and sometimes magnified, focus and energy.

To some, naming their passions also signifies responsibility—something else they have to devote energy to. If it is truly a passion, energy will flow on its own. The passion will bring life to the work, the home, and the relationship. You may have to devote some time to choosing how you will integrate it into your life. Usually people discover that their passions are connected in some way to their values. Sometimes it's hard to distinguish whether values are distilled from passions or passions distilled from values. Either way, once the passion is assimilated into what and how you do things, your actions seem to comfortably align with your values.

Usually passions stem from things that interest us, things that give us energy, feed our soul, light us up. They typically engage our strengths. But, they are different from interests. You'll have a chance to name both, but I am going to ask you to step a little outside your comfort zone and reflect on things that move you, that delight you, that give you a sense of joy, happiness, and contentment. And, if you feel brave, call them your passions. It certainly is a word that has a measure of energy in it. Dare to use the word with the energy it carries!

Now let's talk about strengths, another word that people are a bit shy about. When great organizations embark on a change effort, before they decide on a direction and set a vision, they take an inventory of the business. What are we doing well? What are our strengths? Where are we actually utilizing our strengths? What could we do better if we capitalized on our strong points? What could we accomplish if we connected with our passions and values? The best organizations ask the question, "What can we be the best at?" "What are our driving values?" "What passions, if we could call them forth on a consistent basis, would propel us to be a great company?"

To get at your strengths, these are the same kinds of questions to ask yourself. An analogy to consider is that you are your own organization and you are the CEO of You, Inc. You are in charge of the whole operation. You are the leader of You, Inc. How will you motivate yourself to be your best? What skills do you bring to the table? What challenges will you seek out? How will you develop the skills of self-leadership in order to accomplish your goals and realize your potential? What values would you choose to guide your organization? These questions establish an expectation of performance. They are the building blocks used to initiate performance values to distinguish your level of excellence. You are the leader. You choose.

Over time, we often lose touch with, overlook, or completely forget those areas of strength and passion, as well as the values that underlie our actions. We build our lives around external expectations rather than engaging our talents and strengths to command excellence. When I ask my clients and students to list their strengths, I often get blank, confused looks. Values, passions, and strengths are not areas on which we typically focus our attention. Many of our institutions, including schools, corporations, and youth sports organizations, focus on our weaknesses. For the most part, psychology focuses on pathology—what's wrong with us—instead of asking what's healthy about us and teaching us how to capitalize on that as a priority. The priority for many institutions and disciplines is to overcome, or eliminate, our weaknesses. This creates a culture of mediocrity. Very seldom are weaknesses turned into excellence. They are mostly brought to a level of manageability so they don't take us down.

Fine, let's manage our weaknesses so they don't derail us. But let's capitalize on what we do well—our strengths. If we were clear about our strengths and how to engage them in our lives, we would be moving in the direction of extraordinary. Our strengths usually come naturally to us. They are centered on things we enjoy, do well, and many times, have a passion for. Marcus Buckingham, coauthor of the national bestseller *First, Break All the Rules*, and Donald Clifton, chief designer of the StrengthsFinder and Chair of the Gallup International Research & Education Center, created a groundbreaking program to help people identify their talents and build them into strengths. They found that, when people were able to accomplish this over time and with practice, they enjoyed consistent, near-perfect performance. In their book *Now, Discover Your Strengths*, they found that people who were aware of and able to use their strengths at work were more engaged, happier, and more productive. Organizations who provided opportunities for employees to work in areas that exercised their strengths were able to retain the best people, show greater teamwork and creativity, perform at peak levels consistently, and had employees taking less time off due to illness. All of these had a positive effect on the bottom line of the organization.

Phil Jackson is a coach and a leader who understands the power of capitalizing on a person's strengths. Dennis Rodman, a professional basketball player, seemed to perplex other coaches. He acted out and made poor decisions on and off the court. He was not the productive athlete coaches expected. Why? The teams he had played for all wanted him to make lots of points. They wanted him to be a shooter. When he came to play with the Lakers, Jackson told him he didn't care how many points he scored. He wanted him to be strong "on the boards." Jackson gave him the opportunity to focus on his strength, rebounding. Rodman shined in this position and so did the team, going on to win the National Championship.

Another example is Tiger Woods, a top-level professional golfer. If Tiger had a weakness, it was his bunker play. He struggled to get out of the sand. So, he worked on his bunker game to the point that he could get out of the sand without costing him additional strokes. Tiger was never going to be excellent at sand play without devoting a good amount of practice to that aspect of the game. His goal was to bring his bunker play up to a manageable level so he didn't have to spend too many swings getting out of the sand. His strength was in his full swing and short game. That's where his coach wanted him to focus his practice time. That was the part of golf where Tiger excelled. Managing his weakness gave him more time to focus on his strengths and make his full swing excellent. So, yes, be aware of and manage your weaknesses so they don't derail you or take you too far off course. But you don't have to try to make them excellent. Buckingham's research confirmed that without a great deal of additional practice and time, you are probably not going to move a weakness to the same level of expertise as an identified strength. Focus on your strengths for excellence. And, the research from Gallup also indicated that engaging your strengths allows you to bring energy, passion, and confidence into the activity you are performing. A strength-based focus is more likely to lead people to thrive and live up to their potential, rather than just managing their lives so they don't fail.

We sometimes slip into default mode and go through our days without realizing that we are not living up to our potential. We act in default mode, mindless of how, or if, our actions align with our values and purpose. We may have taken on other people's, our organization's, or society's values without questioning whether they were an accurate fit for us. Now is the time to reflect on who you are in terms of passions, values, and strengths.

Before we move to Cairn VI, where you create your vision, it is important to take the time to highlight your strengths, passions, and interests. Your strengths are things you do well now as well as areas that you are strong in but might not be utilizing currently. You might have talents that you have forgotten about because your current position or environment doesn't call them into play. There may be things you enjoy doing, and do well, that you don't consider a strength. Sometimes we are actively engaged in an activity that we find enjoyable and fulfilling. We may be engaging a strength, but because we are so closely involved in the activity, we are not aware that it is a strength. But, that's why it feels so natural and enjoyable. It's a lot like being in a photo in a beautiful frame. Until we step out of the photo we are not aware of the frame. It's the same with a strength. Sometimes we are involved in performing with a strength but we are not aware it is a strength until it is pointed out to us.

To shed light on strengths and to offer a powerful way to name, define, and clarify one's personal strong points, I provide the book *StrengthsFinder 2.0* by Tom Rath for my clients. The book includes an online assessment that pinpoints your top five talents based on your responses to the questions; there are 34 strengths in all and your top five are listed in an extensive, individualized printout. The book clarifies that these are talents which, with practice, can be elevated to strengths. Many times, if we aren't allowed to utilize our talents, they lie dormant and never really become strengths we can count on. I have found it to be very accurate and my clients really enjoy the process and can thoroughly relate to the outcomes. Most of the time, my clients recognize them as strengths because they have had opportunity to use them and do consider them as a strong point. But, there have been instances where the client really didn't consider an identified talent to be a strength until further discussion and clarification. Either way, the client gained some clarity about why certain things seem to come easy, and if they had a talent that they didn't consider to be strong, they could spend time practicing until the talent developed into a strength.

I particularly appreciate the StrengthsFinder because it uses different words than we normally think of to name a strength such as Input, Connectedness, Activator, and Ideation to name a few. The book and assessment are based on psychological profiles conducted by Gallup with more than two million individuals. This was a 25-year, multimillion-dollar effort from Gallup to identify the most prevalent themes with thousands of combinations. The book also discloses how strengths can be translated into personal and professional success. Because there is such an extensive database, each result is individualized per strength based on responses, even if the same five strengths are listed. So if you and a colleague have the same five strengths listed in your result packet, the words to describe the strength for you and how you use it will be personalized to you and different from your counterpart with the same strengths. Once you have identified which five of the 34 themes you lead with, the book offers exercises and examples to show you how to leverage your specific strengths for powerful results at three levels: your individual development, your success as a professional, and how to put them to use for the success of your organization.

StrengthsFinder measures elements of your personality that are less likely to change as you get older. More and more research is suggesting that our strengths are housed in our core personality traits and remain solid over time. Recent scientific studies have discovered that the essence of our personality might be detectable at a younger age than was previously thought. A compelling study with 1000 three-year-old children in New Zealand revealed that over the course of 23 years these children's observable personality traits were incredibly similar to his or her personality traits when they reached the age of 26. Therefore, StrengthsFinder is based on elements of your personality that are less likely to change. It reveals your talents.

As we all know, talents can go undeveloped if we don't spend time developing and leveraging them. It takes knowledge, skills, and practice to turn a talent into a strength. For example, you may have a talent for music, but if you don't take lessons and actively refine your voice tone and quality, the talent won't be fully advanced. The results of the StrengthsFinder reveal your talents, and the most successful people start with a dominant talent and use their skills and knowledge to evolve the talent into a strength with practice. StrengthsFinder offers this equation to leverage a talent into a strength: Talent (something that comes naturally to you) + Practice (time invested in enhancing your skills, and expanding your knowledge) = Strength (the capability to perform at peak levels on a consistent basis).

The printout from StrengthsFinder has strategies for development and space to develop an Action Plan. My clients choose the talent they feel, if improved, would benefit them the most at the present time and we integrate specific strategies for development that fit with their situation into their Mindful Action Plan.

I would encourage you to invest in the StrengthsFinder as I have found it an accurate and valuable resource for my clients. However, at the end of this Cairn there are several questions that you can use to generate your own list of strengths. Whatever you choose, pick a strength and use your skills, knowledge, and practice to develop it to its fullest. Look at how and when you currently engage your strengths and then make a list of strategies you could implement to further your ability to consistently use that strength to perform at peak levels.

Knowing your strengths, passions, and values is a crucial aspect of engaging mindful living. It gives you a picture of the best you can be and engages your authentic self. Awareness of your strengths offers a reason to be optimistic in your ability to define your own journey—to successfully create the results you want and to distinguish what you deem successful. Clarity around strengths, passions, and values contributes to an intimacy with ourselves. This deeper and broader understanding of who you are and what you want to create for yourself and others continues to place the energy in your hands for determining your perspective and experiences in life. Having a defined understanding of your strengths also offers you the opportunity to establish performance values that have a greater possibility for success.

The final portion of this strategy is to identify your commitments, or obligations. These are things that you are compelled to do to maintain your lifestyle and meet your needs. Commitments are things that you may or may not have chosen. They might be enjoyable or they might be boring and mundane. But, they are things you are obliged to do, such as pay the mortgage, mow the lawn, clean the house, make out the roster for work, and arrange carpooling. You get my gist; they are things that you must do to carry on and preserve the life you are living.

When you can integrate your strengths with your commitments or acknowledge the passions that your commitments allow you to pursue, you can bring a different kind of energy to what used to seem like a boring project or obligation. In the activity section, you will also have an opportunity to name your commitments. The final step will be to decide whether you want to continue to maintain them in your life. You will choose certain commitments and say "Yes," I want to do these things in order to maintain the life I am creating. Through this process, you may realize that there are particular commitments that are not serving you. They don't fit with your values or purpose and really are a misuse of your energy. In that case, you can choose to discard the unnecessary commitments. This moves beyond good time management. It is an investment and an effective use of your energy.

If you maintain unnecessary commitments, you are taking time away from those commitments that engage your purpose and move you toward your vision. Nonessential commitments put a drain on your energy and time. They detract from other commitments that are aligned with your values. Removing these extraneous obligations enhances your focus and simplifies your life.

You may choose to continue to do the very things you have been doing. The point is you will have formally chosen to proceed as necessary. Choosing allows you to bring a more positive, optimistic energy to your commitments because you are acting from intrinsic motivation. The commitments you actively choose to continue to be involved in enable you to live your life along your guiding principles, to be self-directed. They are commitments that fit your values, purpose, and vision and generate a positive energy for living. Your values and purpose form a foundation for your life as guiding principles. They can be used much the same as a hiker uses a compass. They point you in the right direction as you create your life and they provide a path to get back on the right path when you lose your way. Acting from these guiding principles opens up the possibility for you to live a more authentic life, a life where your actions fit within the framework of your values and purpose. This creates a sense of wellbeing and fulfillment. Your passion and strengths provide a source of positive energy to your endeavors.

As we've discussed, your values and purpose are like your personal inner team. They are assets you can turn to for clarity, accountability, and support. They are always available to you as choice-points for effective decision-making. They serve as a compass along your journey. When you add your passions and strengths to the mix, the energy can become palpable. You are truly acting from your authentic self and moving in a self-directed fashion. With these intimate, yet mighty, companions by your side, you can move forward on your journey with confidence. You begin to trust that your experience will be one that involves self-direction, mastery, and purpose.

When you live according to your values, purpose, and vision, and engage your passion and strengths, it sometimes feels as if things are effortless and natural. This sense of ease has been called "flow." Mihaly Csikszentmihalyi, a psychologist and writer, initiated research into a state of being that seemed to transcend time, to feel effortless, which he named "flow." His original findings came from observations and interviews with athletes, but since have been related to any field of endeavor that entails a sense of purpose and passion. Csikszentmihalyi defined flow as "optimal experience, a state of concentration so focused that it amounts to absolute absorption in an activity." When we are in the state of flow, we feel strong, alert, and at the height of our abilities.

Often, when people speak of flow, they relate it to something beyond themselves. They talk about a sense of connectedness to patterns, a sense that their life seems to unfold without much effort. They talk about it seeming natural and being accompanied by a heightened sense of awareness and trust. They say they feel strong and powerful. This is because they are aligning their life with core values, leveraging their strengths, and living on purpose. Flow is a natural, effortless unfolding of our life, extending from our authentic self, moving us towards wholeness, fulfillment, and joy. When we implement our lives through self direction, mastery, and purpose, we enhance the capability for value-based actions, as opposed to emotion-driven,or rule-governed behavior. This opens the door for the experience of flow.

When are you in the flow? What kinds of experiences take you out of flow? At the end of this Cairn you'll find extra pages to complete. They are labeled CORE Evidence and provide space for you to record and describe experiences and activities that energize you as well as those that exhaust you. Combined with your purpose and values, strengths and passions provide another layer as you begin to design your MAP.

APPROACH

Rediscovering your authentic self requires awareness of several critical elements:

- What are your strengths?
- What are you passionate about?
- What are your guiding principles?
- What are your commitments and responsibilities?
- When do you experience flow?

PRACTICE

CORE QUESTIONS

Complete the following questions on the page provided at the end of this Cairn. You can use the questions as prompts to trigger a stream of consciousness and simply write what comes to mind. This is a form of journaling and can help bring clarity to the issue you're writing about.

My CORE Strengths

- What am I doing when people say, "Wow, you really do that well"?
- What do I think I am really good at?
- What do I think I could be the best at?
- What five strengths would get me started on my journey?

My CORE Passions

- If I were guaranteed success in any pursuit of my choosing, what would I go after?
- What fills me up? What contributes to feelings of joy? Happiness? Satisfaction?
- In what things do I invest positive and robust energy?
- What activities am I involved in when I experience a flow state where everything seems effortless and fully engaging?

- What gives me peace of mind?

- In the pursuit of my passions, what would a beautiful day be like?

My CORE Commitments/Responsibilities

Jim Collins was formerly a faculty member at Stanford University's Graduate School of Business and is now the principal of a management research firm in Boulder, Colorado. He and his team identified a cadre of elite companies that made the transition from "good to great" and sustained that ranking for at least 15 years. In his bestselling book *Good to Great*, Collins presents his research about what makes great companies different from just good companies. The primary question shaping the book was, "Can a good company become a great company and, if so, how?"

Relative to our discussion at this Cairn, one of Collins' predominate findings was that the best companies integrated their strengths and passions with a clear understanding of what they were obligated to do. The leaders within those great companies mindfully engaged their employees from the top down in areas where they were strong and showed a high degree of interest. By being given the opportunity to work in their areas of strength, the employees brought a higher level of commitment and engagement to their obligations on the job. When companies enabled their employees at all levels to pursue mastery in areas of strength and interest, there was a heightened sense of self-direction and everyone showed a greater willingness to do what needed to be done in pursuit of "great." It was apparent that employees were able to appreciate a purpose beyond self-interest and much more closely related to the vision of the company and fellow employees. This degree of collaboration, willingness, and focus shifted the company into a higher level of effectiveness and productivity. Those companies who explored and found ways to capitalize on their people's strengths, passions, and values were able to soar to great heights. They moved from good to great.

Another aspect of Good To Great relevant to our overall design and discussion throughout the CORE Journey is Collins' finding that the biggest enemy of great is good. That is one of the key reasons there are so few great companies. Collins writes:

"We don't have great schools, principally because we have good schools. We don't have great government, principally because we have good government. Few people attain great lives, in large part because it is just so easy to settle for a good life. The vast majority of companies never become great, precisely because the vast majority become quite good—and that is their main problem [...] is the disease of 'just being good' incurable?"

As the CEO of You, Inc., this is a question to ask yourself. You may very well have a good life. Are you satisfied with "just being good"? If so, that's okay. And, there will be some of you who want to take your company, your life, to "great." By honestly and thoughtfully engaging in the practices at this Cairn and throughout the book, you can take a good life and create a great life.

Moving from good to great doesn't just happen. It takes a conscious extension of focused energy. As the CEO of your life, you are the principal in charge of making your "company" great. You must pinpoint what your strengths are and how you can engage them on a consistent basis. What is your purpose and can you trust that your actions follow your purpose on a reliable basis? Do you consistently work at your very best? That's how we'll define mastery. Mastery is being able to engage your strengths and purpose on a sustainable basis when it's necessary and beneficial to move your life from good to great. And it's not a comparable enterprise. Your strengths are yours without judgment or comparison to others. They are valuable within the context of your goals, your values, and your purpose. Your charge is to recognize and engage them.

The last concept I want to discuss that allowed companies to move from good to great is the willingness to look at the hard facts. Each company who had set the intention of taking their business to number one had to take a hard look at the brutal facts of reality. Where were they and what would be necessary to move toward their vision? They chose to confront areas of responsibility and commitment and make sure that decisions involving those hard realities would be consistent with their values and vision.

There are also commitments you have that are unique to your life. The purpose of creating the life that you choose is not to necessarily change what you do or where you live or what you have. The purpose is for you to be mindful of your internal power to choose and to make sure your choices are consistent with your values and vision. You are enlisting an aspect of self-direction based on values that work for you within the context of your life. Now, this doesn't rule out that the actual possibility for change may be what works best for your desired outcome. As we move to future Cairns, we will address that possibility. To confront your brutal facts, you must look at areas in your life where you have responsibilities and commitments.

In your life, there are certain things that you must do. For example, you may have a mortgage, you may be saving for your children's college fund, you may be taking care of parents, or you might be paying off college loans. The purpose of these questions is to ensure that these undertakings are of your own volition. Not that you wished for them, but that you are making a mindful decision to engage in these responsibilities for the time being. To gain some clarity around your current commitments, answer the following questions:

- What have you chosen to do to maintain your current lifestyle? LRCCD
- What are things you are doing for others? Kids
- What are things you are doing for yourself? A STD/ DAC
- What are your financial obligations? 5
- What are your familial commitments? 5

Being the creative force in your life means taking responsibility for your life's story and how it unfolds. It allows you to be self-directed, pursue mastery, and live on purpose. It means making mindful decisions about how you spend your time and manage your energy. It means recognizing your strengths and expanding them and finding ways to engage your passions. It is about ensuring alignment of actions and values. Through the process of bringing these things to your awareness, you may discover things you have forgotten or let slide. Recognizing your strengths, connecting with your passions, and living by your values translate into a powerful commitment. It allows for an expression of your authentic self with mindfulness and value-based actions.

Naming Your Strengths

Previously, we discussed the origin and purpose of StrengthsFinder. At this stage of the coaching process, I give my clients the book and invite them to take the online assessment and study the results. As I've said, I have found StrengthsFinder to be an excellent source for helping people name, clarify and understand their strengths.

Earlier I mentioned that it's okay not to take the StrengthsFinder. If you've answered the questions above in the Practice section, you probably have a good idea of the areas where you excel and can name three to five strengths from your answers. Again, however you choose to clarify your strengths is fine. Do what you feel is the best way to clearly articulate your strong points.

APPROACH

To clarify and learn to engage your strengths, passions, and purpose in order to move from good to great.

PRACTICE

- Take the Strengths Assessment
- Choose a strength that would make you more productive, fulfilled, and happier if you found ways to use it more often.
- Track your progress

Let's Review

Cairn III: Values & Cairn V: Strengths, Passions, and Commitments

Listed below are some essential elements that make up your life's story. You might think of them as forming the outline of the story you would tell about yourself and your life. Is your story compelling? Is it interesting? Is it well-constructed, or hit-and-miss? Is it a story you, as a reader, would like to follow? Are you the author or just someone lending your name?

Now is your chance to ensure that the story you are telling about yourself is the one you want to be telling. Now is the occasion to create a story that is authentic, that brings into being your true self. Now is the time to make sure the story you are weaving works in moving you closer to your summit.

As you grow in your awareness and understanding of your story, be aware of any themes that repeat. This practice is a way to increase the clarity of the particular story you are telling about your life and whether it feels right to you. Does it incorporate your values, purpose, and vision? Looking at how you express your life inwardly, as well as openly to others, helps shed light on things that may be keeping you stuck—things that are not workable in terms of goals and aspirations. You truly are the author of your life and you can write a story that engages your full experience, your deepest fulfillment in life. Now, what kind of story do you want to tell? This practice will offer insight into the story, the life, you want to create and the vision you want to live into.

APPROACH

To explore and ensure your autonomy, mastery, and purpose.

PRACTICE

Craft a story using these elements as your guide:

- What interests you? Creating, pos psychol, mindfullnes, producti·
- What things are you passionate about? Same
- What contributions do you want to make to others, the community, the world? → 5 → ⬈
- What kinds of things are important to you? Family
- What do you believe in? Results, Productiv, Honesty
- How would you live into your potential? What would you be doing?
- What kinds of things do you want to accomplish in you life?
- What inspires you? Moves you? Calls you? Pulls you forward?
- What are you willing to take a stand for? Integrity/ Courage
- What things do you want to become better at? Auton, Earning
- Ask yourself within each question above, "For the sake of what?"
- Which values that you chose in Cairn II fit with each one of your answers?

  → Towards what end?
  ↳ What would X do for me?
  ↳ Result in?

Write each value and how it serves your answer.

- How do your answers embrace your vision?

REFLECT AND ENGAGE

- What are your CORE learnings from this Cairn?
- How will you apply these things in your life?
- What have you learned about yourself at this Cairn?
- Based on the practices at this Cairn, what will you do to expand your capacity and ability to be the creative force in your life?
- How will you celebrate the completion of this Cairn?

CORE Answers

Cairn VI

From Concept to Vision
An Invitation to Live Into Your Creation

"Throughout the centuries there were men who took the first steps down new
roads armed with nothing but their own vision."

—Ayn Rand

You have established a compelling energy for being the creative force in your life and named the strengths and passions you bring to the journey. You have reaffirmed the values that guide your actions. And you have clarified your central core or essence, your purpose, a dimension in your life that provides energy and direction. And, in the last Cairn, you clarified what you want to create and mindfully chose to bring specific results into being. Each one of these is a significant area in your life that can increase your motivation to act and can be used as a guidepost for decision-making in order to steer you in the right direction. Now you create your vision! Your vision expands your capacity to think about and plan your future with imagination and wisdom. In many ways your vision becomes the core of your story. It embodies the design and unfolding of your life.

Your vision is the future you desire to move toward, one that is inspiring, achievable, and draws you in. It is an image of the future that you champion as a self-determining principle. The vision will bring into play both your values and your purpose. As you sculpt your vision, it will help to clarify the behaviors that you want to strengthen and encourage as you realize your aspirations and goals. It will also illuminate behaviors that may hinder your forward movement toward your vision and therefore must be changed or eliminated.

The image of the future you desire is alive and dynamic, and as it unfolds it will provide a high-definition picture of the beliefs and behaviors required along the path for success. Your vision should have an emotional appeal and spark enthusiasm and excitement about your future. Your vision will highlight your strengths, passions, and values. It creates a measure of mastery. This allows you to be able to create an image that continues to be motivating and uncovers possibilities as you create your life.

A compelling vision also serves to provide resilience during times of slack and setbacks. Both anticipated and unforeseen obstacles will undoubtedly appear. We all go through setbacks from time to time. The value of holding a vision for yourself is its power to be a guiding light when you find yourself off the path momentarily. If, for some reason, you find yourself unfocused or confused, your vision helps you get back on your created path faster and illuminates the direction to follow. With a vision that you believe in and own in your heart and your head, you will have the enthusiasm needed to engage in the journey and the courage and optimism to persevere through the inevitable challenges along the way.

Shakti Gawain is an author and proponent of personal development. In her bestselling book *Creative Visualizations*, she discusses the power of seeing your vision as if it exists in the present moment. She says, "Imagining what you want as if it already exists opens the door to letting it happen." Designing a vision is founded in imagination. Imagination is the ability to create with our mind, to envision, to see the potential in a concept or idea. It is the ability to see with our mind's eye what we cannot see in reality, yet.

The process of creating begins in our mind. We begin to form a picture of what we want to create. At first you may not see anything. In fact, it may take a substantial investment of time and mental/emotional energy. After sitting with the idea, writing about the idea, or drawing the idea, an image begins to emerge. It is important to keep in mind that your vision may not be as clear as you would like, but over time it will become clearer and clearer. Don't wait until you can define your future with perfect clarity to begin to write it out or describe it. As you move toward your vision, some aspects of it may change, grow, and develop. That's not only okay—it's what will most assuredly transpire. The foundation, which comes from your purpose and values, will not change. But, you may refine the picture of your vision as you move toward it. It is not a question of having your vision written in stone, with complete clarity and definition. The bigger questions to ask are, "Will you know it when you see it?" "Will you know it when you have arrived at the destination you envisioned?"

I use this technique a lot when I work with athletes. I ask them to imagine themselves participating in their chosen sport. I encourage them to use all of their senses. See themselves, feel what it feels like, smell the smells that might be at their event—the wind, popcorn, what ever it may be—and hear the sounds of the event. The more senses you can bring to your imagination, the more "real" it will seem. The same concept can be applied no matter the endeavor. It works for executives, housewives, and salespeople. The approach in any situation is to involve all the senses in order to simulate "real" as closely as possible.

Let's take a moment to look at what I mean by "real." Our brain does not always know the difference between real and imagined. That's why scary movies really scare us even though we know we are sitting in a theatre watching a movie on a screen. It's why when we are mowing the lawn and we see a curvy stick move out of the corner of our eye, we suddenly jump thinking it's a snake. It's why we can think about a special occasion that brought us tremendous joy and we get goose bumps or tears all over again. It's also why the power of our imagination can be used to successfully train people to develop a skill without even practicing the specific movement involved in the skill.

For example, there was a study done in the 1980s with three groups of basketball players from the same team to experiment with which technique brought the highest percentage increase in free throw shooting. The first group physically practiced shooting free throws every day after practice. The second group did not practice free throws at all. And the third group visualized themselves shooting free throws successfully after practice, but didn't touch a real ball. Each group did the same practice everyday following their formal practice for three weeks. Which group do you think improved their free throw shooting percentage the most?

Well of course, because we are talking about the power of our mind, you naturally think the third group. You are correct. The group who didn't practice at all didn't show improvement. The second group who actually physically practiced the skill showed about a 2% increase, but interestingly, under pressure in a real game, they didn't shoot free throws any better than before. However, the third group significantly raised their free throw percentage and was able to make more free throws during competition than they had prior to their visualization practice.

I could give numerous examples like this. Visualization is used in business for salespeople to simulate successful sales calls. Public speakers, leaders, and politicians are taught to use these visualization techniques to "see" themselves giving inspirational deliveries to a difficult audience. It is used to help injured athletes so they won't experience a complete lack of training while they are recovering from their injury. It is used successfully in education to teach students who have a fear of taking tests to imagine themselves answering all the questions in a calm manner, correctly. Visualization is also used to teach people how to relax as well as how to energize. We will talk in specifics about actual techniques for you to practice in a later Cairn on Energy Management. Suffice to say for now that our brains can be powerful and positive tools when we know how to visualize successfully.

How clear does your imagination have to be? It needs to be clear enough that you would recognize the result when it happened. For example, if you decided you wanted to buy a house: you might begin with a general concept of how many square feet and how many rooms you want. You may have a general idea of the exterior you prefer. You might think about how much you want to spend and the location where you would like to live. You might have an idea that you want trees, and that you also want a bright house with lots of natural light. You might want a fireplace, a pool, a spa. You have a result in mind but at the same time you do not have a clear vision of what a house like this might look like. But, as we all know, when you walk into the house you want, you know it. And, there might be things about the house that you like that you didn't know you wanted.

It is much the same when conceptualizing and beginning to formulate your vision. The concept will get clearer and clearer as more specifics come to your mind. The process of designing a vision is moving from the general, the concepts you created at the last Cairn, to the specific, your picture of what you want to create. In the "conceive and conceptualize" process, you were asked to play around with the ideas you might want to create. You dealt with a variety of possibilities, and then you narrowed those down to the ones you actively chose. That is a formative part of the process of creating.

At this Cairn, you move from the general concepts to the specific vision for a specific concept. The focus changes from broad to narrow. As we discussed previously, as you design your vision you are actually limiting your possibilities, creating an intentional focus. This all aids in the decision-making process when choices arise that could throw you off course. Moving from the general to the specific is a powerful part of the creative process. You are harnessing energy.

The next thing to realize and embrace is that there is no right or wrong way for you to create. Remember, you are involving self-direction and mastery. How you proceed in the creative process is based on your strengths, preferences, values, and the results you have chosen to have in your life. You will learn from experimenting. Yes, there is a general path—particular techniques to follow that have proven successful. And, over time you will discover and follow your own path. You will learn how to maneuver the specific practices into your own unique approach. The process is not what works. You are what works. Your energy, personality, and self-awareness is what enlivens your success. You are becoming an expert on what is distinct about how you create. You are mastering your process of creating, which means you are learning how to engage the creative process on a consistent basis, ensuring that you have a life that is self-directed. The path that evolves your sense of autonomy, mastery and purpose is the only one of importance and relevance to your life of creating what is fulfilling and joyful for you.

APPROACH

Where do you want to go? Your vision is both your destination and your journey. It is something solid in your life that you can call on whenever you need direction or guidance. It becomes your guiding light, your lighthouse. You are designing the vision of the life you see yourself living. It is how you envision yourself as a human being. It is the story you author for yourself.

Your vision is an inspiration for your legacy, your purpose and your values, and creates a foundation for your journey. It allows you to see and create possibilities for contributions that align with your purpose. It provides you with a solid sense that you are learning and growing into a life you have created for your fulfillment, joy, and desire to live a meaningful life. Your vision allows for autonomy, mastery, and purpose, three things that have been shown to enhance meaning and joy in one's experience of living.

Whatever you see as being the exceptional experience that you want to design and actualize, this is your vision and it sets the path for your journey.

It yields an energy for you to create the self that you are at your core. Its function is similar to a compass serving to keep you on the path and enabling you to guide yourself back if you stray. And, it is yours and yours alone. Your vision emanates from your purpose and values, and therefore you might say it is a way to bring about your authentic self.

PRACTICE

1. Create a clear vision with the help of these three questions:

    a. What will your life, your thoughts and feelings, your beliefs, and your behavior, look like once your outcome is achieved?

    b. How will you describe the transformation?

    c. What will others say about you once the transformation has been achieved?

2. Imagine. Draw. Write. Visualize. Discuss. Putting it on paper will bring clarity to who you are creating through your vision.

3. Continue to refine your vision to the point that, when you read it out loud to yourself, it grabs you and creates a powerful pull from deep within your being. It should be short and clearly written. You should be able to state and explain it in a short elevator ride.

4. You might begin by stating, "When I have realized my vision, people will be…" For example, one of my clients completed the statement, "People will be maximizing their potential in their chosen field of endeavor." His purpose was to motivate and inspire people to work toward their potential. His vision was seeing everyone realizing his or her potential in a fulfilling career.

REFLECT AND ENGAGE

- What are your CORE learnings from this Cairn?

- How will you apply these things in your life?

- What have you learned about yourself at this Cairn?

- Based on the practices at this Cairn, what will you do to expand your capacity and ability to be the creative force in your life?

- How will you celebrate the completion of this Cairn?

When I realize my vision I will be autonomously (not Los Rios) earning a great livity in a creative, innovative, and enjoyable business I created a guide to ~~greatness~~ self-sufficiency.

– feel sense of accomplishment – that I've worked @ a group to ___ & ___ a ___ .

Why this instead of inside Los Rios.

– ↓ of respect for leadership
– sense of lack of courage & fairness shown

∴ Create something that is ___ ___

~~Create a~~ I am part of a group that ~~solves~~ transforms groups & organizations by showing them the keys (how & why) to allow their ~~people~~ to do their best. (Ugh!

(again)

The CORE Journey

Phase 2
Chart Your Course

The Cairns and practices in this phase are about charting your course to your summit. You begin by checking in with reality to clarify what your life is right now. Your current reality and where you want to go or what you want to create in your life may not be the same. There are probably gaps. This phase introduces a practice to close the gaps between where you are and where you want to be. Then you design your Mindful Action Plan, your distinctive MAP to your summit.

You will encounter obstacles along the path. An integral part of this phase is identifying and evolving past limiting beliefs and actions. The practices in this phase will build your ability to trust that your future is open to what you want to create. You will learn how to live into your desired future rather than having the future already created for you by your past. Once again, you are taking control through self-direction, mastery and purpose toward a fulfilling life experience.

Cairn VII

Interrogating Your Reality

"Toto, I've a feeling we're not in Kansas anymore."

—Dorothy in *The Wizard of Oz*

Once you have your vision in place, the next step is to take a look at where you are right now. This part of the process is left out of many programs designed to help you achieve results. In almost any process for growth and development, the best approach is to start with an accurate description of what an individual's current reality is.

When you go to MapQuest for directions for a trip you are going to take, the first thing you are asked to enter is your starting location. The process is similar when you are preparing to begin the ascent to your summit vision. Before you embark on your journey, you must know your starting point. Where are you currently?

The same process is used when athletes want to improve a skill. Before starting to work with them, the coach will watch them perform in order to assess what the athlete's current skill level is. For example, when I wanted to improve my backhand in tennis, my coach would warm up by hitting a number of balls to my backhand to see how I was hitting the ball, what my form looked like, how consistent I was, what my footwork looked like, and so forth. She wanted an accurate picture of my current skill level before we began to initiate any change.

This is the best way to begin for a couple of reasons. First, it gives you a reference point from which to begin. A reference point offers an opportunity to see exactly what needs to be done to set off in the right direction. A reference point also makes it possible to take a broader perspective. It gives you the ability to look around in all directions and choose the most efficient and direct route to your destination.

Second, it provides a way to measure progress. Defining reality is an ongoing process throughout the journey. At each milestone along the way, you can stop and reassess your progress, make sure you are still on the right path, and make adjustments when necessary.

By designing your vision and defining reality, you have identified the gap between where you currently are and where you want to be. In engineering, this gap is known as a state of disequilibrium. It sets up a tension, which invites resolution. Robert Fritz called this tension "structural tension," describing the variance between the vision and current reality. Fritz developed tools and techniques he felt to be essential to navigate the trail from reality to vision. He is the author of *The Path of Least Resistance: Learning to Become the Creative Force in Your Own Life*. Fritz's most astounding finding is that once an individual chooses to be self-directed and become the primary creative force in his or her life, they are changed forever: possibilities unfold, accomplishments spawn other accomplishments, and their vision for their life seems to flow without effort. Once you make a conscious choice to change your life and then mindfully engage your values and purpose, things begin to fall into place to make that happen. This is the resolution of structural tension.

I've experienced the process of structural resolution in my own life. There have been instances when I made a decision to do something and doors began to open with very little effort on my part. You may also be acquainted with that same sort of event, when things just seem to fall into place after you set an intention. That's exactly what Fritz is talking about when he talks about structural tension and resolution. In discussing this concept with my sister Renee, a mechanical and nuclear engineer, she confirms that tension seeks resolution.

The structural tension that exists between your desired end state, your vision, and your current reality generates action. It supplies an orientation and direction for organizing your action steps and it also yields positive energy for essential motivation. In the beginning, there is a disparity between your starting point and your ending point. As you move closer to your vision, the discrepancy is reduced. When you are successful at creating your vision, the chosen state and your current state are the same. The tension is resolved.

A simple example of structural tension is thirst. Your body wants water. The difference between being thirsty and being satiated with enough liquid to satisfy the thirst sets up a tension—to drink. You find water and you drink until you have quenched your thirst. Another example: say I want to play classical guitar. I want to be able to sit down with a piece of classical music and read the notes so I can play the piece. My current reality is that I have a guitar. I cannot read music, but I do have a teacher. My vision and my current reality are different. There is structural tension. The resolution comes from engaging in lessons one time a week and practicing in between lessons. As I learn to read the notes and play more and more advanced pieces of music, the tension is resolved. Who knows, someday my current reality may be what I have set as my vision.

There is one more thing about structural tension. It may seem a bit mysterious, but I have experienced it myself and I observe it with my clients. When you have tension between your vision and where you currently are, it creates energy. Some would call it serendipity. It seems like things start to happen that you would not have predicted. You meet that certain someone who can help you on our journey. You read an article in a magazine you typically don't read that has an insight into what you are trying to accomplish. You pick up a book off the shelf that you haven't thought of for a long time and turn to just the right page and read something that triggers ideas and actions. I see and experience this kind of happening all the time. In fact, that's exactly what my mom and dad call such events when they are traveling: "a happening."

So, define where you are now compared to what you want to create—your vision. The challenge is to carefully define your current existence as accurately as possible. It's basically about describing what's going on in your life right now. What commitments have you chosen that must stay in place? Interrogate your reality as it is now. This will provide an accurate assessment of where you are starting from on the journey to your summit.

Then, make a list of what you would add to your current reality that would bring it in line with the vision you've designed for your life. Think of all the things we have already discussed. Consider your values and how they relate to your vision. What strengths can you draw on right now to move you toward your goals? In what areas might you need to enhance your skills or acquire new skills? What are you passionate about but not participating in? Carefully consider what would be instrumental to enhance your experience of a fulfilling life. What is it that you would like to experience in order to thrive? There's a space to record this at the end of this cairn.

APPROACH

- Accurately define your current reality.
- Clearly describe each compass according to how it would look if the arrows pointed to north.
- Initiate the structural tension that will seek resolution.

PRACTICE

1. To clarify your current reality and make it visible, let's look again at the CORE Journey Compasses. At Cairn I, you established a compelling energy by filling in each compass with words that described and defined each specific domain of your life. You then ranked how important those values were to you in your current reality and also how well you engaged each quality in your life.

2. At the end of this Cairn you are provided journaling space with two specific prompts to complete this Practice. For each compass describe your life within each domain as it is currently. Write what you are doing and how you see yourself within that specific aspect of your life at this time.

3. Next, according to the vision that you designed at the previous Cairn, list things you want to add that you feel would make you more fulfilled in that area of your life. In other words, for each compass, describe what your life would look like for that domain if each of your rankings were 10 and the needle, or arrow, pointed due north.

4. In the box on the "W" side of each compass write the number between 1 (low) and 10 (high) that represents your satisfaction with

your current reality. In the box on the "E" side of the compass write the number between 1 (low) and 10 (high) that will represent your level of satisfaction when you have been successful at adding your chosen pieces.

The practice of interrogating your reality as accurately and openly as possible is the entry point to establishing structural tension. This tension is intensified as you describe what you will add to enhance this area of your life. This combined effort initiates the structural tension that will seek resolution. The structural tension will become more taut at Cairn VIII, when you design your MAP—your Mindful Action Plan, which will lead you to the summit, the vision, that you created.

As you grow in self-direction and continue to pursue mastery, you will evolve. Your core values may not change, but how you engage those values may shift. You may change the things you want to add half way up the mountain. That's okay. Sometimes we choose to take a different route. That's okay. The point is to continue to adjust your compass to point to true north and adjust your route to ensure it leads to your summit—your vision. This practice is a skill that you can continue to use to create your life now and as you grow and change.

PERSONAL GROWTH

☐ [compass dial: N, E, S, W] ☐

My current reality in this domain is…

I feel like I am awlays "working" on personal growth though without a firm plan.

To create my vision of a fulfilling life, I would add…

1) A real/regular/disciplined mindfullness or sitting practice.

2) A one, two, three, four, five & six year runnin P.G plan

FINANCES

☐ [compass dial: N, E, S, W] ☐

My current reality in this domain is…

Our finances get us by. We our fortunate to be above the median mark & can handle expenses for the most part.

To create my vision of a fulfilling life, I would add…

Know the numbers, stick to a budget & be actively planning for more down 65, 70, 75, 80, 80+

LEISURE

My current reality in this domain is…

I don't take the time, to include leisure in my schedule. Fun things for me individually or @ Mona.

To create my vision of a fulfilling life, I would add…

Find one or more (1+) Individual leisure activity & (1+) for Mona & me that would give me/us pleasure & add to a meaningful life (exercise, beauty, discovery, +++)

HEALTH

My current reality in this domain is…

Pretty good, decent diet, exercise, & weight

To create my vision of a fulfilling life, I would add…

Be at (175/180), ↓ alcohol, cleaner diet & regular exercise & low BP/ chlor…

CAREER

My current reality in this domain is…

Feeling confident & fairly successful in my career, know what I'm doing (for most part) aiding others to succeed

To create my vision of a fulfilling life, I would add…

Take autonomous control of my career to start an independent practice by 66.

HOME ENVIRONMENT

My current reality in this domain is…

Nice home, wonderful relationship w. Mona, but need for more organization & frankly need to take control of beauty in & outside of house

To create my vision of a fulfilling life, I would add…

Beautiful yet simple affordable house in & outside, paint/art/repair (in) & clean, no-clutter junk out

COMMUNITY & ENVIRONMENT

My current reality in this domain is…

My community is my work
or consultant community but 4

To create my vision of a fulfilling life, I would add…

?

FAMILY RELATIONSHIPS

My current reality in this domain is…

Good @ Mona except S, &
time for leisure as easter Cairn,
With each I, E, B there is
a good base relationship

To create my vision of a fulfilling life, I would add…

1So find time for leisure @ Mona
& for each child have One Goal working
all the time
    I - listen/encourage/ talk!
    E - encourage/listen
    B- stay tuned-in

INTIMATE RELATIONSHIPS

My current reality in this domain is...

Earlier stated but need for ↑ S w Mom in order to maintain a strong relationship

To create my vision of a fulfilling life, I would add...

SOCIAL RELATIONSHIPS

My current reality in this domain is...

Need more friends - limited...

To create my vision of a fulfilling life, I would add...

Add an activitie(s) liesure that would add group of friends

REFLECT AND ENGAGE

- What are your CORE learnings from this Cairn?
- How will you apply these things in your life?
- What have you learned about yourself at this Cairn?
- Based on the practices at this Cairn, what will you do to expand your capacity and ability to be the creative force in your life?
- How will you celebrate the completion of this Cairn?

Cairn VIII

Mindful Action Plan
Designing your MAP

"The best way to predict your future is to create it."

—Various forms attributed to Abraham Lincoln,

computer scientist Alan Kay, and playwright Molière

Now you're ready to design and implement your Mindful Action Plan, your map to guide you to your summit. This is the step that creates the structural tension that generates action. It is where you take the ideas you generated in Phase One, devise SMART goals, and execute your plan. SMART goals are defined below in the Approach section. *SMART* stands for Specific, Measurable, Attainable, Relevant, and Time-bound. Similar to a road map, you can use your MAP to indicate your starting point, your destination, and the most desirable path to follow to reach your summit. It allows you to chart your course and provides you the capability to monitor your progress. If necessary, it gives you the possibility to change directions or adjust the speed at which you are traveling. It is your ultimate organizational tool, outlining precisely how to move toward realizing your vision.

This is also an instrument you can use to create confidence and a solid sense of optimism that you have the power to conceive and achieve your best life. It helps maintain focus on your priorities and it is a visual and experiential reminder of the life you want to create. It is a living document and you will refer to it and update it as you realize each goal. During your journey, your MAP will be your avenue to create short-term successes to acknowledge and celebrate.

When you design your MAP, you are making a conscious choice to set the direction and path to your vision. In business, they say that if you don't know where you want to go, someone will gladly decide for you. Your MAP is your ultimate creation tool; it will lead to optimal performance because you are merging the energy and strength of your head and your heart. You are engaging self-direction, mastery, and purpose.

APPROACH

- Prioritize your compasses.
- Formulate and action plan. Design your MAP.
- Establish large goals.
- Construct SMART goals.
- Continue to feel the structural tension.

PRACTICE I

In the previous cairn you interrogated your current reality and chose what you would like to add in order to enhance your fulfillment, satisfaction and happiness for that compass. Now let's place your compasses in priority order. In this Practice you are provided with a blank mountain with cairns. This is where you place your compasses in the order you think best to work your way to your overall summit, or life vision. I've provided an example. This continues the process of establishing structural tension.

1. At the top of the blank mountain in this Practice, fill in the vision that you created at Cairn VI. I've provided an example.

2. At base camp, at the bottom of the mountain, describe your current reality in general—how your life is now.

3. Establish the path you will take to the mountain's summit by placing each of the compasses in the order that you feel will be the best approach to reaching the top. Choose which compass you will work on first, second, and so on in order for your vision to come to fruition.

   You may actually end up working on several compasses at once, but for now place them in the order that you think will most benefit you as you work toward your vision. Give them a priority. In other words, if you think working on your health first, your romantic relationship second and your work third would provide the most benefit, or biggest bang for your buck, so to speak, toward creating the life you want, then place them on the mountain in that order.

   Each part of your life has an effect on the other parts. As you work on your health, it will have an effect on your work, your relationships, and so forth. Priority doesn't mean you'll only be working on that partcular compass. It simply provides a way of managing your time and energy.

4. See and feel the structural tension created by the differences between your summit vision and base camp.

5. Now you are ready to set your large goals and formulate SMART goals for each compass to move you toward your summit—your vision. You'll continue to design your Mindful Action Plan in Practice II.

Life Map

Vision

I am leading a life that is fulfilling at work, loving at home, peaceful with myself, and able to see family at will and travel comfortably.

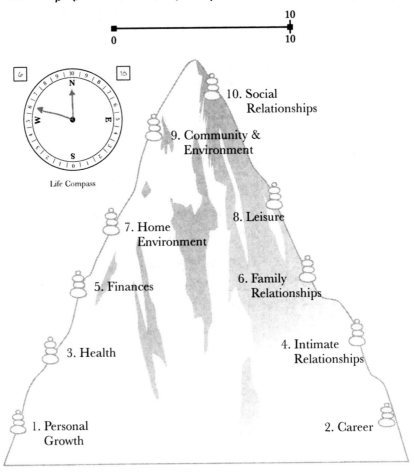

10. Social Relationships

9. Community & Environment

Life Compass

8. Leisure

7. Home Environment

6. Family Relationships

5. Finances

4. Intimate Relationships

3. Health

1. Personal Growth

2. Career

Base Camp

Fullfilled home life; creating my business; active; missing family; learning; growing; not satisfied totally

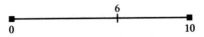

Life Map

Vision

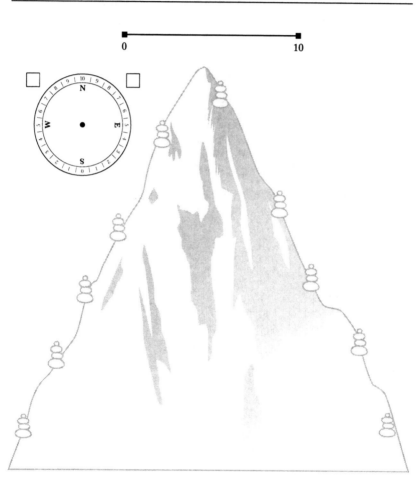

Base Camp

SMART goals are a well-organized and systematic way of managing your activities and plans. Business author Ken Blanchard popularized SMART goals in his bestselling book *Putting the One Minute Manager to Work*. Let's see how it works.

Specific. Your goals must be precise and explicit. For example, "I want to spend more time with my partner" is not specific. This might be an essential element you listed, but to turn it in to a specific goal, write, "I will be home on time three nights during the week to have dinner with my partner." This is specific. It lets you know exactly what you need to do and provides a definite way to know whether you have accomplished that goal. Afterward, you can evaluate whether your current goal is enough, or whether, for example, you want to increase the number of nights.

A specific goal usually answers the "W" questions:
- What: What do I want to accomplish?
- Why: Specifically, what is the purpose or benefit of realizing this goal?
- Who: Who is involved?
- Where: In what location do I work on this goal?
- Which: Identify requirements and obstacles.

Measurable. If you can't measure it, how will you know when you have achieved success? Measurability lets you know how far along you have come and how much further you need to go. It helps to keep you motivated. "Three nights a week" and "on time" are measurable.

- How much?
- How many?
- How will I know when I have reached this goal?

Attainable. Goals must be realistic or you will lose motivation and set them aside. They should also inspire you to stretch your limits beyond your normal ways of doing and being. Goals work much the same way strengthening a muscle works. If we don't stretch the muscle beyond what it normally can accomplish, it atrophies. We get bored. If we work the muscle too hard, we can injure ourselves. We lose motivation. We get anxious. When you identify goals that align with your values and purpose, it should motivate you to act and push beyond your comfort zone. When you identify goals that align with your values and purpose—goals that are important to you—you figure out ways to attain them. You develop the attitude, abilities, and skills necessary to reach them. Sometimes we have to enlarge our financial capacity or will. Theory shows us that goal-setters who set attainable goals sometimes identify previously overlooked opportunitites that when realized, may bring them closer to the ultimate vision.

You may want to be home for dinner with the family every night of the week, but your current position requires you to work some evenings. Your goal to be home a certain number of evenings per week should be within reach. Otherwise it will produce anxiety. Goals should stretch you, but they should also be realistic.

An attainable goal will usually answer the question:
- How: How can I accomplish this goal?

Relevant. Each goal you set should be aligned with your values, purpose and vision. It needs to support your efforts in living your purpose. Your goals should be based on the life you have chosen to evolve into. They should neither be based on others' expectations of you, nor on the life other people think you should be living. You must set goals that will propel you toward your desired summit.

A relevant goal has the answer "yes" to these questions:
- Is this worthwhile?
- Is this the right time?
- Does this meet your needs and align with your values?
- Is this goal moving me toward my vision?

Time-bound. You are busy and life has a way of taking over your day. If your goals are just in your head and not written, or if they do not have a timeline, they get pushed to the back burner, or worse, set aside completely. Dreams can assist in creating a vision. Goals with timeliness assist in making those dreams a reality. They give you a measure of progress. Time-bound goals are a way to establish short-term success and provide the occasion to appreciate and celebrate accomplishment.

- When will I reach this goal?
- What can I do 6 months from now to progress?
- What can I do 6 weeks from now to progress?
- What can I do today to get started?

SMART Goal Example:

Step	Goal	Better Goal
Specific	I want to impact people's lives.	I want to plan educational workshops and programs for adults.
Measurable	I want to do well in my certification class.	I want to learn about the model and how to apply it in my workshop.
Attainable	Earn my law degree within a year.	I want to earn my law degree within 3 years from passing the LSATS.
Relevant	I want to thoroughly review all the research on health in the last 10 years.	I will spend time researching the most recent and impactful work on health and aging within my current scope of practice.
Time-bound	I will earn my certification.	I will earn my certification in 3 weeks online with help from my coach.

Practice II

The compasses you completed at the last cairn are your guides to the summit of your mountain. They not only define the path, but also keep you true to it. They will be helpful as you progress toward the summit to motivate you, help you monitor the direction you're heading in, and help to get you back on the right path more quickly if for some reason you get sidetracked.

Planning hikes and backpacking excursions entails breaking the trek into manageable parts. You plan how far you will travel each day, when you will rest, and where you will spend the night. You also take into consideration parts of the trail that may require a slower pace, for example going over a pass, traversing obstacles and barriers that may require adjusting your route, or descending a particularly steep, rocky trail. Breaking the mountain into segments serves several purposes, from offering a way to manage and renew energy, to offering visible means of measuring progress. As you ascend and successfully traverse each portion of the mountain, your confidence and trust expands. You can see and feel the summit growing nearer and nearer.

Each compass represents a particular section of the mountain, a specific domain or area of your life that must be integrated into your MAP in order to realize your overall vision. You'll want to address and manage each area of your mountain in order to reach your summit. You've just completed the first step in designing your MAP by placing your compasses in the order in which you want to begin to make the necessary adjustments and changes that you named in the previous Cairn to enhance your fulfillment and happiness in that area of your life. The things you listed for each compass are what you deemed important for a full, rich and meaningful life, and they will help establish the goals for that particular section.

Now, the next step is to develop goals for each compass. Accomplishing your goals helps bring that compass, that area of your life, more in line with your vision. As you complete each goal, the structural tension becomes less as you bring your life more in balance with your desired future. Just like following the cairns when you're hiking in the wilderness leads to the summit, completing goals leads you to your summit, your vision.

Remember, each compass signifies a segment of your mountain. Listing overall large goals and dividing those into SMART goals for each compass is like taking a telescopic view of the particular section of the mountain you are climbing. By separating each segment, or compass, you get a clear picture of what that part of the path looks like and what you need to do to move successfully through that area of the mountain on your way to the ultimate summit—your vision for your life. As you work your way through each section of your MAP, that particular compass serves as your true north, keeping you on the right path by working on the goals you set for that section of the mountain. Your overall MAP creates the perfect visual of your actual path so you can monitor and see your advancement through the individual segments, moving you closer to the top of the mountain.

Let's get started breaking each segment, or compass, down into overall large goals and then dividing each larger goal into SMART goals. At the end of this Cairn, you are provided with a page that has a blank mountain for you to complete. This is your telescopic view of this section of the mountain. Remember, each compass represents a sharper image of that segment that you are working on at the moment. It's a way to hone in to that area. Assign a compass for each blank mountain. In the mountain, place your goals in the order you want to accomplish them to bring about the significant changes you want in that part of your life. These are your overall large goals for that compass or area of your life. They're basically the things you listed as things you want to add in order to enhance that area of your life.

For example, every blank mountain will have a Base Camp, which is where you write in your current reality for that compass. The telescopic view page will also have a place for you to write in your purpose for that domain. In other words, how you'd like this area of your life to look to be fulfilling. And, there will be Cairns placed on the mountain. Each segment will vary in its number of cairns depending on how many goals you have, or things you'd like to add. You will follow the same steps for each compass that you did with your life MAP in the previous Cairn. You'll write in where you are starting from in the Base Camp section, where you are going in that area of your life in the Purpose section, and along the way you'll build cairns where you list the large goals that you want to complete to help reach the summit of that particular compass MAP.

For each cairn, or overall goal that you built in the mountain section, you'll now divide that large goal into SMART goals. The SMART goals establish the specifics you'll need to reach the larger goal. You are provided with a space on the mountain to list the SMART goals for each larger one. As you design your SMART goals, take into consideration all the skills and tools we have discussed so far. The more you engage your strengths, passions, and values along the way, the more energy you will bring to the journey and the more likely you will be to produce successful results in a timely fashion. Once you have designed each individual compass section, review the whole MAP once more to ensure that your large goals and your SMART goals are consistent with your values, purpose, vision and commitments.

It's best not to work on all compasses at once. You have prioritized your compasses in the order that you think will be the best way to move you forward toward your vision. This will help you manage your time and energy, so stick to your priority as closely as possible. As previously stated, some compasses will have more cairns than others. Some compasses may be complete as they are with nothing to place as a cairn except to continue on the path you are already on. That's fine. You may add things at a later date. You may get to a certain point and realize that you want something completely different than what you first listed within that compass.

Less is more. Don't get carried away and tackle so many cairns at once that you get overwhelmed. As I said before, the compasses are distinct areas of your life, but working on one will have an effect on other compasses. So you may find yourself working on a goal at one compass and also working on a goal at a completely different compass. That's okay. Some goals in the various compasses will overlap with each other. Once you begin setting and working toward your goals, you'll get a feel for which goals needs to be tackled next. You'll also get a feel for how many cairns/goals you can tackle at one time. Go easy so you don't get overwhelmed and feel like giving up. Be gentle with yourself. Move deliberately. You don't have to think of it as moving slowly, but instead moving with purpose. Trust your intuition. Continue to address your goals. The important thing is to persevere and try to do at least one thing each day that contributes a positive move toward your summit. And don't forget to acknowledge and celebrate when you reach a goal. I suggest not tackling more than two cairns at one time.

Significant to ensuring perseverance with your MAP and reaching your summit is building in short-term celebrations. These are up to you. They represent important milestones on your journey. Sometimes your vision is a two-or three-year journey. Short-term celebrations indicate that you are making progress, serve to keep you motivated, and can reenergize you to push for the next milestone.

They also demonstrate success to your team. The next Cairn is about building the team that will be affected in some way by the journey on which you are preparing to embark. The team you assemble is for support and encouragement, and they can also serve to hold you accountable. Your team will be for you what you determine you want a team to be. The thing to remember is that those close to you will be affected by your journey and you must communicate the changes and growth you are experiencing. We will discuss all the valuable and necessary aspects of forming the right team in the following Cairn. And, if there is anyone who is skeptical about what you are doing or your ability to persevere, short-term celebrations are evidence to the contrary.

As you complete them, you choose which Cairns are events that warrant a celebration. And you can choose to have members of your team join you in marking a milestone. Build the celebrations into your timeline. They can be anything you feel is celebratory, from treating yourself to frozen yogurt to taking your partner out to dinner to taking an afternoon off to do something fun for you.

The final question to ask yourself as you set your goals is, "For what purpose?" Richard Strozzi-Heckler at the Strozzi Institute, a company whose mission is to "produce leaders and teams that embody pragmatic wisdom, skillful action and grounded compassion," emphasizes the question, "for the sake of what?" For the sake of what can be translated as "so that..." For example, "I want to improve my ability to be mindful so that... I can be present to others for the purpose of enriching the relationship." It solidifies the reason and purpose for your goal and activates positive energy. At the top of the MAP for each specific compass, there is a place to write your overall purpose for that specific area of your life. It should align with the overarching purpose you established at Cairn II—the purpose you chose to stand for in your life as a whole.

As you complete the goals/Cairns for each compass, you can look at your main MAP and visualize your journey up the mountain. Of course, as you complete specific goals within a compass, you may start on another goal for that same compass. It doesn't mean you're standing still in that region of the mountain. You have to see it as moving up the mountain section by section, with each section moving you closer to the summit, your overall life vision. It's just like hiking each day to your destination campsite. Sometimes you go up in altitude and other days you descend to a lower altitude to acclimate. You are still working your way to the summit. That's how it is with goals. You complete a goal and start anew with another goal that keeps you moving onward and upward.

Let's look at an example of a telescopic view of a specific compass. Following the example, you'll find the blank telescopic views for you to design to complete your MAP.

Health

Purpose:
Functional Longevity: pursuing hobbies, able to fully paritcipate in life

Cairn V :: Stress Management
- Meditation 1 to 20 mins daily
- Tai Chi 2 times a week

Cairn IV :: Hydration
- drink 60-90 ozs water a day

Cairn III :: Sleep
- 7-8 Hours a night

Cairn II :: Activity
- Peak Eight - 3 times a week
- Strength Training - 2 times a week
- Distance Run - 1 time a week for 30-50 minutes

Cairn I :: Nutrition
- Eating healthy foods (greens, fruits, vegetables)
- Vitamins (Omega 3s, multivitamins, Co-Q10)
- Cooking at home
- Keeping up on nutrition information and research

Base Camp (current reality)
I eat pretty well, but I want to know more about nutrition so I can upgrade my diet. I only run distance—no strength or resistance. I meditate 1 to 5 minutes twice a week

Personal Growth

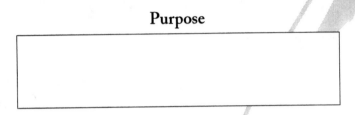

Purpose

Base Camp (current reality)

Finances

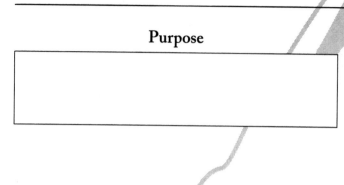

Purpose

Base Camp (current reality)

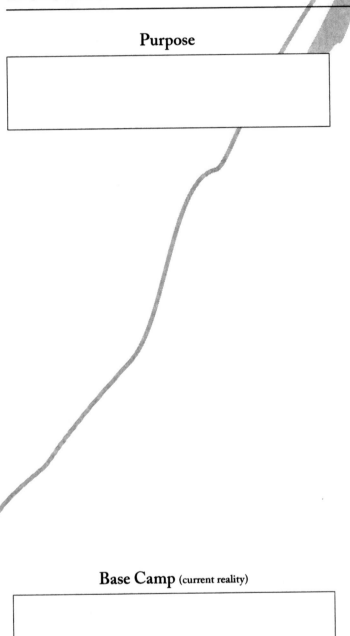

Leisure

Purpose

Base Camp (current reality)

Health

Purpose

Base Camp (current reality)

Career

Purpose

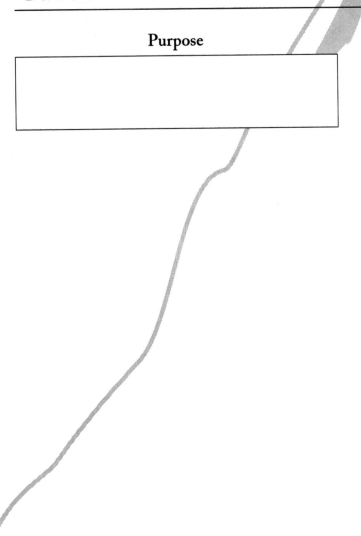

Base Camp (current reality)

Home Environment

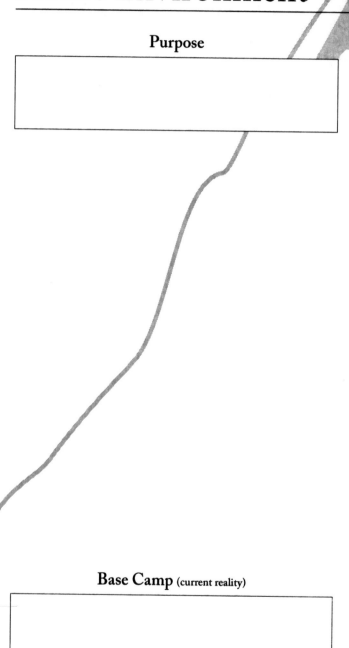

Purpose

Base Camp (current reality)

Community & Environment

Purpose

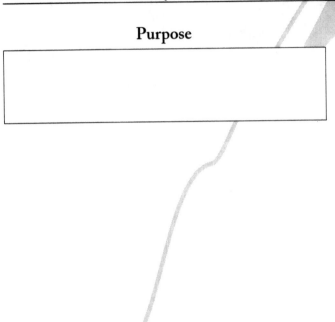

Base Camp (current reality)

Family Relationships

Purpose

```
┌─────────────────────────────────────┐
│                                     │
│                                     │
│                                     │
│                                     │
└─────────────────────────────────────┘
```

Base Camp (current reality)

```
┌─────────────────────────────────────┐
│                                     │
│                                     │
│                                     │
│                                     │
└─────────────────────────────────────┘
```

Intimate Relationships

Purpose

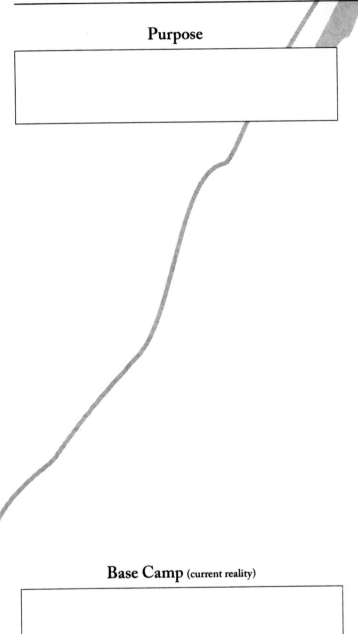

Base Camp (current reality)

Social Relationships

Purpose

Base Camp (current reality)

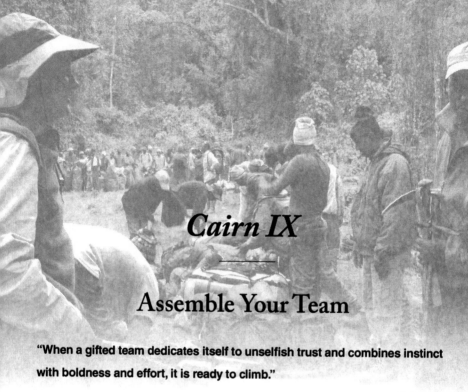

Cairn IX

Assemble Your Team

"When a gifted team dedicates itself to unselfish trust and combines instinct with boldness and effort, it is ready to climb."

—Patanjali

The next step in a successful change effort toward creating your life is to assemble the team that is going with you. No one travels on his or her journey alone. We all make an impact, whether we realize it or not. I like to refer to a quote I read on a bookmark: "You never know when you are making a memory, and you always are." Therefore, it is essential to identify those who will be affected by your change and growth and keep them abreast of your changes and experiences throughout your journey. You don't have to talk with them about every little thing. But you will want to talk about some things. You will be the ultimate judge of what you choose to discuss.

Your team can consist of family, peers, friends, coworkers, and community. They are those who will be directly, or indirectly, affected by your transformation. You are strengthening your capacity to be the creative force in your life and designing your future, but you are not in this alone. There are people in your life that will be affected by and through your transformation. There are also people who can assist and support you on your journey. It will be helpful to those people who can help you along the way as well as others close to you to keep them informed about the evolution that you are experiencing. For the people closest to you who will probably see the biggest change, it is important to communicate where you are going, why you want to go there, how you plan to get there, and the resources you need for your journey. You are building a guiding coalition that can be supportive and motivating, if needed. They can provide accountability and offer a reality test, if necessary, providing valuable feedback.

On my journey to the summit of Kilimanjaro, there was quite a team, consisting of 13 participants, two leaders, and a village of 60 "tough guys" (that's the name the porters preferred). For those of you unfamiliar with some of the lingo of treks, porters are people who the outfitters hire to assist the participants on the expedition. They do all sorts of things to make the trip more enjoyable and comfortable. For example, the porters on my Kili hike not only carried bags, but also set up the tents and placed bowls of hot water to wash our hands when we reached the day's destination. I had been told there would be many people assisting with food, bags, and everything imaginable to make the journey as comfortable and successful as possible; one of the people from Wilderness Travel, the outfitters I signed on with to climb Kilimanjaro, had said there would be a village that would be accompanying us on the expedition. When I got to the trailhead, I was amazed at what I saw. There was truly a village assembled to provide support and supplies on our journey. You might think of the team you are naming as the village that will be with you as you advance to your summit.

Think of teams you've participated on. Maybe they were in school, athletics, or at work. Two key attributes of strong teams are that they have clear roles and a shared sense of purpose. Successful teams have established a process that works for them to communicate in a positive way and build strong relationships. They support each other to help both individuals and the team be productive, contribute their strengths, and celebrate when they reach specific milestones.

Successful teams build and thrive on trust and support. They know each team member is working diligently toward the team's goals. They trust all will go the extra mile to be effective and give their individual best. Their word is paramount. By doing what they say they will do, acting from integrity, they develop a climate of trust and commitment. Even though you are on an individual journey, having people in your life that you can turn to for support and honest feedback is invaluable.

In the business world, without guiding teams, change initiatives are rarely achieved. They don't have the support, speed, or energy needed to implement a change that is sustainable. Harvard professor John Kotter, in his best selling book *Leading Change*, identified and detailed eight steps necessary for successful organizational change. From Kotter's research, the second consideration to ensure a successful change effort was to assemble the proper team from within the organization. Getting the right people on your team is a critical task to ensure a successful change. As you realize and celebrate your short-term successes, more people may want to join your team. That's up to you. Your charge at this point is to invite the right people to the village.

The people you want on your team are those who will be directly impacted by your growth and development. Some of the people you may want to consider are family members, a partner or spouse, and children. You may want close friends or coworkers. You may choose someone close to you who knows you and will be honest with you if you need a "reality check." You may also want someone who can provide feedback to you about how you are being perceived, similar to a "360" in business. Briefly, a 360 is a peer review assessment that many organizations conduct to help managers and executives understand how direct reports, staff, and bosses view them. The 360 assessments are typically used to enhance leadership skills, as well as to help them see where they may not be as effective as they think they are. Just as 360 degree feedback provides clarity in organizational settings, feedback from your team can help you in many ways, including helping to bring clarity to your focus, actions and ideas. If you have participated on an athletic team, think back to the type of team members you really appreciated. This might help you think of the team you are assembling now.

Now, your team may not appear to meet all of these characteristics, but they will have some of them, depending on the level of support and involvement of individual members. Some members will be closer to you and your goals and objectives. Others will be on the periphery. You may have one team member, or ten. Your job at this Cairn is to decide whom you want on your team, the contributions each might bring to your effort, and what you might need from each individual team player.

As you decide on whom you want on your team, you might also consider people who have been through a similar process. You might choose people who have been successful in designing a life of purpose and vision. You might know people who you respect because they exhibit the qualities of self-direction, mastery, and purpose. They may share similar values and certain characteristics that you have. Or they might have habits or essential characteristics that you would like to learn how to assimilate into your character. A smart leader always surrounds themselves with people who bring complementary strengths. You can't know everything, but you can know where to go to get productive feedback and input. Who might be a member that could provide effective direction? As you build your village, think of the resources you would want on your journey and list the people who can provide the necessary support. They will be valuable and trusted allies on your journey.

A central point when choosing allies is to make sure they embody an attitude of "bon voyage" rather than pessimism or fear. Some people in your life may doubt your ability to stick with a commitment, accomplish your goals or create a specific result. You do not want naysayers on your team. You already have plenty of opportunities to doubt yourself, and the last thing you want is someone on your team causing you to further second-guess what you are creating. You want people who themselves value growth and development. You want to choose team members who have an open mind and positive energy, and want the best for you.

This isn't to say you don't want honest feedback. Optimistic realism is a benefit. Offering a different perspective is helpful at times. Questions to help you reflect and provide insight are valuable. Constructive comments regarding your journey are invited to help you maintain authenticity and clarity. This type of support is very different from cynicism and despair, which you might encounter. Being the creative power in your life is a scary prospect for most people. They don't want the responsibility and they typically fail to have the necessary discipline to make their vision a reality. Choose your allies wisely.

If you choose, you will have chances along the way to change the mind of those who may harbor doubts about your motivation, your ability to change, and your capacity for self-direction, mastery, and purpose. Short-term successes will be one way to accomplish this if you really want a particular person's input. Those celebration points we discussed for each compass as you maneuver through that section's cairns are visible examples for people on your team as well as the naysayers that you are moving toward the summit. People see that. In fact, seeing you reach goals and ascend your mountain will be so inspirational to some that they will want to change *their* life. You'll be a model for their choice to embrace self-direction, mastery and purpose, and may become a member of their village. For the time being, focus on optimistic and supportive people that you trust.

Here I have to add a caveat. Some of you are thinking, "Why do I need a team? I'm embracing self-direction. Why would I need someone to ask for assistance or support?" All those questions are valid. Speaking from my own experience, I didn't have very many people on my team at first. For one thing, I couldn't answer a lot of their questions about why I wanted to hike up a mountain that was 19,300 feet. So I just decided to tell my family that I was going without much explanation about why. My partner didn't want to make the trip, so I did have lengthy discussions about whether or not to make the journey. After the decision was final that I was going to Africa by myself, I shared many doubts, concerns, and fears with my partner. That was very valuable to help me see my own strengths and that helped build my confidence. Sometimes our doubts hide our attributes from our own eyes and it takes another person to offer a different way of looking. And, of course, the best part is the phone call to tell your team that you made it to the top safely.

My partner and my family were very supportive. Did I need them to make the summit? No. In the end, it was an act of self-direction, mastery, and purpose. But, am I glad I shared the experience as best as I could with people I trusted, cared about, and respected and who cared about me? Absolutely! Some of these same folks are on my team now as I work through my own CORE Journey.

So, some of you might choose to not assemble a team. That's okay. However, I would encourage you to communicate with those in your life who will see a shift in your way of doing and being. As you change and grow, you are becoming something new and different. You might say you are making a transformation from a moth to butterfly. If you don't communicate some of the aspects of your new perspective as a butterfly, they will continue to relate to you as a moth. Not that there's anything wrong with moths, but that can be a bit frustrating to a butterfly. In the end, it's your choice. And, I still encourage you to build a small team, not only for yourself, but for them as well. It is always an inspiration to see, much less participate with someone who is progressing toward a summit of their own design and determination. You never know when you are making a memory, and you always are. Your achievements may be an inspiration to someone else.

APPROACH

There are several critical elements for your village:

1. Enroll the right people.

2. Establish clear roles and resources.

3. Develop strong relationships along the way with integrity, trust and commitment.

4. Share your purpose.

5. Invite feedback.

PRACTICE

1. List all the people that matter in your life with whom you come in contact on a regular basis. List everyone and don't leave anyone out. The list will be made of people in your family, people at work, those in your neighborhood, in your community, at church, on a sport team or a choir. Just begin to write and let it flow. We will organize later.

2. Now brainstorm the attitudes, strengths, and personality that you want your team members to possess. What resources will you need? What is each team member capable of providing? What strengths does each team member bring to the journey? How many people do you want? What expertise and credibility will each person possess? Do you want a wide range of perspectives? How do you want them to respond to your fears, hopes, and dreams? How do you want to be acknowledged and appreciated for your courage to undertake a transformational journey?

3. The next point to consider is what stake each person holds in your journey. There may be people close to you who will be affected or influenced by your transformation. For example, a partner, spouse, or significant other will be directly affected by changes you will go through. It is at this junction that you name the kind of support and

feedback you want and need from each member. You will need to decide how you will communicate what you are doing, possibly why you are participating in the CORE Journey, and what you hope to accomplish along the path. Your communication may differ depending on the level of involvement of each individual.

Just because you put someone on your list of possible teammates doesn't mean they will accept the invitation. They may not want to talk about it. It might be too scary for them. If you really want a particular person, you may have to enroll them in your vision. To enroll someone is to share your aspiration and inspiration with the hope of a resounding "Yes" from them to participate on your team. As you enroll each member, you will be explaining your journey. As you know, it is an evolution for you too, so you don't know what you don't yet know and may find it challenging to explain. That's okay. Right now, you are building a village of people who bring various support mechanisms to your endeavor. In fact, you may keep your list for a time and not tell anyone until you feel the time is right or necessary.

You must be open to someone declining your invitation. In these dynamic and complex times, people have hectic lives and may not be able to participate the way you want them to. Or, like I said, the whole enterprise might be too scary to them. Or it might mean that they would have to take a look inside and it isn't something they are willing to do yet. Try not to take a decline personally. And remember, as you grow and change, your wants and needs may shift and your team might change as well.

4. Now list each person you have chosen and, beside his or her name, write down the specific contribution you would like from each person.

5. Review your team and make sure you have gone for the qualities you want, rather than quantity.

6. The last thing to consider is when and how often you will communicate with each person. This is an on going process. You will want to keep those closest to you informed throughout the journey. Some will come and go only periodically. Just remember: they are your team and you will want to communicate with them to uphold their trust and commitment to supporting you on your journey.

REFLECT AND ENGAGE

- What are your CORE learnings from this Cairn?
- How will you apply these things in your life?
- What have you learned about yourself at this Cairn?
- Based on the practices at this Cairn, what will you do to expand your capacity and ability to be the creative force in your life?
- How will you celebrate the completion of this Cairn?

THE PEOPLE WHO WILL BE MY VILLAGE ON MY CORE JOURNEY ARE...

Interlude

Energy Systems, Coherence and Structure of Perception

"The soul is dyed the color of its thoughts. Think only on those things that are in line with your principles and can bear the light of day. The content of your character is your choice. Day by day, what you do is who you become. Your integrity is your destiny... it is the light that guides your way.

—Heraclitus, Greek Poet, Philosopher, *The Light of Integrity*

S tanding at 19,300 feet, on the summit of Kilimanjaro, I breathed a deep sigh of both relief and exhilaration as I looked down on the glaciers far below, from which we had begun the final surge earlier that morning. We'd spent the night at 18,500 feet and gazed up at the path that would lead us to the highest mountain on the African continent. Samai, our lead guide for the expedition, and had briefed us each evening at dinner as to what to expect on the next day's journey. The evening before, he had told us that tomorrow morning's trek would probably take about two hours. The faces around the table were expressions of wonder and acknowledgement that we were almost at our destination, and yet the thought of two hours at 19,000 feet and the slow steps that would carry us up the path was still daunting. And, we all knew we would call up the energy to make the final ascent.

Two of our members were not at dinner. They were experiencing altitude sickness and had bad headaches and nausea. We didn't know if they would be able to continue up the mountain. Ron, the gentleman who had celebrated his 70th birthday just two days prior, was not feeling well either. He was close to exhaustion. Three porters had already had to turn back due to extreme mountain sickness. It made me reflect on the spectrum of energy resources required to do what we were doing.

Of course, there is the physical component of hiking at any altitude. Your cardiovascular endurance, leg strength and stamina are all fundamental. Yet even the most physically fit person, no matter their age or experience, can be faced with altitude sickness at higher elevations. Wilderness Travel, a leader in the adventure travel industry, had made it clear that this was a Level 7, the most extreme rating. The journey to the summit of Kilimanjaro would require a high level of physical exertion and therefore one had to train and be at a healthy level of physical fitness. We all had trained in various ways. I felt that I was in excellent physical condition. Hank, a marathoner who was part of our group, was also in good shape. That being said, we were the first to experience altitude sickness for three days beginning at 11,000 feet. I felt miserable. I wondered, if I felt this bad at this elevation, how would I feel as we ascended to a higher altitude? At that point the thoughts and emotions were secondary. I had self-doubting thoughts and negative emotions, but I couldn't let them cause me to deviate from my goal. I had to muster the energy to go on. My priority was taking care of myself physically as best as I could and continuing the journey up the mountain.

The information sent out prior to the climb had also addressed the mental and emotional aspects of altitude. It had addressed the need to be a team player and the openness and tolerance which would be required from each person, as well as the required willingness to suspend one's own perspectives so we could work together as we made our way up the mountain. Altitude can effect your emotions. Samai had told us not to be surprised if we felt a heightened level of emotion as we ascended higher and higher. Sure enough, my tentmate and I both had a similar experience. A couple of times around 15,000 feet, at the end of the day we would enter our tent, sit down and just cry for about 60 seconds. When we were done, we felt better. It was odd. Other people said they had similar experiences—exaggerated feelings of emotion from irritation to sadness. One gentleman had intense dreams and feelings of delusion that the guides were going to leave him behind. He would wake up in the middle of the night in a panic and get up to make sure everyone was still there. It was interesting how the altitude affected our thoughts and emotions. We all had to call on a different level of mental and emotional energy than was typical.

But, no matter what, we all gathered ourselves each morning for the day's journey. At one time or another, the climb called on all of our energy systems. This type of venture calls for an immense output of physical energy. But I don't think any of us really knew how we would be challenged mentally, emotionally and spiritually. Sick or not, you had to recruit energy from your whole being in order to persevere through the challenges. There were times when I was physically miserable, wondering if I could go one more step. Overcoming that took mental and emotional toughness and a determination that called on my experience and training as an elite athlete. I know the experience of pushing through pain and exhaustion in sports helped me persist through what I was experiencing on the mountain. And, when I was feeling awful at 15,000 feet, I had to dig deeper than I had ever done before.

Emotionally, the challenge for me came when I got sick. I had serious doubts about whether I would make it to the top. I felt terrible, and we were only at 11,000 feet. The summit at 19,300 feet seemed a very long way off. I had to touch a trust that I hadn't experienced before. I had to trust that the guides knew what they were doing and if I needed to go down, they would say so. Some guides have been known to push the travelers past a healthy level to increase their summit percentage. I trusted that Samai would not do that. Then, I had to rely on an inner trust in myself. I think that was the easiest. I had pushed through discomfort and beyond my comfort zone many times as an athlete and a backpacker. I knew I could do it again. That being said, emotional energy was a key ingredient for success on this journey.

The investment of spiritual energy is probably unique to each individual. For me it was part of a lifelong pursuit and value system that included personal growth, a passion for exceptional experiences, a desire to test the further reaches of my self, and quite simply a desire to see the view from the top of the hill. It may sound silly, but when I was asked why I wanted to climb Kili, I really didn't have an answer except to say, "Because, I just do. I've seen pictures and I want to have the experience." Nothing deep. No profound personal insight. I just wanted to do it. And, when it came right down to it, the experience transformed how I thought of myself. Words wouldn't do it justice, so I won't try to extrapolate the experience. Again, it changed me—my perspective of who I am and what I'm capable of achieving. I would say it gave me a glimpse of self-actualization—an unparalleled perspective into the best I could be, and a glimpse of how deep I could dig under challenging circumstances.

Throughout the entire journey, I called on all four energy systems every day. We all did. At times, I was able to move within a coherent field with my head and heart aligned. I'd say that there were times when I was so absorbed in putting one foot in front of the other and breathing that I was in a flow state. There was a sense that the only time that was important was *now*.

I had to be cognizant at all times about how my perception of the outside situation and events was being influenced by how I was feeling inside. It was an exercise in realizing that, despite doubts and fears, I could push onward. The negative thoughts and emotions were not going to keep me from going on. We all engaged all four energy systems throughout the trip in order to survive. But, we did more than survive. We thrived on that mountain. Even with the wind chill below zero, people were smiling with the awareness of what they were accomplishing.

From conversations I had with members of the team, I can say without a doubt that everyone in our group was changed by the experience. My energy in all systems served me well and I grew in each domain because of the event, the place, the mountain, the people, and my own internal power. And, I am still growing in the ability to manage and renew my energy. It's not easy. It takes a willingness and a commitment. The ability to manage and renew your energy in all four systems, physical, mental, emotional and spiritual, is fundamental for the successful completion of your CORE Journey.

Just like climbing a mountain, life demands the acquisition and expenditure of energy. When we learn to manage and renew our energy, we are increasing our capacity to do our best on a sustainable basis. When we learn to bring our energy systems into coherence, we are extending our capability for excellence. Our grasp of our own mastery in terms of our individual freedom and autonomy begins when we learn that our perception is an outside reflection of an internal experience, and that it is a matter of our choice. When we realize that we always stand at a choice-point no matter what the situation, we are breaking down barriers that may have limited us in the past. This enhances our self-leadership ability and our capacity to create a value-based, purpose-driven life that we find fulfilling.

The next two Cairns, Energy State Management and Structure of Perception, will involve a detailed discussion of three significant concepts—Energy Systems, Coherence and Structure of Perception. These are integral components of your journey, expanding your capability to engage a mindful approach for self-direction, lifelong learning and living on purpose. The concepts we've been exploring throughout the CORE Journey have built on one another, and are interrelated and dynamic. Now we want to optimize your capacity to consistently engage those concepts beyond just an intellectual understanding. We want to integrate them into your life as skillful actions wherever and whenever they are needed. Let's begin with energy systems.

ENERGY SYSTEMS

Human beings are interrelated and dynamic energy systems. This is no longer a notion only espoused through spiritual literature, but one that has been demonstrated through research from such diverse disciplines as physiology, biology, psychology, sport sciences, neuroscience, and quantum physics. As we go through our day-to-day lives, we draw from four separate but analogous energy systems that make up human beings—physical, mental, emotional, and spiritual. To participate fully in our lives, two things become advantageous: to expand each system's capacity to function at its optimal level, and to generate coherence between each system.

All four energy systems function separately and they are also intertwined, each drawing vitality from and supplying influence upon the other. Each system's impact on the other in many ways determines how efficiently and effectively the systems function as separate networks and as a connected force. Independently, each system functions at its optimal level when it is strong and flexible. With robust and limber energy systems, we are able to call upon and sustain energy levels as necessary. To fully engage in our daily activities at home and at work on a sustainable basis, we need to strengthen and renew each system throughout the day.

Dr. Jim Loehr is a world-renowned performance psychologist and founder of The Human Performance Institute, a firm dedicated to improving the productivity and wellbeing of elite performers in business and athletics. The Human Performance Institute offers a science-based approach for fully engaging people's talents and skills to enable consistent and sustainable peak performance. In 2003, Loehr joined forces with Tony Schwartz, president and founder of The Energy Project and a bestselling author and professional speaker with over 30 years' experience working with leaders to teach them to thrive amidst change, to co-author New York Times Bestseller *The Power of Full Engagement*. In the book, Loehr and Schwartz suggest that it is not time we must manage, but rather, we must master our energy systems for greater productivity and health. It's not how many hours you spend on a project. Time is a constant. There are always and only 24 hours in a day no matter how much we manage the day. Time only has value when we are able to merge it with energy. Human energy is a sustainable and renewable resource. *The Power of Full Engagement* speaks to the science and discipline of energy management.

At Cairn X, I combine the research behind energy management, emotional intelligence, and performance psychology to help you learn how to effectively cultivate your energy systems for maximum productivity and health.

Energy state management is about enriching the quantity and quality of your energy. It is about understanding the power of your energy systems and becoming proficient in directing the focus of your energy. Managing your energy systems is a skill that can be developed and enhanced the same way athletes expand their strength, endurance, and flexibility for maximum efficiency. The process of building the muscles in our body pushes the muscle beyond its comfort zone for a given amount of time and then allows that muscle, or group of muscles, to recover. In other words, you stress the muscle and then allow it to relax and recoup. The more deliberately and consistently you do that type of workout, the more the muscle grows in strength, endurance, and range of motion. To ensure sustainable and consistent optimal performance, you will learn how to do the same thing with all four of the body's energy systems. This allows for a heightened sense of wellbeing, balance, creativity and engagement.

It's easy to think in terms of building our physical muscles through a disciplined strength-training routine. Loehr and Schwartz suggest that the same principle applies to the other three energy domains: mental, emotional, and spiritual. To strengthen any energy system, you must regularly expose it to regulated stress and recovery periods for optimal growth and expansion. As Loehr and Schwartz wrote, you might consider that each energy system has its own set of muscles that can be made stronger, more flexible, and to have greater balance and endurance. The more we develop each system's strength and flexibility, the more we are able to experience better balance and endurance and sustain full engagement in our daily schedule with optimal energy levels.

It is not enough that the muscles of each energy system are strong and flexible; to use them to their full potential they must function in a coherent fashion. When the systems are balanced, we are more capable of drawing on each necessary system for a specific task or circumstance. When systems are coherent and able to resonate with each of the other interconnected systems, it allows each system to operate optimally. Through this coherent functioning you are able to rely on the greatest quantity and highest quality each energy system has to offer.

Where did the notions of energy systems and coherence originate? The 80s and 90s produced a body of research that opened up previously unknown possibilities with the introduction of the idea that our bodies have various systems of intelligence. All systems of intelligence throughout the body are in constant communication with each other. Communication between two systems in particular has a huge effect on our emotions, thoughts and perceptions—the heart and the brain.

Prior to any action, our heart and our head transmit messages that regulate and affect our behavior. A highly adaptive and beneficial intelligence system is located in our heart and it profoundly affects how our brain functions. When the two are out of balance, it creates unproductive responses that can be harmful to others, the environment and ourselves. Bringing the two systems into balance, or coherence, provides an opportunity for a more thoughtful, balanced and positive approach to our relationships and our ability to function at effective levels. The coherence created when we learn to engage both our heads and our hearts for decision-making and problem solving serves to engender wellbeing and happiness.

Coherence also lends itself to greater creativity and productivity. Mindfully managing your mental and emotional energy systems can produce amazing results for you both personally and professionally. By forging a coherent system in the moment, you are able to choose the type of energy you extend to people and the environment in which you live and work. Your interactions are no longer driven by triggers, mechanical responses and knee-jerk reactions, but instead are more attuned to your values and purpose. You choose how to act and the type of energy you will extend to your relationships and your external environment.

As we proceed, you will learn more about what coherent functioning is and how to create it, but for now let's consider the definition we will be using. For our purposes, the definition of coherent is "united as, or forming, a whole." When energy systems function in coherence, they are functioning as a whole, allowing us to draw on the strengths and full capacity of each system as needed. Let's look a bit more closely at this thing we're calling coherence and why it's integral for our overall wellbeing and fulfillment. What is coherence? The dictionary defines coherence as a "logical and consistent way of being; united as or forming a whole." In physics it's defined as "having a constant phase relationship." Another way of looking at it is as an internal harmony throughout the components of a system, extending to related components of another system.

The Institute of HeartMath is an internationally recognized nonprofit organization involved in research and education to help people reduce stress, manage emotions and build energy and resilience for healthy, fulfilled lives. HeartMath has developed technology to teach people to understand and trust the intelligence of their heart in conjunction with their minds at work, home, school and play. HeartMath has conducted extensive research, training and practice with coherence in athletics, business, and education. They are instrumental in establishing a worldwide movement for heart-based living and global coherence by inspiring people to reconnect with the intelligence and wisdom of their own hearts. When people tune in to the symphony between their hearts and minds, they are better equipped to act with integrity. HeartMath has played a significant role in increasing the awareness of energy systems and the significance of coherent interaction between systems. They define coherent functioning as "the tendency toward an increased order in the informational content of a system or in the information flow between systems."

All of these definitions share the idea that being in a coherent state of energy provides a consistent and interconnected flow of information that can be used for greater creativity, better decision-making, and healthier and more positive ways of interacting with one another, contributing to everyone's overall wellbeing and happiness. Coherence also lets us steadily engage all of who we are to a much greater extent. It enables us to integrate information from our heart, our brain and our gut. Neuroscientists have found that the brain houses specific circuitry that is directly connected to the gut. The brain circuitry that is in communication with the gut provides us with information that we call intuition—messages coming from our gut. When we can use the awareness of our intuition and the information our emotions are giving us and join both with rational and logical analysis from our brain, we respond from the greatest amount of information and resources available. When we discount any of those areas—head, heart, or gut—we are limiting our resources and our information, and therefore our response. Creating coherence between systems manifests awareness, clarity and trust and actually makes us smarter and more effective with others and ourselves.

STRUCTURE OF PERCEPTION

We've talked about energy systems and coherence. The last concept I want to touch on here is Structure of Perception. Our Structure of Perception is built over a lifetime and includes our values and intentions, personality, life experience, family, society and culture, as well as our thoughts and emotions. It is our foundation for relating to and interacting with the world we live in. Our language, actions and overall way of being are a direct consequence of our Structure of Perception. It is a primary factor in our ability to access and utilize our talents, knowledge and expertise, all of which contribute to our capability to consistently perform at peak levels.

Because our Structure of Perception has been developing throughout our lives, it provides us with a sense of certainty and safety. It feels comfortable and familiar to us and we maneuver within the structure with ease, almost at an unconscious level. As our security grows, our language and actions offer consistency and our Structure of Perception becomes subconscious, and we see our perception as the truth. We develop stories around our Structure and these stories become who we are. Sometimes these stories work well for us. They provide a consistent way of addressing the world and those around us. But sometimes our stories are built on misconceptions, assumptions and falsities. It is then that this Structure of Perception becomes a limiting factor in our lives. This manifests itself when we feel unfulfilled or stuck. The problem is that, because our Structure of Perception works at a subconscious level, we are unaware that our perception is really the limiting factor, rather than anything external.

The feeling of "stuckness" is one of the primary reasons people come to me for coaching. They have tried everything in their repertoire of resources and nothing seems to provide a sustainable change. Life has lost its meaning, or at best it has become dull and mundane, and they need help to sort things out, make and engage a plan, and integrate it into their life for sustainability. This can also happen in the middle of the CORE Journey. Sometimes people create their MAP, begin to work toward their summit and find themselves confronted with self-doubts and barriers to moving along their chosen path. That's why, at Cairn XI, we take an in-depth look at Structure of Perception, what it is, how it manifests in your life, and whether it supports and encourages you or restricts and thwarts your goals and your progress. We look at how and why your Structure of Perception may be keeping you from creating the life you want based on values and results that are fulfilling to you. We begin to realize that our perception is a mirror, not a fact. Our internal world is what is projecting either an unfriendly, sometimes fearful world and keeping us from aligning values with actions, or a world where we see possibilities and avenues for achieving fulfillment and happiness.

Cairn X is a presentation of our four energy systems. You'll learn what they are, why they are important, how they interrelate, and what you can do to manage your energy on a consistent basis for productivity and wellbeing. At Cairn XI, you will learn how your Structure of Perception is either a limiting or supportive factor for you on your Journey. You will learn ways to be mindful of your actions to ensure that they are aligned with your values and purpose. This is a very important step in reconnecting to your innate capacity to create, self-direct and consistently enhance your life.

Cairn X

Energy Management
Step 1: Physical Energy Management

"Keeping your body healthy is an expression of gratitude to the whole cosmos—the trees, the clouds, everything."

—Thich Nhat Hanh

When I was coaching volleyball players, I trained them in all four energy systems. Physically, we used sport-specific training techniques, very similar to the concept of functional training today. For example, to develop jumping ability, the players would do a variety of jumps. Some were from a squat position, jumping straight up as if they were blocking the ball; some were doing an approach and jump, preparing to hit the ball, then backpedaling and repeating. At times I had them jump in place with a partner on their back; some jumps were from a full squat, while others were a stance where their thighs were parallel to the ground. I used a variety of jumping positions to stress each muscle group that was involved during a game of volleyball. As the players developed strength and endurance, we added more weight and repetitions to continue to stress their muscles. Exertion was followed by a timed period of recovery. Following these protocols, the result was expanded strength, flexibility, and endurance.

Each day, the players also had specific physical exercises to strengthen their arms, core, and cardiovascular endurance. Exercises for arm strength included push-ups, tossing a weighted medicine ball with a partner, and various lifts and pulls with dumbbells, ropes and sandbags. The exercises combined a low number of repetitions for power and a higher number of repetitions to increase arm speed and endurance. Power and speed were combined for a more forceful and efficient swing.

All of the exercises mentioned above also helped strengthen their core. Specific core training involved planks. Planks begin with the body in a prone position, holding your back straight, resting on your elbows and toes for a specific amount of time. We did a variety of these such as a straight plank, making sure the back is kept straight. Then we would add one leg lifted off the ground. As the players got stronger, we would add lifting an arm off the ground; sometimes the arm on the same side as the lifted leg, other times with the opposite arm and leg lifted. This type of exercise is not only great for strengthening your body's core, but works to increase overall balance.

In order to build the type of cardiovascular endurance needed for an anaerobic sport like volleyball, the players ran a variety of high-intensity intervals. We did line intervals, a specific type of short sprint that incorporates fast starts with short distances. For example, they would start at one end of the volleyball court, sprint to the 10-foot line, touch, and return to the end line, then turn and immediately sprint to the net line, touch and return to the end line, touch and sprint to the other side of the net and touch the 10-foot line on that side, return to the original end line, turn and sprint to the far end line, touch, and sprint back to the original end line. We would do a series of these. There are all kinds of ways to involve different lines and lengths of sprints. I tried to mix it up by providing various combinations of interval training to keep things interesting, both to the athletes themselves and their bodies.

At the start and close of each practice, we did a slow jog to warm up the muscles and then did flexibility exercises. This aided in the players' ability to go all-out during practice and helped limit injuries resulting from tight muscles. Throughout practice, various drills would also include strength, flexibility and endurance exercises. In this way, practice simulated what a real volleyball game was like—intense periods of activity with a brief rest between points.

The goal was to develop the players' overall strength, flexibility, and breathing capacity so they could practice and perform at their optimal level. Building in a system for expending and recovering energy assured that their energy levels remained fairly consistent. By pushing past the players' comfort levels and allowing for recovery, they expanded their capacity to perform at sustainable high levels during competition.

The point of this detailed explanation of a volleyball practice is to show the importance of training the whole person for the task at hand. We were a volleyball team, so we could have just played volleyball. However, we could not have played at peak levels without participating in a system to increase the strength, flexibility and endurance of the players' muscles and the cardiovascular systems. It's the same for you as you move through your day. You may not be preparing for competition, but the same principles for consistent and sustainable performance apply to all of us. One cannot consistently participate with full engagement in the tasks of daily living at work and at home without caring for their physical energy.

The best way to do this is to integrate periods of physical expenditure with a time for stretching and recovery. It's easy to see the relationship between expending energy and recovery when we talk about our physical body. And as we will see, the same holds true for the other three energy systems. But let's continue to look at the importance of developing your physical energy system.

Physical energy is the fundamental resource for all of our energy systems. If we expect to be able to remain calm under pressure, sustain focus and creativity during critical times, and align actions with our values when confronted with difficult decisions, situations and people, we must manage the expenditure and recovery of our physical energy first and foremost. Without adequate levels of physical energy, our capacity to fully engage the other energy systems is greatly diminished. We are unable to sustain the degree of strength and stamina necessary for optimal participation in our chosen task.

As I've said, the importance of physical energy seems obvious for athletes, but in our daily lives we have a tendency to overlook the physical domain, and yet still expect ourselves to perform at our best. If we want to be able to fully engage in our daily lives, we cannot neglect the importance of physical vitality. Physical wellbeing is just as important for performing our normal day-to-day functions as it is for athletic performance.

I can hear you now, though. "I'm not a performer. I'm a mom, a teacher, an executive. I don't need to perform—I need to work." Let's distinguish what being a performer means in every day life. I consider all of us to be performers, whether we are parents, salespeople, business executives, artists, supervisors, contractors, dancers, soccer players, doctors, nurses or teachers.

You name the profession; each of us is performing tasks throughout our day or our area of expertise. In this instance, performance is defined as "the action or process of carrying out or accomplishing an action, task, or function." In the context of this definition, we are actively involved in a variety performances throughout our day. We are all performers. By strengthening our physical energy system, we can become capable of being elite performers within our specific tasks, be it teaching, parenting, selling, managing, or dancing, what ever our chosen field of action might be. Managing our physical energy system enables us to rise to the occasion and perform at optimal levels on a consistent and sustainable basis.

Let's look at the components of our physical energy system.

Nutrition, movement, hydration and sleep are all important components of the physical energy system. They can be a problem for anyone and they are often a challenge for college students such as my volleyball team. Educating the players on the importance of balanced and nutritious eating habits, the appropriate amount of sleep and optimal hydration levels was part of the coaching process. We discussed how to eat healthy at home, at school, and while traveling for competition.

Eating a nutritious diet helps keep energy levels at the optimum and aids in optimal weight maintenance. Eating is one of the most important regulators of physical energy. We could spend a whole book discussing what eating correctly in this day and time means. Our knowledge and understanding of nutrition is expanding on a daily basis. Extensive research in the field of nutrition is ongoing with results that call into question traditional ways of eating and thinking about food. Like I said, there are entire books written about what, when and how much to eat. I have studied nutrition for a number of years, primarily for my own understanding and utilization so I could maximize my athletes' training and performance as well as my own. Over the past year I have chosen to expand my coaching practice to include health and nutrition. I have formalized my study by going back to school to become a certified health and lifestyle coach.

Through my study, my knowledge and understanding of nutrition has grown in leaps and bounds and I am still learning and assimilating the research I'm reading about and my own experience with the performers I work with and myself. My primary focus is on sport and performance nutrition focusing on what and when to eat so that we get the maximum benefit from the food we eat. In my coaching practice, I work with people who cover the full spectrum of performance activity from elite athletes to people who participate in a variety of sports and leisure activities to people who want to begin to include some form of movement in their life. I also work with people on healthy weight management. It all revolves around what, when and how we eat. It sounds like a simple concept, but one not easily incorporated into our everyday lives primarily due to the plethora of information that floods the airways every day. It's challenging enough keeping up with the information as a professional, much less as lay person trying to figure out whom to listen to and believe.

What I now understand completely is that no way of eating works for everyone. Bio-individuality must be a starting point when you are considering what to eat that will nourish your entire energy system and prepare it for the optimal output required for your specific activity—from bodybuilding to cycling to tennis to an executive to a parent trying to keep up with an active youngster. You cannot say "that diet worked for Susie, so it will work for me." Each person's physique, genetics, metabolism and lifestyle are unique and must be taken into consideration when choosing a way of eating that fits their body type and individual distinctions.

Another key component at the heart of nutrition is that nourishment is about the whole person. Nutrition has to do with more than eating. It comprises being healthy and well in all of our energy systems, making time for exercise and movement, having healthy relationships, a fulfilling career, and a spiritual path that speaks to your chosen values. You can have the healthiest eating style and be involved in a job that's not engaging or a negative relationship and your energy is going to suffer. Likewise, you can have a fulfilling career, a positive relationship and a sound spiritual path, but without proper food intake, your efforts in those other areas will eventually be less than optimal. Nutrition is about your life and being fully engaged and present to those your care about and the things you enjoy doing.

In my experience what you eat will transform your body toward optimal output and energy, or it will contribute to limited energy production and confined energy resources. What, when and how you eat will drastically influence your opportunity for peak performance no matter what your level or area of performance. All that being said, let me repeat that this is not a book about nutrition. In the context of your journey, I will offer some general guidelines and include resources for your further exploration in the Resources section.

The old saying "garbage in, garbage out" is good to keep in mind when choosing foods to put in your body. There are several excellent books about nutrition and food that also take into account that people have preferences as to the kinds of foods that appeal to them. Some people eat meat. Some people are vegetarians. Some people are allergic to grains or sensitive to dairy products. A lot of proper eating has to do with being in tune with how your body handles various foods. In addition, how you eat is important. Do you eat on the run? Do you eat out or cook at home the majority of time? Do you buy local and organic foods? It also has to do with *when* you eat.

Many people let too much time go by between meals and their energy drops so they can't concentrate or focus. Some people eat very little in the morning, preferring to grab a cup of coffee and a bar and then eat a large meal in the evening. If you were raised on a farm, chances are you eat a large dinner mid-day and lighter fare for supper, or the evening meal. Again, a lot of this has to do with where you live, your lifestyle, and your culture. There are entire books written about when, how and what to eat and there's not enough space in this book to do any specific topic justice, but here are some general rules to think about:

Eat a variety of fresh fruits and vegetables. Fruits with a low glycemic index such as pears, strawberries, grapefruit, and apples provide a slower release of energy because they are converted to sugar more slowly and therefore give you more consistent energy levels, leading to better performance. That's not to discount bananas, grapes, and fruit with a higher glycemic index. They provide minerals and other nutrients that the other fruits don't provide. Again, it's good to know when to eat which types of fruit. But, this much I do know: the average population doesn't even come close to eating the proper amount of fruits. And, let's be realistic. No one's going to sit down and eat 10 bananas or 10 oranges. Moderation is always the key.

Vegetables speak for themselves. Most nutritionists will agree that there are no bad vegetables. Any time you can eat fresh, organic veggies, do so. Our knowledge about nutrition and what constitutes a healthy diet is growing, but one consistent theme is that you can't go wrong with fresh vegetables and fruit.

One of my favorite books on nutrition is *The 150 Healthiest Foods on Earth: The Surprising, Unbiased Truth about What You Should Eat and Why.* It is a unique reference guide written by Jonny Bowden, Ph.D., C.N.S., a nationally-known expert on weight loss and nutrition. Bowden debunks old-school food myths and offers facts from his and a variety of other experts' research findings so you can make wise, health-conscious decisions about what you eat.

Bowden discusses the latest research and recommendations about the health benefits of eating whole foods. He addresses 150 whole foods in categories such as vegetables, grains, fruits, nuts, seeds, dairy, meat, and specialty foods, and rates each food. For the foods that are the best in their category, he gives a star. These are foods that are so uniquely loaded with nutrients, fiber, antioxidants, cancer-fighting phytochemicals, or a combination thereof, that they deserve special mention. Some examples of star foods are oatmeal, avocados, almonds, broccoli, swiss chard, butter, eggs, tea, garlic, carrots and coconut oil. He also includes discussion regarding omega-3 fats, antioxidants, fiber and glycemic index.

The book is a wealth of research-based information. Although he brings in research from around the world, the book is accessible and actually enjoyable to read. It lives on a shelf in my kitchen and I often refer to it. I have included Bowden's website and information in the Resources section.

The frequency with which you eat is important as well. It would be great if we all started eating like Hobbits, with five to six small meals throughout the day. This way, we maintain performance levels and avoid low blood sugar, which can cause irritability, lack of concentration, and low energy. Eating small meals throughout the course of the day helps avoid both the uncomfortable feeling that comes from overeating, as well as feeling like you are famished, which often in turn leads to overeating. However, the subject of the number of meals you should eat for maximum health is also a source of disagreement. Some nutritionists say eat two meals with a snack; others say eat only three meals a day and no snacking. With all the varying ideas and ideals in the area of nutrition, you can see why it might be beneficial to work with a health and nutrition coach to help sort through the information and research and figure out what's right for you.

Drinking adequate amounts of water is important for a healthy body. Research suggests that at least 64 ounces of water during the day is beneficial for good performance. Lack of hydration can negatively impact concentration and coordination. One study from Australia found that people who drank five eight-ounce glasses of water per day had less coronary heart disease than those who consumed less than two glasses a day.

Why is water so important? 75% of your muscles are water. Your brain is 74% water and your bones are 22% water. Water is necessary for every metabolic process in your body as well as digestion and absorption of minerals and vitamins. It also helps get rid of toxins and fats. Water can improve energy for physical and mental performance and it aids in keeping your skin healthy-looking. No one knows exactly where the "eight glasses a day" rule came from, but suffice it to say that most people do not get adequate amounts of hydration. So, drink up. A bit of advice from Jonny Bowden: "Divide your weight in two and drink that number of ounces a day. There's no firm science to back that up, but I've been using it for years, and as a basic guideline, it works quite well."

There are many ways of thinking about food. For example, the Paleo Diet, which suggests we go back to our ancestry of being hunter-gathers and advocates eating the proteins in meats and vegetables and limiting intake of grains, legumes and dairy products. There is the Raw Food movement, which leans heavily on herbs, grasses, vegetables and fruit. Many of its resources stem from ancient medicinal foods found in Asia, South America and the Native American heritage. There is the macrobiotic diet, the heart-healthy diet, the South Beach diet, the Blood-Type diet, the Atkins diet, the Zone diet. The list goes on and on.

In school I am studying over 100 different diets so I'll be familiar with the pros and cons of each depending on the bio-individuality of my clients. Again, I will provide resources, but one thing to consider is that, if you think eating healthy is going to deprive you of things you love and can't live without, you will not even try it. So, have an open mind. Do some reading and research. Be aware of where the research is coming from. And, if you're serious about maximizing your health, wellbeing and performance, it is a good idea to seek a trained professional who has an expertise in nutrition to work with you and your goals around nourishment and living a healthy and active lifestyle for functional longevity. Functional longevity is not about just living a long life. It's primarily about fully engaging in life as we age so that we flourish and can generate and sustain energy to do the things we love to do for a very long time.

Something to consider if you are thinking about changing the way you currently eat: rather than eliminating things from your diet, start to add healthy stuff more and more, for example more fruits and vegetables. Before long, the foods that may have been limiting your energy will begin to be crowded out. Without feeling like you are missing something, the healthy foods will start to become the mainstay rather than the occasional. Many times nutritionists will give their clients a handout on foods they must eliminate from their diet. That turns most people off immediately. They feel like they will have to deprive themselves to be healthy. They think that being healthy means eating things they know are good for them but that they don't enjoy. By simply adding some of those healthy star foods Bowden discusses in his book, your body will naturally adjust. It's hard to eat the recommended amount of vegetables and fruits each day and still crave a gallon of ice cream at night. Your body is very intelligent. It knows what supports it and what depletes it.

The problem is that we don't listen to our bodies. We simply put things in and then wonder why we don't feel well. Then we typically take a pill and proceed down the path we were already on. Begin to listen to your body. Many ailments can be diminished or even eliminated through healthy nutrition. I'm not saying that you shouldn't seek medical advice when you feel ill. I am advocating, however, starting to be aware of the information about nutrition that is accessible so you can make informed decisions about whether a shift in what you eat might help you feel better. Start to be aware of the information your body is giving you about what you're putting in it. Your body will provide you with info, such as gas, low energy and mood swings. This is all information on what foods work well for you and which food causes an issue.

Nutrition is an evolving science and an art with new research findings coming out on a regular basis. It's challenging to know what to believe and who to listen to. If the information seems overwhelming, you might choose to find a certified nutritionist and let them assist you in making informed choices. Either way, knowledge does begin to add to our self-governing even in the area of nutrition. We want choices. Then you can decide how you want to celebrate—with a cookie or an apple. No judgment! I love when Girl Scout cookies are in season. What we want is to have choices and not a mindless reach-and-stuff approach. And, moderation is key. If you want an occasional cookie, have one. Just don't have the the whole box.

There are some general guidelines for healthy weight management. Some of them are: eat a healthy breakfast, make sure you stay hydrated by drinking more water, cook at home and make your own lunch, get the right amount of sleep, integrate some form of movement into your lifestyle at least 4-5 times a week, reduce your stress, and be mindful of what you put into your body. Become a detective and be aware of clues your body gives you as to how it reacts to particular foods. Keep track. Modify as you go along. Your body is very intelligent. You just have to be mindful of what it's telling you.

Another important regulator of energy is breathing. Regular aerobic exercise, such as walking briskly, running, cycling, or swimming, strengthens the heart and helps to maintain proper weight. There are a variety of other types of exercise that you can choose from to enhance aerobic capacity, including machines such as StairMaster, elliptical machines, rowing machines, stationary bikes and functional fitness. Weight training and certain types of yoga also increase cardiovascular proficiency. An aspect of physical fitness to consider as well is whether to invest in a personal trainer. Personal trainers can design a specific program that is particularly geared to your goals, time and lifestyle.

Functional fitness is transforming the training techniques used by many personal trainers. It is geared to life activities that we regularly participate in rather than isolated events. Functional fitness involves a workout that prepares your body so it can perform routine activities such as walking, bending, climbing stairs, and lifting without pain, injury, or discomfort. Functional fitness is becoming the direction of the fitness industry. The challenging part of choosing between the various types of physical training is finding what works best for your schedule, time, and body as well as choosing an activity and routine that you will stick with over time.

As an aside, my brother, Jay Wright, is a personal trainer and the founder of a multi-faceted company, The Wright Fit, a design and management company of high-end training facilities for upscale residential properties nationally and internationally. A major component of the facilities Jay designs is functional fitness. Jay would add that a choice to integrate physical fitness into your life is a lifestyle decision. It isn't something you do for a limited amount of time. Physical fitness becomes an integral aspect of your daily living that aids in stress reduction and enhances optimal performance at all levels and in all areas of your life. It influences all the other energy systems and positively affects all aspects of your life. I've included Jay's website and other entries in the Resource section on exercise and personal training to give you some ideas on a variety of possibilities to incorporate exercise as part of a healthy lifestyle.

As a person who has competed at a high level and always had physical activity as an integral part of my life, I consider movement to add value to life in general. So, keeping up with the latest news in the strength and conditioning industry is interesting and fun. It is an ever-expanding field. Research continues to increase our knowledge about how the various types of movement each impact our physical health and our overall wellbeing. Part of my job as a nutritionist and health coach is to stay abreast of the research so I can help my clients sort out what will work for them and be the most beneficial. Another aspect of my work is exploring who's out there doing what so I can be a referral resource for my clients. My clients are unique; so are personal trainers. Not one personality clicks with everyone. I like to establish a working relationship with several personal trainers in the area that I respect so I have a variety of people to choose from when referring my clients. If you choose to engage a personal trainer, visit several and choose the one that best fits your personality, lifestyle and belief system.

One of the areas that has changed our understanding of how certain types of activity affect our bodies is high intensive interval training, or HIIT. Phil Campbell is an exercise physiologist who has done extensive research on the effect of HIIT on muscle fiber and metabolism. The old way of thinking was that you were born with two different types of muscle fiber, fast and slow twitch. Common knowledge also indicated that each individual had either a majority of fast twitch or slow twitch muscle fiber. Fast twitch is the type of muscle fiber sprinters have, for example. An example of slow twitch fiber is the fiber found in those who are good at long slow distance running. The experts thought that you could increase your fast twitch muscle fiber by doing short, intensive sprint-like training and that long distance training would decease you fast twitch muscle, thereby making you slower. For many years experts also said that long slow distance, or LSD, was the best way to train and offered the most benefit for your heart.

Recent research has shown that we actually have three different types of muscle fiber: fast twitch, slow twitch, and super fast twitch. And, we have all three types of muscle fiber when we are young. Over time, if we don't use our muscles, they will begin to atrophy, or get weaker. An additional finding is that, not only do our muscles atrophy, but we also eventually lose the fast twitch fiber we had to begin with. Phil Campbell has found that we actually have two types of fast twitch, one and type two, and we develop both types by incorporating high-intensity training into our physical routine. An additional benefit of gaining fast twitch muscle is an increase in our metabolism. In other words, fast twitch muscle burns more energy than slow twitch so you are actually raising the intensity of your metabolism. Campbell's' research has indicated that, following a high-intensity interval workout, our metabolism continues to be elevated for at least two hours after exercise. He says the increase in metabolism is like a heat-seeking missile and continues to search out and burn fat even after you have completed your exercise routine.

Campbell has found that short, high-intensity intervals are actually better for your body than long slow distance. It benefits your heart, weight and muscle tone. He has named the program that he recommends Sprint Eight. The more common name for it on most websites is Peak Eight. It consists of a warm-up period of three to four minutes, then eight intervals for a duration of 30 seconds followed by a recovery period of 90 seconds between each interval. The routine is completed by a cool-down period of about 4–6 minutes followed by stretching. The goal for the interval periods is to get your heart rate to your maximum. You calculate what your maximum heart rate is by subtracting your age from 220. For example, if you are 57 your maximum heart rate is 163. What I do is take my heart rate after the fourth, sixth, and eighth interval to make sure I'm exercising at the right intensity.

Phil recommends doing the Sprint Eight either on an elliptical machine or a recumbent bike. You can do it with any type of exercise, swimming, running, etcetera, as long as you are getting your heart rate to the desired count. If you choose to use running as your exercise, you have to be careful not to pull a hamstring. I do my HIIT by running and I haven't had any problems. I make sure I warm up and I ease into the sprints. For example, I may not get my heart rate to its max during the first or second interval. But after the second sprint I'm going full throttle. In the Resource section I have included several websites for companies that have specific machines designed for Peak Eight. I have also included several YouTube sites that show how to do the Peak Eight and have Phil Campbell being interviewed by Dr. Joseph Mercola on the research and how Campbell trains elite athletes using his Sprint Eight.

Dr. Mercola has named his version of Campbell's exercise routine Peak Eight. Dr. Mercola was a long-distance runner but, because of some research he had been reading about the benefits of interval training, he decided to try some interval training techniques. After reading Campbell's research, Mercola tried Peak Eight and found it to be the one that works best for him. Mercola is a true believer because of the results he has seen in his own body in just six to eight months. I have included links to a video demonstrating Phil Campbell coaching Dr. Mercola through a Peak Eight routine on a recumbent bike.

After a thorough review of the literature, I decided to try Peak Eight. After two months I could see and feel a significant change in the way my body felt and looked and the increase in energy I experienced. Peak Eight is now a regular part of my exercise routine. I do it twice a week, sometimes three times a week. The recommendation is two or three times a week. I used to run distance four to five times a week. Now I do Peak Eight twice a week and run distance one or two times a week just because I like it and it soothes my soul. I also incorporate a strength training routine twice a week. My speed in my distance runs has actually improved and my cardiovascular health is stronger then whan I was doing more distance.

I don't want to sound like a commercial, but in my experience the HIIT has a definite impact on muscle tone, metabolism, and cardiovascular health. Take a look at the resources I have included and see for yourself. It is also a good alternative for those who have limited time. Literally you are spending only about 25 to 30 minutes twice a week with very beneficial results. Again, every body is unique so you have to be the judge of what works for you. And, as with any intensive physical training, you must ensure you are healthy enough to participate in that type of routine. If you have any type of heart problems or physical limitations, it is best to seek professional help and to see your family physician before doing that kind of exercise.

Lastly, we cannot overlook the importance of getting proper sleep. Lack of sleep can affect concentration. It can lead to increased anxiety, high levels of stress and low levels of energy. Research suggests that most people need seven to eight hours of sleep per night for optimal performance levels. I realize there can be extenuating circumstances such as babies, pets, and work schedules that can prevent even the best-intentioned individuals from getting the right amount of sleep. Whenever you can, though, get the recommended amount of sleep. My sister and sister-in-law made it a rule that when the baby took a nap, so did she. Whether she was sleepy or not, she made herself lie down and rest. I'm sure the moms and dads out there have come up with novel ways to get some sleep. Take a look at your sleep habits and make sure you are doing what is necessary for you to engage mindfully during your waking hours. It will help you feel refreshed and ready to fully participate with optimal energy throughout the day.

APPROACH

Let's develop a system to manage and renew your physical energy.

What type of physical energy do you have? Do you exercise regularly? Do you have healthy and nutritious eating patterns? Do you intersperse your work day with some time to rest and rejuvenate? Let's take a look at your physical energy management and choose what aspects you want to continue doing, what you might want to stop doing, and what you want to start doing in order to develop strength, endurance, flexibility and balance in the area of physical energy.

Practice

Physical Energy

- How would you describe your overall physical health?
- Describe your exercise habits.
- Describe your eating habits.
- Describe your sleeping habits.
- Based on what you've read in this Cairn, how well do the habits you've just described lend themselves to effective management of your physical energy?
- On a scale of 1 to 5, where would you rate your ability to feel deeply relaxed?

    1   2   3   4   5

- When was the last time you fully let go and felt fully disconnected from the stresses and pressures of life?
- Describe a time when you felt low energy, difficulty maintaining concentration and/or low stress tolerance. What time of day was it?
- How did you renew your energy? What do you think contributed to that experience?

This is a lot of information to track on your own. Optimal fitness involves attending to the whole body and mind. It has become an industry that includes a variety of expertise and experience including personal trainers, nutritionists, message therapists and performance coaches. To fully understand and optimize your physical capacity, you may want to consider a personal trainer with a solid background in exercise physiology, a nutritionist with a focus on sport and performance nutrition, or joining a small gym geared toward an integrated approach to fitness where you can get personalized attention and a well-rounded training program specifically designed for you.

I realize that some people balk at the word *exercise* so let's just call it movement. The important thing is that if you already incorporate movement in your life, continue to make it an important and integral aspect of your lifestyle. If you do not have a movement routine, say walking, yoga, or any type of motion that gets your heart going, seek out a routine that you will enjoy and sustain, either on your own or with help from one of the professional resources provided in the Resource Section.

Physical energy is fundamental as a source of fuel. Some people think that exercise will make them tired, so they don't exercise at all. Interestingly, physical exertion actually increases our body's energy stores. Over time, our cardiovascular system improves and we are able to exercise more frequently and for longer periods of time. Exercise also enhances our ability to recover in less time. Exercise also reduces distress and can relieve symptoms of depression and melancholy. How does aerobic exercise do all these things? One of the theories is the release of endorphins.

Exercise increases the amount of endorphins in our brain. Endorphins are little chemicals called peptides, which are produced by the pituitary gland during exercise, excitement, and love, which resemble opiates in their ability to create a feeling of wellbeing. They have analgesic properties. A widely known effect of endorphin production is what we know as the "runner's high."

It generally takes about 90 days to become comfortable with aerobic exercise. Go at it slow and steady. A rule I use for my clients is to jog as fast as you can while still holding a conversation. You may be breathing hard, but you can still talk. The goal is not to kill yourself. The goal is to learn to enjoy the time you spend moving, no matter what type you choose, otherwise you won't continue.

To build and sustain a healthy physical lifestyle, you must take into consideration what you eat, your cardiovascular condition, the flexibility of your muscles, your sleep habits, and your ability to balance expenditure with recovery throughout your day, at home and at work. Loehr suggests that we should approach each day as a series of sprints rather than a marathon. The marathon concept seems to suggest drudgery and a drive to just keep going even if you're tired. The sprint concept Loehr suggests is to engage in your chosen activity for 60–90 minutes, then take a break. The break can be short; a couple of minutes is all it takes. It can involve a walk around the room or down the hallway, or a simple relaxation technique while still in your office or at your kitchen table. I discuss this technique in the Practice section below.

Athletes such as tennis players use this relaxation technique. When you see tennis players changing sides of the court, they sometimes sit down and put their heads under a towel. Many of the elite players have become proficient at being able to put themselves in a relaxed state of mind in a matter of seconds. Research from sport psychology shows that even 60 seconds of this type of relaxation can be beneficial in renewing energy.

Some examples of ways to rejuvenate during your day will be discussed when we talk about Mental/Emotional Energy. Below are a few to consider building in to your daily ritual.

1. Take a break every 90 to 120 minutes to allow for recovery so you can be fully engaged throughout your day.

2. Eat a healthy breakfast. Have a snack around 10:00 and 3:00 consisting of things like a low glycemic energy bar, a handful of almonds or walnuts, fruit, or protein drink. Stay away from high-fat snacks such as donuts, cookies, crackers, candy or chips.

3. Simply sit back in your chair, close your eyes, and focus on your breathing for 60 seconds. As you are focused on your breaths, think of something or someone that creates feelings of compassion and love. This can even be a pet. Whatever you decide, let the image fill your heart. Breathe through your heart and allow those compassionate, loving feelings to move smoothly through, in and around your heart with each breath. You will be amazed at the rejuvenating power this simple and brief practice has. You can do this longer, say up to three, five or ten minutes, if it fits in your routine. Even Einstein was known for taking catnaps. What a smart guy!

4. Consult the resources listed at the back of the book in the Resource Section.

Whatever you decide to do, do it consistently and give yourself at least 90 days. It usually takes that long to develop a new habit. I also invite you to remember *Desiderata*, a poem by poet and attorney Max Ehrmann and a big influence on the life of Adlai Stevenson. Adlai Stevenson was the United

States Ambassador to the United Nations from 1961 to 1965. As a politician, he was known for his intellectual demeanor and eloquent oratory. In 1952 and 1956 he was the Democratic nominee for president; both times being defeated by Dwight D. Eisenhower. Then, in 1960, he ran again only to be defeated by John F. Kennedy, who appointed Stevenson an Ambassador to the United Nations. He was an avid reader and a Princeton graduate in history and literature.

Desiderata was a piece of literature he felt had an impact on how he conducted his life. It is said that a guest in Adlai Stevenson's home found a letter attached to a copy of the poem by Stevenson's bedside shortly after his death in 1965. The letter said he was planning on using it in his Christmas cards. The publicity from this finding gave widespread fame to the poem. It has been a favorite of mine since I was a child. I don't remember when I first read it, but it had an impact. It comes from the Latin word *desideratum*, which means "desired thing." This is one of my favorite lines from *Desiderata*: "Beyond a wholesome discipline, be gentle with yourself."

REFLECT AND ENGAGE

- What are your CORE learnings from this Cairn?
- How will you apply these things in your life?
- What have you learned about yourself at this Cairn?
- Based on the practices at this Cairn, what will you do to expand your capacity and ability to be the creative force in your life?
- How will you celebrate the completion of this Cairn?

Cairn X

Energy Management
Step 2: Emotional Energy Management

"Courage is not about being unafraid. Courage is the willingness to be with fear."

—Ezra Bayda, *Saying Yes To Life (Even the Hard Parts)*

This step is an integration of performance psychology, neuroscience and Emotional Intelligence (EI). We will explore:

- What is performance psychology?

- What is Emotional Intelligence?

- What emotional states are working for you and which ones are limiting you?

- Practical action steps for personal transformation.

- How you can rewire your brain.

- How you can engage in emotionally charged situations in an effective manner for greater success at home and at work.

In this section, the accent will be on emotions, what they are, why they have such an acute effect on behavior, and how we can learn to manage them in support of our ability to create a rich, full and meaningful life. We will first look at neuroscience and the way the brain is wired. Next we will focus on how our emotions impact behavior from a performance psychology perspective, followed by an investigation into Emotional Intelligence and its overall significance in our ability to successfully cope with our environment. We will complete the picture by looking at the concept and experience of coherence. In the next section, Mental Energy Management, our focus will be on the other aspect of our cognitive functioning, thoughts. Together, these two sections further our ability to recognize and engage our internal power as we expand our awareness of the power of our minds. So, let's start with emotions and the limbic system.

We are predisposed physically, mentally, and emotionally to respond to our environment in ways that assure our survival. Our brain houses a highly adaptive and intelligent system equipped with mechanisms to keep us safe. The part of the brain that is charged with alerting us to danger and then positioning us to cope with that danger is known as the limbic system. Our limbic system is encoded with a basic set of nerve patterns that fire when we encounter certain events, thoughts, people or situations. Neurotransmitters are chemicals that conduct messages between nerve cells, triggering a pattern of responses in our body, leading to the actions necessary for us to survive a threat.

Early on, our brains recognized the threat of a saber-toothed tiger and sent the appropriate signals across nerve cells to fight or take flight. These signals served to keep us safe and over time became hard-wired, or default, patterns in our brains. Our environment has changed, however, and it is no longer necessary to respond to saber-toothed tigers. However, the identical physiological mechanisms that enabled us to survive primitive threats are still active in our brains. We have the same physiological response to apparent danger because of the hardwiring in our brain. Physiologically, we react to a saber-toothed tiger, when in reality the "perceived danger" is an event, situation, person, or experience. We may want to run or fight, but those are not the most effective responses. The difference is that we now have much more sophisticated brains in terms of our awareness and ability to realistically and rationally identify and respond appropriately to the apparent danger.

As we have evolved as a species, our brains have adapted to changing environments. Our brain is not static. It is malleable and has an inherent capacity to change, which scientists call "plasticity." Research by neuroscientists has documented how our brain designs new patterns in response to new information. As we learn from our new and ever-changing environment, we are literally reconfiguring the neural pathways in our brains. As a result of learning, the signals from our neurons are able to travel a different path. We are changing our wiring so we can respond in a more fitting manner. Even though we may have a similar physiological reaction to a perceived threat, the message in our brain travels new pathways and creates opportunities for a much more skillful response. We don't have to flee or fight. We can now intentionally choreograph behaviors that are appropriate to our modern-day environment.

This marvelous feature of the brain is the genesis of our capacity to transform our minds. This transformation includes both emotions and thoughts, but for now we are focusing on emotions. By identifying emotions that have previously caused undesirable behavior, we can begin to redirect the patterns traveling over our nerve cells and change the way our brain works. Inner transformation begins with awareness, which then contributes to our learning and involves a disciplined approach to rethinking ineffective conditioned responses. This is what I refer to as a systematic training of the mind. By becoming cognizant of our internal states, whether it's a perception, sensation or notion, we can begin to shift our automatic, or default, responses to ones that provide a more skilled approach in support of our values and purpose.

The energy that our cognitive center puts out is powerful. However, the limbic system, our emotional center, puts out a higher frequency of energy than our cognitive center. The HeartMath Institute has documented findings that the heart emits an energy field that measures 60 times greater than that of our brain. One of the initial steps that forms the bedrock for our ability to tailor a more skillful response to a stressful environment is to bring these affiliated and powerful systems into a coherent unit. When these two potent systems are united in terms of their energy, it cultivates a sense of equanimity which yields increased wellbeing, deepened relationships, expanded creativity, and more masterly conduct in our daily and work lives.

By creating coherence between the brain and the heart, we are able to draw on the information from both energy systems. Being able to use both our head and our heart in tandem brings clarity and focus to our situation and we are better equipped to act in an effective, value-based manner. With both systems operating in coherence, we have full access to our knowledge, wisdom, experience, and expertise. Coherence within these two powerful energy systems actually makes us smarter and more skilled because we are now firing on all cylinders. We are using our full capacity for decisions, problem-solving, and actions. Ultimately, through a coherent inner condition, we can consistently perform at the upper reaches of our potential.

The thoughts and emotions experienced when you are in a coherent state are similar to those that athletes experience when they are in the zone— the flow state. To call upon a coherent energy state at any given moment is a skill. Athletes practice their mental skills just like they practice their physical skills. And, just like physical skills improve over time with consistent practice, so do mental skills. When you practice creating coherence, you will be able to create your own flow state in any given moment just like the best athletes can create their flow state under pressure.

"Flow" is a term proposed by University of Chicago professor of psychology Mihalyi Csikszentmihalyi as the mental state of someone absorbed in a feeling of energized focus, complete engagement, and success in the process of an activity. According to Csikszentmihalyi, flow is a "single-minded immersion" and characterizes the ultimate in harnessing the emotions. Flow is fully-focused motivation. In the flow state, or "the zone" as it is sometimes referred to, time seems to slow down and people experience surprisingly higher physical performance. The trademark of flow is a feeling of spontaneous joy, even rapture, while participating in an activity or while executing a task.

In sports psychology literature, flow represents our optimal performance state. Each of us has an optimal performance state that is distinct to us, depending on our personality and how we approach competition and mastery. You can learn to enter the zone, the flow state, through visualization. Visualization is a skill often used by elite athletes who want to learn how to create their optimal performance state on demand so they are able to perform consistently at peak levels. Using visualization to engage the flow state is now being applied in business, sales, education and the performing arts to help people reach the "top of their game" when needed. The skill of visualization gives you an edge in a competitive environment.

The more you hone the skill of visualization, the faster you will be able to create an internal environment that fosters good performance. When you have learned to compose the right constellation of emotions unique to you, performing at your best at any given moment is possible. However, you don't have to have a particular "zone" state to have a good performance. In coaching athletes, business people and other performers, I've learned that even when you're not feeling positive, you can still perform well. You can be frustrated, anxious, or even angry and still perform well. The skill here is to be able to accept how you're feeling and refocus your energy to your values and intention.

Looking back over the years that performance psychologists have spent attempting to improve performance, we've learned that the overall constellation of positive emotions is beneficial for optimal performance, but not necessary. What is necessary for high performance is the ability to direct attentional focus while engaged in an event or situation. Attentional focus is being able to attend to the task at hand no matter what you're thinking or feeling. If you're so concerned with what and how you're feeling that you can't focus on the specific task, your performance will suffer. Your attention is directed inward instead of outward, where the performance is taking place.

In the past, we've been taught that, to perform well, we have to be feeling good and thinking positively. That's why, when we're in a negative state of mind, our energy is typically directed at trying to change, fix, or eliminate the negative thoughts or feelings. But this inward orientation prevents us from focusing externally, where the performance is taking place, thereby distracting our attention and impacting our performance negatively.

So, there are two skills essential to perform consistently at optimal levels. The first is to understand your individual ideal performance state and use skills such as visualization and self-talk to practice creating that internal state whenever you want to. This provides you with the knowledge that, when you know you have to perform well, you can prepare ahead of time to create your optimal performance zone. You can also use visualization and self-talk to maintain that internal state throughout the performance event.

The second skill is being able to redirect your focus to the performance task at hand when you are having negative thoughts and emotions during an event, situation or interaction with a person. The performance is taking place in the external environment—the situation, event or person we are interacting with. We want to be able to accept internal unrest, turn our attention outside ourselves in the moment and direct our attention to the task at hand—the performance. When we can do this, no matter what our internal state is, there will be a minimal negative impact on performance.

This gives us the ability to control our attentional focus. When we can successfully do this in the midst of internal conflict, we can perform with poise. Poise is the capacity to direct our attention to the event, situation or person at hand and manage our response in a value-driven manner, no matter what is happening in our internal or external environments. When we can do this, our thoughts and feelings have less impact on our performance. It puts us in the driver's seat, and rather than having an emotionally-driven reaction, we have a value-based response. Following the event, you can reflect on the thoughts and emotions that arose during the situation and choose whether to address them. This is part of our capacity to rewire our brain to think in more positive and less limiting ways. We'll address this skill at the end of this cairn, and in the next cairn on mental energy.

To reiterate, one skill necessary for optimal performance is the ability to create our optimal performance state on demand. The other skill necessary for optimal performance is the ability to accept your emotions, thoughts, and bodily sensations as passing events rather than absolute reality, or something that needs eliminated or fixed right then, and focus rather on the task at hand. This skill makes optimal performance possible despite internal states of worry, anxiety, or self-doubt. Another way to look at this skill is as the ability to feel the fear and proceed anyway. Either way, you can develop the ability to enter the zone of optimal performance whenever you choose to do so and attain your flow state.

Flow is characterized by strong, positive emotions and is based on the ability to create a positive, task-specific focus. Realizing your flow state, your zone, whenever you need or want to requires the ability to create and maintain a positive approach to a competitive environment despite any situation or challenge. This is a practical skill to develop and have at your disposal no matter what you are engaged in, whether it's parenting, teaching, managing, or any circumstance that involves focusing on a person, task, goal or situation. Being in a coherent flow state provides greater clarity and a more robust internal environment for effective, value-based action.

Let's look briefly at how the limbic system, the body's emotional regulatory system, functions within the parameters of flow. The sciences of neurophysiology and biochemistry have given us valuable insights into our understanding of emotional states and their effect on performance. One of the first disciplines to conduct and apply research on emotions, coherence and their effect on how we function under stress was athletics. Why did some of the best athletes exhibit exceptional performance on one day when, a week later, their performance was less than stellar? Let's look at one example of a brilliant athletic career that had its ups and downs, that of John Elway, the quarterback for the Denver Broncos who led the team to two Super Bowl victories.

My parents live in Denver and I've watched the Broncos play football many times with my mom and dad. There were times when Elway couldn't do anything wrong. His passes were right on the mark. When he was under pressure, he ran effortlessly for first downs and touchdowns. And his play-calling and team leadership were beyond reproach.

You would assume that, after a great game, followed by a week of recovery, rest, and practice, Elway's skill level would improve over the previous week's outstanding performance. Not always so. There were times when the next week's performance was sub-par—nowhere near Elway's capabilities and talents. He was the same person externally, yet something had shifted internally. His head and heart energy were not in coherence and he was unable to use his strengths and skills to their potential. Where in the former game, Elway's performance seemed to be in the flow, the following week his efforts seemed disjointed, and not in sync with the team. His entire production that day was simply off the mark.

Findings from Performance Psychology and motivational literature indicate that it is not the talent or skill level of the athlete that varies from performance to performance. It stands to reason that practice improves one's skill level. So, what is the culprit behind a less-than-skilled rendering of talent? Research confirms that it is the athlete's mental/emotional state that is out of sync. When they feel focused, confident, at ease, they play to their potential. When they have positive feelings, they have outstanding performances. When the appropriate emotional state is in place, a good performance is the result. Why?

At the core of these findings is our old friend, the limbic system. Housing our emotions, it controls the emotional climate of our bodies. On top of all that, it is also a switchboard where messages from various parts of the body pass through on their way to other parts of the body. These messages are carried in the form of neurotransmitters and hormones. Neurotransmitters carry signals between cells. Hormones flow in the bloodstream. Different neurotransmitters produce different experiences in the body.

For example, norepinephrine produces an energized state. If you don't know how to regulate the output of norepinephrine, it can make you edgy and anxious. Serotonin, another neurotransmitter, causes feelings of calm and relaxation. Therefore, your emotional state can determine whether you can perform the simple act of holding your hand steady. You can see how your emotional state can have a dramatic effect on performance. You are physically and chemically different with different emotional states. When you change emotional states, happy to angry, bored to excited, uptight to calm, you change your biochemistry and your ability to perform a task.

If you are unaware of your emotional climate, you will experience less-than-effective performances or behavior. As we will see in our discussion about Emotional Intelligence, we can get hijacked when we are unaware of our inner condition. This can lead to a downward spiral, taking us further away from any semblance of effective action. The good news is, with awareness and understanding, we can develop significant control over our emotional balance. With practice, we can learn to shift our emotional climate and develop control over our performance state. We can achieve our optimal performance state by learning to create a unique emotional environment that is within our control.

Emotional management ensures that you can reach the upper reaches of your capacity on a consistent basis. You can learn how to move between energy states, giving you the capability to engage effective behavior, no matter what your "performance arena" or the activity you in which you are involved. Emotional control gives you the ability to summon your best effort when it is needed. It also gives you a greater ability to create a positive inner condition for enhanced wellbeing and happiness. Developing emotional awareness and control puts us in a position to choose our feelings. It basically gives us the capability to recognize unwanted or harmful emotions, and then choose to replace them with more positive feelings so we can cope with our situation in a healthier, more effective manner.

Listed below are some of the sensations, feelings, and thoughts that have typically been observed in people during their experience of "flow" or a peak performance. These are typically referred to as positive mental and emotional states. When we look at the emotions extended from a coherent state, you'll immediately notice the similarity between that list and the list of thoughts and emotions listed below.

Positive Energy States

Energized	Joyful	Curious
Compassionate	Appreciative	Open-minded
Willing	Engaged	Trusting
Kind	Relaxed	Purposeful
Enthusiastic	Passionate	Mindful
Connected	Flexible	

Next I have listed some emotions, feelings, and sensations that some psychologists refer to as "hot" emotions. These feelings tend to detract from our ability to create coherence. They are sensations, emotions and thoughts that can lead to negative consequences and can be harmful to those around us as well as ourselves. They are usually experienced as triggers leading to distress and less-than-optimal performance.

Negative Energy States

Weary	Jealous	Annoyed
Fearful	Envious	Irritated
Anxious	Resentful	Burned-out
Angry	Overwhelmed	Disconnected
Frustrated	Bored	Sad
Vengeful	Uninterested	

The skill is to notice the emotion and not to judge yourself for experiencing this feeling, but simply to ask, "What is this sensation telling me about my inner condition and my perception of the outer environment?" Rather than judge your internal backdrop, it is best to observe and describe it with mindfulness and clarity. Then you can use the description of what you are thinking and feeling as information so you don't get hijacked into actions that may limit you or slow your progress toward your goals. We can then use that information to change our thought patterns and choose to focus on positive, beneficial emotions and thoughts. Choice gives us the ability to short-circuit our typical responses to "hot" emotions, which might lead to negative consequences. When we are aware of the emotions that trigger ineffective behavior, we can override those actions by choosing to behave in a value-based manner.

When we mindfully engage in this process, with practice we are able to assure that our actions are aligned with our values, giving us an increased sense of peace of mind. With practice, we gain the ability to recognize the triggers that typically would cause a default negative reaction and choose more effective behavior. We are changing the very structure of our brains by reconfiguring our hardwiring. This transformation in our thinking gives us the ability to engage actions that are beneficial and effectively promote happiness and wellbeing and serve to enrich our relationships.

A caveat for this section is that some say that emotions such as anger or fear can motivate and heighten action. I acknowledge that they can increase our level of energy, but it is neither positive nor coherent. Business and athletic research indicates that this level of performance is unsustainable and will lead to burnout very quickly. The performance and actions that ensue from these emotions is not only inconsistent, but does not lend itself to a coherent, or flow state.

The key is to "experience" the emotion, identify the source, accurately interpret the information the emotion is transmitting, and then direct our behavior toward a productive, skillful response. We can actually create an internal environment consisting of the emotions, sensations, and thoughts that constitute the constellation for our unique flow state. But why would we want to do this outside the arena of business and athletics? It becomes almost commonsense that managing emotions is linked to living a full, rich and meaningful life.

A school of thought that is gaining recognition and popularity in business and other disciplines is Emotional Intelligence, or EI. Emotional Intelligence provides a scientific, as well as a practical, backdrop for why managing our emotions is critical, not only to optimal performance, but also a healthy balance in our everyday lives. The field has significantly contributed to our knowledge and understanding of the impact of our emotions on our health and wellbeing. The domain has also provided a method of measuring and developing our intelligence around emotions. This gave the theory a foothold in the scientific community and raised the concept to the level of IQ. In fact, findings indicate that Emotional Intelligence is the separator between those who are adequate at what they do and those who excel. Let's take a deeper look at this burgeoning field.

EI represents our innate genius. It encourages our capacity to be our best. It houses our ability for self-awareness, self-actualization, and self-regard, as well as our ability to feel empathy, compassion and kindness for others. Without Emotional Intelligence, we become mechanical and reactive to external circumstances to the point of feeling that we have no choice. EI is about choices. It is one of our most powerful skills, and necessary if we are to not only survive, but also thrive, as individuals and as a society. Through our awareness and management of emotional energy, we can positively influence our behavior and the impact we have on others. We can also develop the skills of empathy and social responsibility to better understand and relate to the people in our life and make a positive contribution to the human community. We will focus on how Emotional Intelligence is a key component to living, working, and relating at our best.

The idea of Emotional Intelligence has been around since the early '70s, with the original research coming from the disciplines of psychology and education from Harvard and Yale. When the concept of Emotional Intelligence was initially introduced to the academic community, most of the world remained unaware of the influential impact EI has on our success in our personal and professional lives.

In his 1995 bestselling book *Emotional Intelligence: Why It Can Matter More Than IQ*, Daniel Goleman introduced the concept of Emotional Intelligence to the general public. In it, he reported breakthrough neuroscience and business research indicating the importance of awareness and management of emotions as the critical factor for success, rather than just our cognitive abilities. During times of a heightened emotional state of agitation, our knowledge, expertise and experience become a moot point if we are unable to access the necessary information for an intelligent response. We need to learn to notice and interpret our emotional state so we can integrate our analytical abilities and choose a response that parallels our values and purpose. This is the foundation of emotional energy management.

Since the release of Goleman's groundbreaking book, there has been a multitude of books relating the research from the fields of neuroscience, organizational development, performance psychology, and motivation to Emotional Intelligence. Now there is a solid body of research indicating that EI is key to our success in all types of relationships, personally and professionally.

Emotional Intelligence is defined as a collection of skills that we use to be aware of and manage our relationships and ourselves. Goleman and other researchers have clearly demonstrated that those who effectively engage the competencies of Emotional Intelligence have higher levels of wellbeing, personal fulfillment, and success at home and at work. Research from the

HeartMath Institute reveals that, more often than not, lack of success in our personal and professional relationships is directly related to mismanagement of emotional energy.

Emotions motivate us. The root word for emotion in Latin is *motere*, "to move." Emotions move us in one direction or the other. They can take us in a positive direction and create coherence, or they can send us in a downward spiral. When we are not aware of our emotions, they can hijack our intellectual functioning. That's why even smart people can do and say stupid things. To avoid being hijacked, we need to be aware of what we are feeling in the moment and be cognizant of other people's emotional energy as well.

When we are aware of our emotions and the emotional energy of those around us, we can regulate our responses and behaviors to positively impact and enrich our relationships. Emotional Intelligence begins to develop at an early age. We all have a certain talent for Emotional Intelligence, but whether or not we develop the talent into a strength so we can access it under duress is another story. That's why it's important to understand what Emotional Intelligence is and recognize the competencies involved. Awareness of our emotions and the emotions of others is a skill that can be developed. When we set an intention to expand our skill in Emotional Intelligence, the direction of our development grows exponentially. Being able to call on this skill in highly-charged, stressful situations requires a mindful approach to our interpersonal interactions. If we fail to be mindful, our emotions can overwhelm us and cause negative results within relationships at home and at work.

Remember our old friend, the limbic system? Let's look at still another reason why a cursory understanding of this system may prove beneficial in our quest for optimal performance and wellbeing. The limbic system is the part of our brain that houses structures such as the amygdala and the hypothalamus. Our hypothalamus is home to all of our memories and the amygdala stores the emotions attached to those experiences. This is why certain situations can bring up feelings instantly. They remind us of an experience from the past. For example, if I were to mention the events of September 11, 2001, several things start to happen for you. You can probably remember exactly what you were doing and where you were when you first became aware of the tragedy. Most likely, the mention of that date provokes an emotional response. The memory of that event is stored in the two organs I mentioned: the hypothalamus remembers where you were and the amygdala houses the emotions attached to the memory. This is why certain words, gestures, or sights trigger emotional responses without us even knowing it is going to happen. Once again, this was initially meant to keep us safe so our species could survive. However, sometimes we have an emotional trigger that sends us down a negative path even when the situation is not threatening. Our limbic system is a powerful force in our lives. To use that faculty to cope successfully with life, we must be aware of our internal environment.

By remembering what a particular experience was like and how we responded to it, we can utilize those emotions to recreate the internal environment necessary for another successful experience. For example, we can remember a successful race where we experienced a peak performance and can use that past experience to create a flow state for optimal performance whenever we're faced with an event where we want to do well. Remember, this methodology has been used successfully with athletes for years so they can learn how to intentionally fabricate an internal experience of flow.

One of the primary reasons imagery is so compelling is because the amygdala and hypothalamus have stored experiences of joy, happiness, or any experience of success we have had as well as the related emotions. To reiterate, we can tap into this past knowledge through remembering what this state felt like, and then recreating the feelings that accompanied the original occurrence. We can trick our brains to think we are actually participating in that joyful experience. Certain brain structures literally don't know the difference between reality and imagination. That's how powerful our thoughts, emotions, and imaginations are. We will discuss this topic further during the Practice section of this Cairn. It is a useful skill no matter what your chosen endeavor may be. Our cognitive and emotional centers are powerful tools, but they can only be used successfully once we learn how to mange them.

Our emotional-cognitive structures are interconnected. They are highly adaptive and intelligent systems. They are meant to keep us safe. That is why they engender the "fight-or-flight" response. For example, when you are walking along a path and see a curved stick out of the corner of your eye, you might jump because you think it is a snake. That initial feeling of the urge to flee comes from our limbic structures and is meant to take us out of harm's way. Another example: imagine you are walking back to your hotel room after dark in an unfamiliar city and you hear footsteps quickly approaching you. Most of us would have a feeling of concern, maybe even fear. Our brain is telling us it might be time to run, or prepare to defend ourselves. Once we realize it's just a jogger out for their evening run, we settle down. Once again, our limbic system has reacted to keep us safe. And it does so very quickly, mostly without us realizing it. You might say we are hard-wired to react in specific ways under certain circumstances. For our purposes, what you need to know is that the amygdala reacts much faster than our cognitive brain. That is why intense emotions can hijack us if we are unaware of what we are feeling. Some memories are so subconscious that emotions can seem to come from nowhere and send us in to a downward spiral very quickly.

When our emotions take over, we cannot access our cognitive strength. We are simply functioning at less than optimum. We are not acting with our full capacity. Awareness and understanding of our emotional states gives us the ability to regulate our response so we can combine both our analytical and emotional mind. This literally makes us smarter.

Emotions are powerful motivators. They originate in the brain, but they seem to live in our heart. Candace Pert, a neuroscientist, is internationally known for her discovery of the opiate receptor, the cellular binding site for endorphins in the brain. For a time, it was hypothesized that these receptors were only found in the brain. However, Pert's extensive research found similar opiate receptors both in the brain and in the heart. Her findings showed that these molecules store emotional memory and circulate throughout the body. In her book *Molecules of Emotion,* she expounds on her theory that "molecules of emotion integrate what we feel at every level of what I call our bodymind." Our brains and our heart are powerful tools that can be used to create health and wellbeing. Bringing these two powerful sources of energy together so they function in a vibrant, connected pattern offers the greatest opportunity for us to call on our deepest learning and experience, not only for optimal health, but also for optimal performance. The energy of both the brain and the heart is vast. Our aim is to create resonance between these two related fields so they can work in tandem, complementing the other energy systems, generating healthier relationships and greater effectiveness in our daily and work lives.

All of this information offers a solid understanding of the benefits of a coherent state. The bottom line is that, when we integrate our cognitive and emotional resources, we can use all of our intelligence to make us smarter and better able to successfully cope with our environment. The gathering of the whole of our intelligence into a coherent pattern contributes to our overall wellbeing and balance. Being able to acknowledge and use the information from our emotions and intentionally integrate it with our cognitive knowledge in a healthy and positive manner is at the heart of Emotional Intelligence.

The first step in acknowledging emotions is awareness. In many ways our culture has denigrated emotions to second-class citizens. Emotions are a nuisance to be ignored, averted, or eliminated. In the business world, emotions are treated like dirty shoes. Please leave them at the door. Do not, under any circumstance, bring them to work with you. We now know that leaving emotions at home is not possible. They are with us every moment of every single day. So, we must learn to be smart about our emotions and how we use them.

Being smart with our emotions comes, first, by being aware that an emotion is happening. Learning to be aware of emotions involves two processes: noticing and clarifying. First, we must be able to notice what emotion we are feeling and how our body manifests that emotion. What does it feel like? Is it constricting, hot, tingling? Do you feel it in your shoulders, neck, stomach or jaw? Are you able to feel it as it begins to emerge, or is it a full-blown mood when you finally recognize it?

The next step to enhance awareness is to clarify the emotion. Be specific in naming the feeling. Many times we say we are angry, but we are really irritated or frustrated. Having a good repertoire of feelings is helpful. Feeling angry usually doesn't start right from anger. Feelings typically grow in intensity along a continuum. We usually start out feeling annoyed, move on to irritated, then become frustrated, then angry and then enraged. Part of the benefit of first developing the skill of noticing is having the ability to register that something is welling inside of you, name it, and clarify what information the feeling is giving you before it triggers a reaction out of anger or rage. The importance of being clear about the specific feeling is that each feeling gives us different information. Frustration gives us very different information than rage, therefore offering a different interpretation and response. If we are unable to notice and clarify our emotions, they can easily elicit unproductive behavior.

There are several reliable measures of Emotional Intelligence. The one I prefer is the SEI—which is the Italian word for "six". It stands for Six Seconds Emotional Intelligence Assessment. The Six Seconds model is practical, action-oriented and simple and is designed to help people change. It is development focused and geared to getting results. It is a rigorous, best-in-class psychometric measurement that has been standardized, normed and validated worldwide. It is an on-line assessment and takes about 20 minutes.

The SEI consists of learnable competencies that focus in three areas: Know Yourself, Choose Yourself, and Give Yourself. There is a SEI-360 and a

SEI YV-Youth Emotional Intelligence Assessment. It consists of eight competencies. Under Know Yourself there are two competencies: Enhance Emotional Literacy and Recognize Patterns. Choose Yourself consists of: Apply Consequential Thinking, Navigate Emotions, Engage Intrinsic Motivation and Exercise Optimism. Give Yourself encompasses: Increase Empathy and Pursue Noble Goals.

The SEI assessment is built for learning and growth in emotional skills. The report provides both summary and detail, plus reflection questions and goal-setting processes so participants are encouraged to take action. You can learn more about the SEI model and competencies in the book *The Heart of Leadership: How to Get Results with Emotional Intelligence* by Joshua Freedman, co-founder of the company Six Seconds.

Included in the Resource Section are a number of good books written about Emotional Intelligence, some of which offer assessments that can give you a cursory idea of your Emotional Intelligence. Of course, if you're serious about understanding and developing your EI, it's a good idea to seek professional assistance in administering an assessment and interpreting the results.

Approach

- Expand your emotional literacy, clarify what coherent energy feels like for you, and develop rituals so you can create coherence.
- Develop a system to manage and renew your emotional energy.
- Assess and develop your Emotional Intelligence.

Practice

Following is a list of six families of emotions. I offer them as a way to expand your awareness of the various emotions that one can feel—a way to expand your emotional literacy. The psychologist Albert Ellis created this list as a way for his clients to gain a more accurate picture of what they were feeling, so he could help them understand their subsequent behavior. In this way, his clients could assess with greater clarity what they were feeling and then choose appropriate ways of responding to the emotion.

Under each category is a list of feelings that fall under a specific emotional umbrella. For example, anger is one of the basic human emotions, and within the idea of anger, there is a continuum of feelings that vary in intensity. Remember, emotions aren't good or bad. They offer us valuable information about our internal environment. This information helps us respond in a more effective manner than if we clump our feelings together. It can also protect us from getting hijacked and reacting in an unskillful way. This increased clarity gives us a way to distinguish between the information each feeling offers us and navigate the array of emotions we're experiencing. For example, under the umbrella of the emotion "anger," *irritated* gives us different information than *irate*. The information gleaned from *annoyed* differs from that of *livid*. Different feelings offer contrasting data and will engender divergent behavior.

Most people clump whatever they're feeling under one emotion. "I'm angry." But the question to ask is, To what extent are you angry? Is it anger or frustration? Are you feeling impatient or are you really feeling incensed? To be able to clarify more clearly what you're actually experiencing internally will illuminate the feeling and help you understand your emotions and the reactions they generate.

I give this handout to my clients for two purposes. First, it simplifies the six basic emotions we experience as human beings. With that knowledge we can see the myriad feelings that could be spawned by a specific emotion. Second, the continuum yields a way to visualize a wide array of intensities that a client might encounter from one emotion. This helps them see that they have a broader array of words to choose from other than simply saying, "I'm angry." Now they can clarify what it is they're really feeling and garner the information that specific feeling gives them. It is a way to expand emotional literacy.

I ask clients to study the feelings listed under each emotion, and during the next week, be mindful of the explicit feelings they are experiencing, name them, and check in with themselves to see if their naming was accurate. Just attempting to put a name to a feeling can tell us if it is true. You've probably had that experience. You feel something but you're not quite sure exactly what. You say, "I'm furious." But you realize that *furious* isn't quite it. No, "I'm not that angry; I'm just annoyed."

The caveat to this is that emotions can escalate, and they usually do so along a continuum. For example, at first you might be annoyed, and if you don't acknowledge that feeling it could escalate to irritated and then to furious. I'm sure you've experienced how a feeling can grow in intensity if not acknowledged. This awareness helps us act in a more emotionally intelligent fashion because we have been precise when naming the emotion and therefore ascertained more accurate information so we can respond in an effective way.

Over time, this practice broadens our emotional literacy. We now have an expanded awareness of the variety of possible feelings and can therefore receive more accurate information from each feeling. We can understand and choose our behavior in a more skilled manner when we are more precise in naming what we're feeling. We are less likely to get hijacked by a feeling we understand than by a feeling we can't name.

THE TWO PHYSIOLOGICAL SENSATIONS

LOVE   **FEAR**

The Six Families of Emotions

Happy	Creative	Surprised	Anxious	Angry	Depressed
Content	Imaginative	Shocked	Fearful	Enraged	Sad
Ecstatic	Resourceful	Dumbfounded	Worried	Sarcastic	Suicidal
Joyous	Artistic	Startled	Concerned	Annoyed	Melancholy
Pleased	Inspired	Astonished	Nervous	Furious	Grieving
Cheerful	Innovative	Amazed	Uneasy	Irritated	Gloomy
Blissful	Ingenious	Stunned	Restless	Irate	Miserable
Exultant	Inquisitive	Flabbergasted	Fretful	Livid	Heartbroken
Delighted	Playful	Astounded	Frightened	Incensed	Distressed
Enthused	Pioneering	Taken Aback	Panicky	Cross	Poignant
Caring	Encouraged	Alarmed	Guilty	Rage	Burdened
Comforting	Brave	Helpless	Numb	Vindictive	Disgrace
Concerned	Capable	Perplexed	Inept	Impatient	Empty
Honored	Curious	Shame	Reluctant	Harassed	Lost
Tender	Open		Suspicious		Resigned
Secure	Engaged		Overwhelmed		Regretful
Passionate	Peaceful		Queasy		Lonely
Gentle	Optimistic		Frantic		Discouraged
Joyful	Energized				Miserable

PRACTICE

List emotions you feel on a regular basis. Think of a variety of situations at home, at work, and during leisure activities. Now distinguish the feelings that you feel in each of those situations. Be aware that, in different situations, you may experience different levels of emotional intensity. This will help you name the feeling. With practice, you'll be able to name a feeling in the moment with more and more precision. This accuracy expands your emotional literacy and places you at a choice-point rather than a reactionary state.

The development of mindfulness is a means of self-regulating attention and intention, and de-centering from one's own internal experience; value identification is a means of determining direction for actions; development of poise is a way to expand experiential acceptance as opposed to experiential avoidance; mindful awareness and mindful intention are ways to promote behavioral change; awareness and understanding of our own internal rules helps to broaden our choices.

Here are some definitions that may help this practice.

- Mindfulness—paying attention in a particular way: on purpose, in the present moment, and non-judgmentally
- Sensation—a physical feeling or perception resulting from something that happens to or comes into contact with the body; an inexplicable awareness or impression
- Emotion—a natural instinctive state of mind deriving from one's circumstances, mood, or relationships with others; instinctive or intuitive feeling as distinguished from reasoning or knowledge
- Feeling—an emotional state or reaction

PRACTICE

Visualization is a powerful tool for bringing internal energy states into balance, or coherence. When you are acting within a coherent framework, you can bring clarity to stressful thoughts and emotions, transforming actions so they are more efficient and effective. Mastering mental/emotional skills takes practice just like it takes practice to learn a new physical skill. With practice, you will be able to move into coherence quickly and in the moment choose a more proactive, positive response rather than one that is mechanical and negative.

Here is a process for creating coherence:

1. Be still a moment and bring your focus to your breathing. There is no need to be anywhere else right now except with your breath. Gently breathe in through your nose, letting the breath fill the area of your chest around your heart. Softly exhale, letting the stillness expand to fill your whole being. You do not need to force any type of breathing. Simply let yourself breathe.

2. Focus on your breathing and notice your breath as it comes in through your nose and out through your mouth. Take a few deep breaths and as you exhale, let any tension that you feel go out with your breath.

3. As you breathe, imagine the area around your heart. Breathe into that space surrounding your heart. Let each breath expand the spaciousness of the center of your being around your heart, allowing it to open more fully. Be aware of the spaciousness each breath allows.

4. Intentionally engage an image that engenders a positive, compassionate, or loving feeling. It can be from any part of your life—someone or something that you love, a partner, a pet, an image from a spiritual tradition that you embrace, or a place that creates a sense of ease, calm, and peace.

5. Begin with any image you can see easily. See the image with your eyes open and closed. If your attention drifts, simply refocus on the image. It may take some time to be able to visualize the image clearly and firmly, but as you practice, you will be able to create the image with great detail. Once you begin to visualize the image, make this feeling as "spacious" as you can and see it as light filling your entire being. Feel the positive energy the image generates around your heart. Allow that feeling to rest in the center of you heart and be aware of a sensation of ease and serenity that flows through you. Notice your experience of the sensation of peacefulness and, with intention, let that feeling radiate through your entire being. Let the image fill you

completely and create a feeling of courage, compassion, and calm. This is your experience of peace and wellbeing.

6. Dwell in this state of consciousness for a while. Realize that you can embody this feeling as it permeates every cell of your body. Now, with that feeling securely anchored in your being, begin to see the world through quiet eyes—eyes of calm, ease, and peace. Practice this exercise on a regular basis, two or three times a day, until the feeling that your image arouses becomes a natural part of the center of your being, surrounding your heart.

7. At the end of your visualization, let the image drift free outside of your body. See it in front of you. Recognize that you created the image and brought it into your being to foster feelings of calm and peace. Observe how your consciousness created this image and let it go as well. Realize and accept that you create and free all images in your mind. Rest in this awareness. This recognition allows for freedom and peace. As you become more astute in your visualization practice, you begin to know that you can allow this image to reappear whenever you desire.

Once you have practiced this and have the experience of what the calm and spaciousness within feels like, at any moment during your day, you can breathe into the space surrounding your heart and create your experience of peace. This sensation offers stability, openness, focus and freedom.

Now you are ready for reflection and/or action with enhanced clarity and creativity. You can use the spaciousness as an opening to look at behavior patterns, thoughts, emotions, and any resistance you might be experiencing. You can also use this "heartspace" breathing as a conscious pause during your day to simply bring awareness to where you are in the moment. It can be used to renew your emotional energy. And it can also be a positive exercise to engage when you need focused attention because it is calming, clears your mind and broadens your perspective and ability for increased focus.

To increase your ability to move to a coherent state of being, practice the "heartspace" process several times a day. You can practice at any time, standing in line at the checkout counter, sitting at your desk, doing the dishes, or walking your dog. Be aware in particular of when you are experiencing some of the feelings of incoherence such as anxiety, frustration, impatience, whatever might cause an emotional trigger for you. By using this practice at these times, you'll be able to shift those feelings to a more positive, coherent experience. From there you'll be better positioned to act from your values and purpose. With practice, you will be able to put yourself in a coherent, spacious space even in a stressful situation.

The lists previously mentioned of thoughts and feelings for positive and negative energy states mirror the thoughts and emotions associated with coherence and incoherence. Incoherence can be associated with action, but it will eventually drain you of energy and make it impossible to be fully engaged or functioning with poise at optimal levels. Usually, incoherent feelings cause us to close up, shut down, or become defensive.

It is interesting that the feelings that emerge from a coherent state are closely related to the same constellation of emotions that transpire within a flow experience, or the zone. These feelings give a sense of openness, flexibility, ease and connection. If you refer to the list of Positive Energy States, you can use an image of any of these words to create affirmative, open energy states. You will realize the greatest benefit as you begin to describe the texture of these words for yourself. What are the sensations you perceive when these emotions happen? Try to paint a vivid picture for yourself for each word. As you develop an awareness of what these words feel and look like for you, the bodily sensation they manifest and where you hold them in your body, with practice you will be able to create the desired energy state at will, regardless of external circumstance. Through mindful intention you'll be poised to engage in a coherent state of being and much more apt to produce positive outcomes.

Imagery is a powerful tool and can be used to create a coherent energy state for optimal performance or a state of relaxation, freedom and peace. Becoming proficient in the ability to create a coherent state is foundational for managing our emotional energy. Coherence elevates our ability to quiet our mind, open our heart, and discover our internal freedom to respond in ways that foster wellbeing for ourselves and others in our lives.

Coherence is the first step. From that internal calm we can begin to feel where and how we experience emotions. The next step is to enhance our awareness of what triggers those emotions. Once we recognize the emotion and understand the trigger, we can begin to discover the thoughts the emotions engender. We can understand whether or not these emotions and thoughts support or limit our ability to live a fulfilled life with value-based actions. We will continue to explore this discipline of energy management in the next section, Mental Energy Management.

If you are interested, this is the point at which I would suggest that you seek out someone who is able to administer, debrief and coach you through an assessment of your Emotional Intelligence. Identifying and taking action to grow your EI will be beneficial regardless of your area of endeavor. Remember, EI is the differentiator between good and great performance, and it benefits every aspect of our lives at home, at work, and at play.

Increasing your awareness of your emotions and how they prioritize your ways of thinking is the beginning for the enhanced ability for self-determination. You recognize that your consciousness creates images, and with awareness, you can begin to control which images you will focus on and which you will let go. The next step is to bring awareness to your patterns of thinking and then to bring both your head and your heart into coherence for an expanded capacity for full engagement. At the following Cairn, I'll introduce several visualization practices you can use to create a state of relaxation or a heightened state of energy for positive, effective action.

REFLECT AND ENGAGE

- What are your CORE learnings from this Cairn?

- How will you apply these things in your life?

- What have you learned about yourself at this Cairn?

- Based on the practices at this Cairn, what will you do to expand your capacity and ability to be the creative force in your life?

- How will you celebrate the completion of this Cairn?

Cairn X

Energy Management
Step 3: Mental Energy Management

"We already have the capacity to deal with challenges. But we need a calm mind to draw on the resources locked up within."

—Eknath Easwaran, *Strength in the Storm*

A s a sport psychologist, I recognize the importance of the mental and emotional aspects of high-level performance. Once you get to a certain level, having the skill to manage your mental and emotional states provides an edge. This principle applies to business, education, parenting—almost any endeavor. People who learn the skills to manage their internal states are the ones who will achieve above and beyond the ordinary and experience an amplified sense of self-determination and mastery. Through an awareness of your cognitive and emotional states, you are better able to manage your behavior and interactions with others so your actions parallel your values and your purpose. Once you can perform this skill on a consistent basis, you begin to experience a greater sense of calm and ease within yourself. Your focus and intentions become much more clear, allowing you greater flexibility to live a life of autonomy, mastery, and purpose.

To ensure that your actions are aligned with your purpose and values, you must develop an awareness of your inner condition at any given moment. This seems simple, but it's not easy. It's during stressful situations that old habits, triggers, and conditioned patterns of reacting take over. Managing our private behavior—our thoughts, feelings, sensations and memories—allows us to anticipate and master our public behavior, i.e. our words and actions. It allows us to be patient during trying times, to tap into our creativity when needed, and to engage the appropriate focus for the task at hand. Developing that level of awareness is an artistry that can transform your ability to make good decisions, to motivate yourself and influence others, and to interact positively with those around you.

In the previous section, we looked at Emotional Intelligence—what it is and how it can be used to direct your emotional energy. We looked at the workings of the brain and the authority of emotions as a motivator. We learned of the commanding connection between our head and heart, as well as how to use visualization to bring them into concert in order to facilitate coherence and wellbeing. In this section, the emphasis will be on a specific area of cognitive functioning—our thoughts, and how they affect our experience, our perception, and our comfort and security. Here the major focus is on identifying positive and negative habits of mind so that we encourage a grounded outlook of optimism and positivity and use it to expand our ability to sustain our coherence, peak performance and continued wellbeing. Bringing emotions and thoughts into league with one another promotes a steady transformation in our ability to self-direct our daily lives while embracing the journey of a rich, full and meaningful life.

In order to achieve a genuine inner transformation, we must practice a systematic training of our mind. With deliberate design, we can cultivate a positive mental attitude that allows us to realize more expansive periods of clarity in focus and freedom in creativity, thereby nurturing peace and wellbeing.

In review, we are born with a system in our brain that is genetically hardwired to keep us safe. We are predisposed physically, mentally, and emotionally to respond to our environment in ways that assure our survival. Our brain is encoded with a basic set of nerve patterns that fire when we encounter certain events, thoughts, or situations. Neurotransmitters are chemicals that conduct messages between cells throughout the body, triggering a pattern of responses that lead to the actions necessary for us to survive a threat. As the neurons travel the same pathways over and over, the paths become well-worn, eventually forming habits, sometimes unknown to us, and our behavior, both private and public, becomes mechanical, without conscious direction.

The findings from modern neuroscience provide proof that when we do something repeatedly, it becomes a natural response. When we replicate thoughts and actions, they actually influence our nervous system. With each action, synapses fire, neurotransmitters are released, and neural pathways are formed and strengthened. We construct a neural hard-wiring that becomes the path of least resistance. It is much like practicing golf. When you intentionally practice your swing over and over, you are forming a neural pathway so you can consistently perform the swing without consideration. Ideally, your golf swing becomes unconscious. Similarly, if we feel angry on a regular basis, it's like practicing being angry, and, therefore, we develop a strong pathway for anger. It's almost like becoming addicted to the emotion of anger. It becomes our default, unconscious reaction and the slightest trigger will set the pattern of anger in motion because it is now our path of least resistance.

At this Cairn we are concerned with identifying our mental states of mind, both negative and positive, along with the consequences of each that have become unconscious pathways of least resistance, limiting our capacity to self-design our lives. We will identify thoughts that generate negative and limiting consequences and then learn to intentionally shift those thoughts to a positive mindset, enabling us to evolve a sustainably positive style. This, again, is like practicing a golf swing. It will take mindful intention and, with practice—repetition, patience and time—it will become our natural swing because we are reconstructing the tracks in our brain. Even though the task of rewiring our brains might seem daunting, the outcome is well worth the effort.

Research from performance psychology and the positive psychology movement supports the premise that mental energy derived from positive thinking precipitates perseverance and sustainable levels of skilled energy. A positive style generates effective performance. Positive mental attitudes promote the ability to focus, generate heightened levels of creativity, encourage better decision-making and problem solving, and best of all, promote an enhanced sense of overall wellness.

Psychologist Martin Seligman spent several years studying the relationship between positive thinking and successful performance. He found that salespeople who had an "optimistic explanatory style" were more persistent over time and in turn had greater success than their cohorts who tended toward doubt and pessimism. Rather than turn their negative experiences back on themselves, blaming and judging, the top sellers chose to appoint a positive approach, to see what they could learn from the previous encounter and what they had control over in order to fix and improve the next situation. In the language of Emotional Intelligence, this is called "realistic optimism."

Again, the question always arises about negative energy also being an impetus for a surge in productivity. Adverse emotions such as anger, resentment, fear or jealousy can spawn an increase in strength and stamina. After all, negative energy is still a form of dynamic vigor, yet the outcome from this type of energy is typically detrimental and destructive to our relationships and ourselves.

Sometimes we don't recognize the deleterious and exhausting effects of negative emotions until we start to increase our awareness of our physical body. Negative energy can propel us into a sense of energetic frenzy along with sustained levels of cortisol. An elevated amount of cortisol over time from repressed or enacted negative emotions is known for having unhealthy effects on our body. Cortisol is a steroid hormone released in response to stress. Its primary function is to increase blood sugar and suppress the immune system. It decreases bone formation and releases substances in the body that cause inflammation. Cortisol also aids in fat, protein and carbohydrate metabolism. Cortisol levels are increased in response to stress. However, prolonged secretion of cortisol due to chronic stress can result in significant physiological changes that can cause improper functioning of some of the body's systems including weakening of the immune system, increasing the chance of stomach ulcers and shutting down the reproductive system. Any way you look at it, raised levels of cortisol are unhealthy and negative emotions that are not managed in a healthy way will eventually drain our energy stores and contribute to burnout and disengagement. The energy from negative thinking is depleting and almost invariably leads to counterproductive and compromising behavior.

Conversely, a shift toward realistic optimism offers physical benefits. Not only can it help to lower cortisol levels in the body, which helps put the body back in homeostasis, but optimism also increases mental clarity and emotional balance. Realistic optimism contributes to our ability to enact all of our intelligence. It provides us with the openness to access our cognitive functions and we are able to use the valuable information from our emotions. In combination, those attributes allow us to act effectively. Effective, value-based action alone can help lower stress and alleviate its negative consequences.

Some of my clients begin to realize the detrimental effects of their negative emotions when they see how they may be manifested physically as headaches, back pain, stiff necks, and stomach trouble. They realize that when they were in a negative state of mind, their focus was diminished. Their negative self-talk caused them to be less motivated. Over time, they became less persistent.

Negative attitudes also limit our scope. We may feel energy, but this type of energy surge feels more constrictive than liberating. Our whole body seems to recoil. Negativity confines our focus to the point that we are not able to access all of the skills we typically could take advantage of. We are in such fight-or-flight mode that our reactions are far less skillful than if we were dealing through our full repertoire of competencies.

One of the best examples of how negative energy can take its toll is in the premier tennis career of John McEnroe. McEnroe had a volatile temper on the court. The least little thing—a perceived bad call, a slow ball boy, a noise in the crowd—would set him off. His own mistakes caused him to yell and scream. He didn't look like he was enjoying any part of the game. McEnroe retired from tennis when he was 34 years old. Even though he was able to win several Grand Slam tournaments and held the number one ranking worldwide for several years, McEnroe admits that if he had learned to control his negative moods, he would have achieved greater heights and been able to play the game longer and had more fun while playing.

Contrast this with award-winning tennis player Jimmy Connors. He also had a bad temper, but as he got older, he learned to control his angry outbursts. Connors looked like he was having fun and enjoying himself. Sometimes he reminded me of a kid, bringing a sense of appreciation, interest, and curiosity to competition. Like McEnroe, Connors also gained the top ranking several times and won many Grand Slam tourneys. While many sportscasters argue that McEnroe was the more talented of the two tennis players, Jimmy's career lasted longer. He reached the semi-finals of the US Open at the age of 39 and retired from the game at 40. I remember watching that match. Jimmy smiled more than I had ever seen him smile. I recall the announcers commenting on how much it looked like Connors was enjoying the game. It was really fun to watch.

McEnroe did redeem himself when, after suffering a devastating loss at the French Open because he blew up and spiraled out of control during the rest of the match, he decided he would not let his emotions overtake him again. Later that year, he managed to curb his anger and win Wimbledon. He was able to shift his negativity to a more positive explanatory style, which, he later wrote in his autobiography, gave him greater focus and increased his capacity to persevere throughout the match.

You might be thinking that these athletes have nothing to do with your situation. They had to learn to manage and direct their emotions during intense physical competition. But, when you are in a stress-filled environment, whether at work or at home, your body has the same reaction as Connors and McEnroe in their high-level competitive environment. Our body doesn't differentiate between the two situations. It reacts to stress in very similar ways, whether it is a challenging remark flying at you or a hundred-mile-an-hour tennis serve. The challenge remains the same: to shift your focus to a positive style which facilitates an external focus on the task at hand so you can deliver your most skillful response during intense circumstances.

The more consistently we can shift our thinking to a positive explanatory style, the more persistent we are and the more capable we become of achieving our desired outcomes. This requires an awareness of what we are thinking, feeling, and wanting in the moment so we can then choose our language and actions. This takes practice, and over time we learn to trust our ability to act in a positive and value-based manner.

First, we have to become aware of how our negative thoughts are harmful to us, causing us to react in unskillful patterns. This negative behavior has harmful consequences for us, as well as those around us. As we develop awareness of what our negative thoughts feel like, what our physical response is to the unfavorable thoughts, how they prioritize our thinking, and how it affects our perception, we can prevent the reactionary behavior triggered by negativity. We can mindfully reframe the thought and replace it with a positive strategy. Mindfulness is really the ultimate power tool. It allows us to recognize possible unhealthy triggers before they take us over and then, in the moment, adopt a more positive frame of mind, which increases our chances for skillful action.

Secondly, we learn the beneficial aspects of positive thoughts. We learn what they feel like, where they come from, and how they affect us physically, mentally, emotionally, and spiritually. The goal is to reconfigure the hardwired negative pathways to be more receptive to positive ways of being. By replacing negative thinking with a positive approach, we make the favorable wiring the path of least resistance. Over time, we are more and more likely to approach situations, people, and our environment with an affirmative mindset. We can engage our focus and creativity with much more clarity and purpose. Our decisions and actions seem much more coherent with our values. The foremost advantage of affirmative thinking is the trust in ourselves that we are acting in an authentic, autonomous manner through our core values in order to create a life we direct, not one directed by exteral happenings.

We'll discuss some of the literature and research that has increased our understanding of the benefits of positivity for our clarity, creativity, and overall sense of wellbeing. Through the intention to redirect our minds toward a more value-based approach to living, we gain a secure knowledge that our experience is within our own hands. When we engage mindful living, we take leadership of our life's direction, our pursuit of mastery, and living on purpose.

This is not simply saying positive affirmations to yourself in the mirror or plastering post-it notes on your desktop. This is a mindful approach to transforming how you think about what you are thinking, what feelings you choose to engage, and the possibilities you see for your life. It is a redesigning of your mind and internal state of being—a restructuring of what you deem relevant to your focus. You begin to understand that you don't have to identify with your emotions. They are not who you are. In fact, you learn to accept whatever physical sensations, thoughts or feelings you are experiencing in that moment as simply that—physical sensations, thoughts, or feelings that will change in the coming moments.

This is known as metacognition. Metacognitive awareness is the ability to fully experience whatever you are feeling, thinking, and wanting simply as that and not as absolute realties that must be acted on right now. You see thoughts, emotions, and sensations as passing events that occur naturally and shift according to the environment. Your core values and purpose do not change. They are consistent over time and under varying circumstances. Therefore, you can respond in a value-based manner no matter what the situation. Even under the most difficult challenges, with a clear understanding of your values, you can respond effectively. Knowing that you can respond to any situation according to your values enhances the experience of autonomy. Autonomy lends itself to a more optimistic approach to life. When we feel we have a choice, we approach life in a much more self-assured, positive manner.

Scientists have known for a long time about the physical and mental benefits of a more optimistic approach to life. Now the research expands our understanding to show that positivity brings increased focus and creativity, better decision-making and problem solving, enhanced performance and an overall sense of choice in our actions. The aim here is to develop the skill to mindfully engage your mind for a more favorable and skillful approach to daily living. This involves employing workable approaches and solutions to situations that lead us closer to our goals.

By engaging mindful living, the ultimate goal is to enhance our ability to guide our attention and respond with grace and self-possession according to our values and purpose. Attention is defined as being present to information relevant to the task at hand, whether it is a person, situation, or activity. Grace is defined as the ability to respond in the service of values, purpose and goals despite negative internal states triggered by thoughts, emotions, and bodily sensations. Previous approaches to changing behavior have attempted to teach us ways to think and feel better by eliminating negative thoughts, emotions, and physical sensations. A recent review of over two decades of research in sports psychology and some types of therapy indicates that the current ways in which we are attempting to enhance performance are not successful the majority of time. Eradicating negative thoughts and emotions is not possible for the bulk of people.

I've been working with individuals for over 25 years and I don't know one person who has totally eliminated negative internal experiences. Some people might be able to reduce or limit negativity for a while. But, again, these internal experiences are meant to keep us safe. When something appears to threaten us, whether it's a person or situation, we will experience fearful sensations. It's a natural response. The key is to recognize the negative experience for what it is: a naturally occurring event. Now we are better poised to attend to task-relevant information and respond with grace and self-assuredness in an effective, value-based way. We don't need to judge or control these negative experiences. The skill is to observe and describe them in order to increase our understanding of the information they are giving us. The negativity doesn't cause us to react. Rather, we can successfully respond to the external environment even when the negative feelings or thoughts are still present. This is a great example of being self-directed and not allowing the limiting thoughts and emotions to dictate our behavior.

Throughout the CORE Journey, our approach has been geared toward developing a present-moment self-awareness of our internal environment, to be able to name, understand, and accept whatever thoughts, emotions, and bodily sensations occur. With understanding comes an increased ability to tolerate negative internal states. Mindful living expands our ability to simply "be" with our thoughts, emotions, and physical sensations, viewing them as passing, transitory events rather than absolute realities that we must act on. Therefore, there isn't a need to expend energy to reduce, limit, or extinguish naturally-occurring internal experiences. We can focus on the task at hand and the important information related to the task so we are better able to respond effectively in the moment.

As was noted earlier, one of the biggest contributors to understanding the benefits of a positive approach to life is the discipline of positive psychology. Prior to this new scientific movement, psychology was based on a disease model primarily devoted to describing what was wrong with a person. It was concerned primarily with discovering ways to alleviate human suffering and depression. Martin Seligman, then-President of the American Psychological Society, decided to focus his study on aspects of what makes life worth living. He founded the movement of "positive psychology." We previously cited some of his findings: positive thinking enhances performance and creates greater chances for consistent success.

Positivity is an important field of research and a powerful component of coherent functioning. Barbara Fredrickson has been conducting research over several decades on the relationship between a positive approach to life and a person's overall sense of wellbeing. She was at the forefront of the positive psychology movement and coined the term "positivity" as it relates to the field.

Fredrickson conducted studies with randomly-assigned participants to watch films that caused positive emotions such as contentment and joy, and films that caused negative emotions such as fear and sorrow. Compared to the other groups, participants who experienced positive emotions demonstrated increased creativity, novel thinking, and a broader perspective. Further studies revealed that positive emotions play a role in resilience and flourishing. She developed her broaden-and-build theory of positive emotions, which argues that positive emotions lead to novel, expansive, and resilient behavior. Her research also suggested that over time, these actions lead to meaningful and fulfilling resources such as knowledge and healthy social relationships. With the publishing of her book *Positivity*, a general audience became aware of the concept of positivity and the idea has crept into the everyday lexicon.

Fredrickson also hypothesized that positive emotions undo the deleterious cardiovascular effects of negative emotions. Under stress, people experience increased heart-rate, higher blood pressure, immunosuppression, and other adaptations optimized for immediate action. Unregulated, these experiences can lead to illness, such as coronary disease. Positive emotions help people who were under stress relax back to a healthy physiological basis. Her findings show that positivity not only has an impact on our health, but gives us a more robust ability to successfully cope with environmental demands. Over a period of ten years, positive psychology assembled a wealth of research on the possibilities that stem from a positive mindset. The examination of this mindset has imparted volumes of information on why and how to unlock positivity.

Fredrickson and her colleagues found that people who experience specific positive emotions more often have more creativity, are better at problem-solving and decision-making, experience more concentrated focus, and posses an enhanced sense of control over their experience. Fredrickson has named ten emotional states that contribute to positivity. They are hope, inspiration, joy, serenity, pride, gratitude, interest, amusement, awe, and love. Linked with Emotional Intelligence, positivity is a powerful way to manage your energy as it contributes to an elevated capability for peak performance regardless of the circumstances. We learn to command our cognitive patterns. With the knowledge and understanding of which thoughts contribute to an affirmative mindset, we can begin to nurture specific ones that fit for us. With patience and practice, our catalogue of positive thoughts, sensations, perceptions and memories become our touchstone for engaging mindful living.

What is thought? As the Buddha said, "Thought is your friend. Thought is your enemy. No one can harm you as much as unwise thought. No one can help you more than wise thought." Our life is structured and governed by our thought. The drawback is that we are not consciously aware of how our thoughts dictate our lives. We accept them as the way things are, and the more consistent and invasive they become, the more we begin to interpret them as the truth. We become attached to our thoughts, eventually believing they are who we are. They become our identity, our story, and our truth.

I do a lot of hiking and backpacking. I remember that during one hike I smelled something that did not smell good. Every time I took a break, I'd get a whiff of something in the air that just smelled awful. For some reason during one rest stop, I checked my boots, and sure enough, I had stepped in deer droppings sometime back and that was what I had been smelling the whole time. I'd been carrying the smell with me. I had to laugh because it reminded me of a story about a Buddhist teacher who had a way of using plain language to challenge his students to look within. The teacher's name was Ajahn Chah. Ajahn had a student who was never satisfied with where he chose to study. One place was too cold. The next place had bad food.

Another place was too remote. So finally he came to study with Ajahn Chah. Even at Ajahn's monastery, the student found nothing was ever quite right. One afternoon, after watching the student with amusement, Ajahn said to him, "You have put your monk's bag down in shit but you don't know it. Now, wherever you go, you say the new place smells bad!"

Our thoughts inform our experience throughout our day without us knowing it. It's like putting in a music CD and hitting repeat. It starts playing the same song over and over, eventually becoming background noise, and fading from our awareness. Our thoughts are like that. Some are thoughts about a problem: "I need to replace the filter on the heater." "I need to call Walt about the leak in the bathroom." Some thoughts are evaluations: "I will never learn to play this piece of music. It's just too hard for me." "I keep messing up. I'll never get this book done." And some are just ongoing planning about dinner, tomorrow's meeting, and what's on the TV tonight. They are the voices in our heads that talk to us constantly whether we are aware of it or not, and whether we listen to them or ignore them.

The voices in our head are like the air, always with us but seemingly right beneath the surface. Unbeknownst to us, they influence our perception and behavior. They are pervasive; we can't see how they are everywhere we go and impacting our way of being and interacting with our world. When cleaning my boots, some stuff comes right off without much effort and sometimes I have to take the boot off and scrub with a big stick. It's the same with thoughts. Some are more pervasive than others and will take more work to understand and accept.

We've all been there, when our thoughts lead us into fear and create tremendous anxiety and discomfort. We feel the fright running through our body. I remember when I was working in the corporate world: I was late completing a project. I turned it in late on a Friday evening and went home. That weekend I received an email from my boss saying he wanted to see me first thing Monday morning. All weekend I knew I was done for, probably fired. You know how it is. The thoughts go on and on down the negative spiral. The anxiety led to insecurity, which led to thoughts that I would never get another job, I'd lose my house, and I'd be poor the rest of my life. Needless to say, by Sunday evening I couldn't eat or sleep. I just knew the worst was coming. Stewing in an overwhelmingly pessimistic mood, Monday morning I went to my boss's office only to hear words of appreciation for the excellent presentation I had prepared. It was so good that he wanted my permission to use it as a model for other departments. All my worry and related symptoms were for naught and they were all created in my head. None of them were real.

Our fears many times don't turn out to mirror reality. They are just a story we are telling and we see the tale in our heads as a true depiction of reality. Recognizing that the thoughts are a story and not who we are is a freeing realization. Through the use of mindfulness, we can begin to identify patterns of thought that lead to discomfort, unrealistic expectations and unskilled action.

The practice is to become aware of when we get caught up in our thoughts without realizing it. When we have negative thoughts over and over, they form pathways in our brain. Thus, when we find ourselves in certain circumstances, our thoughts default to those well-worn paths. They color our perception and influence our behavior. We want to be able to catch the first glimpse of negative thoughts before they take over and lead us down that well-traveled path of anxiety and insecurity.

The first step is to recognize how the thoughts appear. Do they create a constricting sensation? Do you feel an ache in your neck, acid in your stomach, or tension in your shoulders? Wherever you notice the onset of negativity, register it and remember that this is where you hold tension. Then look at what triggered the thought initially. Was it a mood, a gesture, a word or tone of voice? Once you recognize this, you are in a position to act before your mind even gears up to control you. Now you can do several things. The first might be to enact the coherence practice we worked on in the previous section. Take that pause and breathe. Let the breath fill your heart space. Visualize the image of love, calm, or compassion that you chose. With the sensation of calm, you are in a better position to consider your response. This is a simple version of being mindful in the moment. With this mindful approach to each situation that could possibly trigger negative thinking, you can instead choose skilled, value-based action.

Engaging mindful living is, again, simple, but far from easy. Negative and painful thoughts occur automatically without our ability to see them. They are following a well-constructed highway that we have created over our lifetime. We are in the process of reconstructing a different path for our brainwaves to follow, and restructuring our brain takes practice, patience, and energy. With practice you will be able to recognize potentially harmful thoughts and redirect them to more beneficial ones which will eventually lead to value-based action. It's kind of like shopping for fruit in the grocery store. You pick up several pieces to see if they are ripe. If they are not what you want, you put that piece of fruit back and choose a different one until you find the right one for you. Choosing which positive thoughts work for you is much the same as choosing which piece of fruit you want to eat.

Some thoughts are stickier than others. These are the most difficult to change. They come from a deep-seated belief about ourselves. We will take a closer look at that in the next cairn, which is about belief systems and perception. But, for now, the more ingrained thoughts must be met with an even more powerful intention. Gearing up for the need of a powerful intention comes from awareness of people, situations, or moods that possibly could trigger a negative reaction. Knowing that as you enter that particular situation, you can be on alert for the signs in your body as we discussed above. You have to be tenacious in your desire to change your brain. Through awareness, you offer yourself choices. With time and experience in your ability to respond in a skilful manner aligned with purpose, you'll develop trust in your ability to act mindfully, even amid the most challenging circumstances.

When we mindfully engage in this process, with practice we are able to assure that our actions are aligned with our values, giving us an increased sense of peace of mind. With practice, we gain the ability to recognize the triggers that typically would cause a default negative reaction and instead choose more effective behavior. We are the architect of our minds and we are reframing our brains to house more positive, robust and boundless possibilities for a rich and full existence. This transformation in our thinking gives us the ability to design behaviors that are beneficial and effectively promote happiness and wellbeing and serve to enrich our relationships.

The section that follows is a little different from past Practice sections. Whereas I have typically offered one Practice, in this section I am going to offer several activities that can be used to manage and renew your mental energy. The reason for this departure from the norm is that the skill of relaxation can be used as a jumping-off point for a variety of ways to manage and renew energy.

The first Practice will be a simple exercise to replace limiting thoughts. Then I'll provide a relaxation exercise. From this foundation of relaxation, you'll be given ways to use relaxation to renew your energy. We will also review how to create coherence.

The final part of this section is a discussion about mindfulness. I've mentioned mindful living throughout the Journey and I feel that a brief look at how it is defined and its benefits would be useful.

APPROACH

- Develop a system to manage and renew mental energy.
- Identify those thoughts that cause negative or limiting behavior. To identify positive sensations and thoughts that may kindle a sense of peace and wellbeing.
- Learn to be able to use visualization to facilitate your ability to focus task-relevant cues to enhance performance and create greater wellbeing and happiness.

We all have habitual sensations, thoughts and emotions that arise from various triggers, be they events, people or situations. The reason they are habits is because they can cause us to react without thinking. In many ways, habits cloud the fact that we have choices and can take responsible, value-based actions. Becoming aware of both our external and internal environments is key to behaviors driven by values. Mindfulness is the foundation of awareness.

Developing the skill of mindfulness refines our ability to become aware of what we are thinking and feeling in the present moment. Jon Kabat-Zinn was the first Western scientist to study and show the benefits of mindfulness. In his book *Full Catastrophe Living*, Kabat-Zinn discusses the psychology of mindfulness and his program called Mindfulness-Based Stress Reduction, or MBSR. He developed an eight-week MBSR program for patients who were experiencing pain, stress, loss or illness and observed that the participants had a significant reduction in blood pressure, cholesterol, and other stress-related illnesses. But his observations didn't stop there. In interviews with post MBSR patients, Kabat-Zinn noted that they were more content with who they were, less anxious about their current condition, and more proactive about continuing to live their lives in a positive, proactive manner. They said the experience of mindful practice had raised their level of consciousness as to what was still possible for them to create and experience in their lives.

We all posses consciousness. It is our ability to fully experience our whole environment, both our inner and outer worlds. Consciousness allows us to think, feel and act beyond our habits and instinctual drives. It is one of the primary constituents of autonomy, or our ability and desire to be self-governing.

Consciousness means to be mindful and enables us to engage mindful living. To engage mindful living means to be open to seeing the world we live in and the world within us, to understand the context in which we live, and to choose how to respond to them in ways that respect our purpose, values, and goals, beyond judgment. Mindfulness yields openings for us to expand our conscious awareness in a non-judgmental way. It provides us freedom, personal power, and the dignity of value-based behavior.

When we can invoke the power to choose our actions, we are successful. Some might argue that success is winning and reaching our goals. I'd like you to consider that there is a success beyond success, a term introduced by Fred Kofman, MIT Teacher of the Year and author of *Conscious Business*. Success beyond success is about bringing values to bear on all of our endeavors. You may not meet your goals, or get the client, or win the race. But if you've acted with integrity and applied values to your actions throughout the event, no matter whether the event was a personal interaction or a professional pursuit, you have achieved success. True success is not about winning or achieving your goals. True success, or authentic success, is about feeling happy and at peace with who you are for yourself and others. You might think of it as not being about the outcome, but about the process. It is more about purpose and values. Engaging mindful living is about that kind of success.

There is significant research from performance psychology that people who consistently engage value-based efforts tend to realize their goals and objectives faster and more consistently then those who don't act with intention. So the notion of value-driven behavior I've been talking about isn't just a good idea, it will help you reach your goals more often than emotionally driven reactions.

The practices in this section weave the thread of mindfulness throughout. They provide ways to be more and more aware of your inner and outer worlds and to respond with value-based actions. They offer ways to know and understand yourself more deeply, to recognize your authentic self, and to become awake and conscious of who you are in the world and for yourself.

PRACTICE I

Reframing Unskilled Thoughts

Unskilled thoughts can minimize your ability to be consciously aware of your inner and outer worlds. They have a tendency to narrow your focus and limit your ability to see the whole picture. The following practice is designed to help accept unskilled thoughts for what they are, simply thoughts which need not necessarily be acted upon or have any energy applied to them. With awareness of the fact that the thoughts are not effective, you can then move beyond any limitations they might impose by focusing on a more productive thought so you can enact your values and purpose.

First, become aware of the thoughts that are flowing through your head. They are like a radio in the background with a constant murmur of voices. What are they saying? What do they sound like? Feel like? Look like? When are they the loudest—at night, during the day, when you first rise in the morning, at work? Take note of the situations that trigger them. For some it is social events; others have these unhealthy thoughts during family functions. At times our partners, work, friends and leisure time can elicit a plethora of unpleasant voices in our head.

Notice how these voices make you feel. Notice whether they are destructive, creating an unhealthy perspective of self-judgment, shame, and unrest. Start to be aware of how they prioritize and narrow your thoughts and your ability to focus on the activity in which you are participating. Typically these types of thoughts direct our focus inward and distract us from our activities. When this happens, we lose the ability to attend to external signals that might be relevant. An inward focus inhibits the possibility for an experience of flow.

Design a phrase or word that confines the negativity and imparts a more healthy structure for action. Use the word or phrase like a mantra, repeating it over and over, even if, for the time being, you don't believe it. For example, you can use phrases like, "I will use this day to its fullest." "I appreciate my life." "I trust life." "I hold myself in compassion." "I will love myself as I am."

These are not simple affirmations. This type of phrase is more in line with an intention. In a sense, the phrase takes your mind off of the negative thought and allows you to refocus your attention. If you recall, we spoke of this earlier in this section. The goal is to shift from an internal to external focus of attention, so you can be aware of task-relevant cues and contingencies that call for action. In this way, you are engaged in the activity rather than self-absorbed. Self-absorption can increase worry, anxiety, or anger.

Choose a phrase that seems right for you—one that sets up a positive intention. You may not believe it when you are surrounded by the nasty little voices that create negative self-judgment. You are reframing the negative thought with a positive thought as a form of release from an internal focus. It is like picking up a piece of fruit that feels too soft. The point is to replace the spoiled fruit with a piece of ripe fruit that you would like to put in your mouth—a piece of fruit that provides nourishment, not a stomachache.

For the next month, whenever a negative thought enters your head, substitute the thought you've chosen as a healthy replacement. You can start by initiating the coherence practice, breathing into your heartspace, we discussed previously. I will give you another, shorter version later in this section. The feeling of coherence clears your mind so you can make the substitution. However you decide to do this practice, do it with intention, firmly and deliberately. This gets you out of the worry zone so you can focus on what needs to be done—right action.

A word of caution. Be gentle with yourself. Hold yourself in compassion. What you are attempting is an advanced focusing skill. It is difficult. Persevere. Reflect. Persevere. Practice. Practice. Practice. If you don't remember to do it at first, just do it when you remember. It usually takes about three times to recall that you actually do have a new tool to use. The first time you find yourself in a challenging situation, you may not remember. Upon reflection, you recall this practice. The next time you are in an unhealthy storm of thought, you remember, "Oh yeah, I can do that practice now." Do it. You went a little down the rabbit hole, but not all the way down like the first time.

The next time you find yourself confronted, your awareness of the skill will be further developed and you'll be able to use the practice without getting caught in the negative spiral. It's all about awareness and choice. Once you gain some skill in this, more and more it will become a natural response. Before long, you will have rewired the negative pathway and your considered path will be a positive one that allows for value-based action. You will have successfully formed a new path in your brain.

PRACTICE II

Relaxation

The skill of relaxation is a cornerstone for managing and renewing energy in all four domains. The practice below can be used as a simple exercise to make yourself ready for sleep. It can also be used as the foundation from which you can generate an energized frame of mind so you have the right kind of energy that you need to fully engage in a task or activity.

The ability to place ourselves in a state of relaxation optimizes our chances of clearly being aware of our inner condition. Relaxation in this context is a state of mind without tension or distress. This state of mind provides the optimal environment for the clarity and focus needed for the desired performance. When we are relaxed and focused, we stand a better chance of being able to choose which thoughts and emotions to keep and which to replace or let go.

Begin by noticing your breath. Gently let your breathing become calm and natural. This is your time. There is no need to be any place else or to do anything else. Simply be still and let your awareness of your breathing create a sense of calm and peace. If thoughts enter your mind, notice them and watch them pass. Notice any feelings and let them pass as well. Focus on your breath and feel your body gently easing into your chair.

Now place your focus on your forehead and feel any tension you might be holding there. Take a deep breath and release the tension with an exhalation, letting the tension go out into the air. Move on to your cheeks and mouth and do the same thing. Take a deep breath and exhale, feeling the tension dissipate completely. Move to your neck and then your shoulders taking a deep breath as you scan for any tightness. If you sense tension in these areas, release it as you breathe out, releasing the tension into the air. Imagine that it is broadcast out into the air and dissolves completely.

Work your way down through your core, your back, stomach and buttocks, as you inhale, feel any tension and release it with a complete exhalation, dispelling the tension outward. There is no need to force your breathing; simply inhale and notice and exhale calmly and see the tension release.

Continuing the scan down the body, inhale and sense any tension in your thighs, your hamstrings, your calf muscles. Let it go with a breath out. If you feel any tension in your feet, let that go too. See any tension in your legs or feet dissolve into the floor. Now scan your entire body and check to see if there is any tension left, focus on where you feel it, take a deep breath and let the tension go with a calm, complete exhalation.

Focusing on your breath, allow this state of calm and peace to spread throughout your body and notice what it feels like to you to feel completely relaxed. You might sense feelings of warmth. You might feel a tingling sensation. You might feel heavy and feel like you are sinking comfortably into the chair. Whatever you feel, acknowledge and identify the feeling as what it feels like for you to be in a calm, relaxed state of being.

Now sit quietly for several minutes in this relaxed state, breathing normally. Continue to notice what your state of calm feels like. If any thoughts or emotions enter your mind, simply notice them as they pass by. Notice them as temporary, passing events that do not call for any action. Redirect your focus to your breath. Enjoy this state as your heart and your mind merge into coherence.

This is the initial practice for creating an experience of relaxation. From this state of awareness, you can regulate your energy for full engagement in any task. If you want to use this peaceful state as a way to relax or reenergize, simply let yourself soak in the experience of this feeling of calm. A brief period in this state is an excellent way to revitalize your energy during the day. It doesn't take long; five to ten minutes is optimal and 60 to 90 seconds can be useful as well.

Following this time period, you will feel revitalized and able to continue in your day with more clarity, focus, and vitality. At the end of the time you have chosen to spend in this relaxed state of mind you might say to yourself, "Now I have the necessary energy to continue through my day with optimal focus and clarity." Then open your eyes slowly and reorient yourself to your environment. You're ready to go.

This is a good exercise to employ following an intense or stressful interaction. This state of relaxation gives the body an opportunity to dispose of harmful chemicals that are released into the body during times of stress, the traditional fight-or-flight response. Cortisol is the chemical released to prepare us for action. Relaxing after this type of interaction gives your body a chance to dissolve the cortisol. If you don't give your body a chance to let it go, the cortisol continues to circulate and can cause deleterious effects in the body. Research shows that a constant state of cortisol and tension is a primary contributor to heart disease and high blood pressure. Learning to create a relaxed and calm state of mind is a valuable skill, not only for optimal performance, but for overall wellbeing and optimum health as well.

With practice you will be able to create this internal state of calm faster, with less effort, and with more clarity. A practice to consider is to develop an image of a real or imagined place that brings with it feelings of calm, peace, and serenity. It can be an ocean walk, sitting by a stream, or walking through a field of waving grasses. Whatever your relaxation image is, develop the internal picture as clearly as possible using all of your senses.

For example, if your place is a stroll along the ocean, you might feel the mist off the waves, smell the ocean air, and hear the seagulls flying overhead and the waves hitting the beach. You might feel the sand on your feet, the warmth of the sun on your skin, and the cool ocean breeze blowing through your hair. Whatever you imagine, make it as vivid as you can by involving all of your senses: sight, hearing, smell, taste and touch.

The picture you envision becomes your image for relaxation. Now connect the feeling you get when you are actually walking along your favorite beach to those familiar feelings of peacefulness and serenity you realized during the relaxation exercise. Feel your muscles melt into your chair and the warmth move throughout your body. Now focus on your breath, slowly in through your nose and out through your mouth. Just breathe naturally and listen to your breath.

With practice, you can create this image of the place you have chosen and, with a few intentional breaths, put yourself in a state of relaxation without going through the whole process of scanning the body. Over time and with practice, you will be able to use this image as an anchor for relaxation and create that sensation in a matter of seconds regardless of the circumstances.

If you are preparing for a particular activity, or anticipate a situation that will require you to be at your best with positive energy, the relaxation exercise can be used to create a state of being that primes you to engage imagery to energize your body for optimal performance and action. Use the same procedure as above in the relaxation exercise. Let yourself experience the relaxed state. Now think of a time when you performed at your optimum—a time when you felt your actions just flow without effort. It could be an athletic event, a bike ride, a run at dawn, or a presentation, a great meeting, or a wonderful conversation with your partner or child. It is any experience you've had where everything seemed to flow. Whatever your image is, use all your senses to recreate the internal environment you felt during that experience in preparation for the activity you are getting ready for now.

Practice III

Energizing Imagery for Optimal Performance

I'm sure you are familiar with the saying "A picture paints a thousand words." An image in our mind is a powerful way to manifest the emotions you want and need. I remind you of what we discussed earlier: our brains don't always recognize the difference between reality and fantasy. Remember that bit about seeing a stick in the yard while mowing and the jolt it gave you? This practice involves creating an image that will be a useful tool for experiencing "flow" and moving into the zone.

Develop an image of a past performance where you were in the flow, in the zone. Like I said before, it can be anything you've experienced that gave you feelings of joy or excitement. What was your internal environment? What feelings, emotions, and sensations were you aware of? Utilize your senses. What was going on with all of your senses? Where were you? What did you smell? What did you hear? For example, if you were at an athletic event, was there popcorn? Was the temperature hot? What was the crowd saying and doing? Develop the image using all five of your senses to make it clear and "real." Write it out if it helps develop clarity.

Recalling the feelings, sensations, and thoughts you had during the actual event, use the image to recreate the same internal environment now. Feel the hair stand up on your arms. Feel the excitement in your stomach. You may have felt a calm excitement. Let that be the feeling you feel now. Use your picture to compose the internal condition you desire for optimum performance. Again, our mind does not recognize the distinction between "real" and imagined experience. With images you can create any internal environment you desire as if it were happening in reality, right now. This is the power of visualization that athletes have known for quite some time, and now salespeople, leaders, managers, and performers in the arts are learning to utilize visualization to harness the power of their minds.

This is a skill, and like any other skill, it takes practice to master. With time you will be able to use this image whenever you need to perform at optimal levels. Again, with time you will be able to breathe deeply into a relaxed state and then imagine your "energizing" image and within seconds create the internal environment necessary for your ideal performance.

Practice creating the inner conditions that you actually felt during that "performance." With practice, you will be able to create an inner environment for optimal performance with a touch, image, or word. This is called an "anchor." Choose an anchor that is comfortable for you, something that you can do without notice, such as squeezing your fist, touching the side of your leg, putting your fingers together, or silently speaking a chosen word or phrase. Whatever you choose, this anchor becomes a signal for your mind and body to create the necessary feelings and mindset that you created in your energizing imagery. You can use an anchor for energizing or relaxing without tension. Each anchor will be different and will be a signal for a specific internal environment.

Practice IV

Heart Breaths

We've done the long version of this activity in the previous section. Here is a short version which you can engage in 20 to 30 seconds for a quick energy renewal. To reiterate, this practice is an excellent process for enhancing your capacity for creating calm, peace and wellbeing through mindfully engaging positivity.

When we focus on our heart, we automatically adopt a slower pace. The Western world has done a good job of numbing us to what we experience through our heart. When we allow ourselves to listen to what we are feeling and thinking through our hearts, we gain valuable insight and clarity. Focusing on the "heartspace" engenders coherence between our hearts and minds. From this vista, our choices, decisions, and actions are more aligned with our values and purpose.

Take a moment and experience what it feels like to "breathe" through your heart. As you feel your breathing move with your heart, focus on the good things in your life. Think about the people, places, and experiences for which you feel love, appreciation, or gratitude. Think about the compassion that has come your way and the kind acts you have done lately. Feel the calm and peace that these thoughts promote. Focus these thoughts with your breathing and allow the experience of gratefulness and love to expand with each breath. Now simply notice what you are feeling and let yourself experience it fully. Keep taking one more breath into the center of your chest and letting it dwell in the area of your heart. Each breath creates more spaciousness around your heart and allows for more openness and freedom.

This is a practice to create coherence between your brain and your heart. When you have practiced and identified specific experiences, people, or situations that promote thankfulness and love, you can call upon them whenever you want, or need to establish coherence.

Practice V

The CALM Model

I developed the CALM Model for people to use whenever they want to stay composed and even-tempered and engage a value-based response in a situation that may be confrontational or trigger a negative reaction. It is based on the acceptance-based performance model that we've discussed earlier. The process involves a mindful decision in the midst of a demanding circumstance to check inside yourself, accept what you're thinking, feeling and wanting, look at your values and intentions, and manage your response in a value-based manner.

This is a mental exercise that with practice becomes a skill you can trust in any situation. It expands your ability to ensure consistent value-oriented behavior and can contribute to peace of mind following a difficult event or interaction because you didn't let yourself get hijacked by unwanted emotions or negative thoughts. Instead you were able to direct your words and actions according to your values. When you're able to act with integrity and enrich the relationship, rather than being self-absorbed and dead-set on being right no matter what the consequences, you are establishing and/or furthering the foundation for trust. When people see that you are able to act on your values instead of self-indulgence, they'll begin to trust your words and value your response.

The CALM Model can be used whenever you sense the occurrence of a heightened emotional state. It is a mindful approach for self-awareness and self-regulation regardless of the physiological arousal or emotional reactivity you may be feeling. Experiential acceptance on your part is critical to optimal performance. Performance outcomes depend on your ability to acknowledge and accept your internal experiences as natural and normal occurrences, to be willing to persevere with the task in spite of these experiences, and sustain focus on the circumstance, event, or person instead of your internal emotions, thoughts and physical sensations.

The presence or absence of disquieting thoughts or emotions, or uncomfortable physiological arousal such as anxiety or anger, does not predict how your performance will unfold, nor does it forecast the end result; instead, it is the degree to which you can accept these experiences and stay centered and behaviorally engaged in the task at hand. Through awareness, you simply notice what you're thinking and feeling without fighting it, controlling it or fixing it. When you

can do this, the possibility for a negative impact on the results of your performance will be minimized. You choose your response based on values and intention, not on emotional reactivity. Over time you build trust in yourself that you can direct your behavior, or performance, despite internal challenges that previously could have derailed your intentions.

The outcome of exercising the CALM Model in difficult situations is consistent value-based ACTS. You develop an enhanced Awareness of your feelings and thoughts. You expand your ability to notice and clarify what's going on inside yourself no matter what the situation is. You increase your capacity to make a mindful Choice by pausing and then intentionally directing your response. Trust evolves over time that you are able to engage your values and purpose despite uncomfortable internal and external challenges. And, regardless of the discomfort, you are able to Sustain value-oriented behavior. You learn to let go of these unwanted thoughts and feelings in the moment and be present. You direct your focus toward the relationship, the situation or the event rather than on yourself. When you are present to the task there is a possibility for a flow experience. You develop the skill for value-based ACTS.

Here is the simple, yet effective process to ensure that you live your intentions through value-based ACTS.

CALM

Check in with yourself. (Internal focus) What am I thinking, feeling, wanting?

Accept how you are feeling *without judgement.*

Look at the task according to your values. (External focus)

Manage your response with intention.

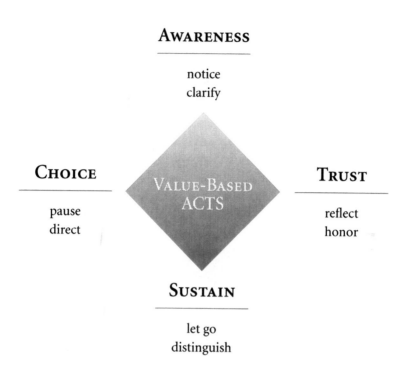

AWARENESS

notice
clarify

CHOICE

pause
direct

VALUE-BASED ACTS

TRUST

reflect
honor

SUSTAIN

let go
distinguish

REFLECT AND ENGAGE

- What are your CORE learnings from this Cairn?
- How will you apply these things in your life?
- What have you learned about yourself at this Cairn?
- Based on the practices at this Cairn, what will you do to expand your capacity and ability to be the creative force in your life?
- How will you celebrate the completion of this Cairn?

Cairn X

Energy Management
Step 4: Spiritual Energy Management

"There is a vitality, a life force, an energy, a quickening that is translated through you into action, and because there is only one of you in all of time, this expression is unique. And if you block it, it will never exist through any other medium and it will be lost. The world will not have it. It is not your business to determine how good it is nor how valuable nor how it compares with other expressions. It is your business to keep it yours clearly and directly, to keep the channel open."

—Martha Graham, quoted by Agnes DeMille,
Martha: The Life and Work of Martha Graham

The amount of energy that we bring to our daily tasks and routines is largely a manifestation of our physical energy. When we take care of our body by eating nutritious foods, exercising regularly, getting the proper amount of sleep and staying properly hydrated, we are capable of bringing forth the necessary quantity of energy for the performance, or task, at hand. Although all energy systems impact the quality of our energy, the spiritual domain evolves from our innermost self and has the potential to transform the quality of our effect in the world. Our spiritual energy is what prompts us to be fully engaged in the experiences, including people, places, and things, in our life. When we employ our spiritual energy, we maximize the potential of all the energy systems. When we are able to draw upon our spiritual energy, we are enrolling our intrinsic motivation to realize our full expression, our life force. This encompasses all other energy systems. As Daniel Pink confirmed in his book *Drive*, our internal appetite comes from our innate commitment to autonomy, mastery and purpose. It comes from an inclination to fully and completely advance our unique self expression. We possess a predisposition for self-actualization.

"Spiritual" in this context does not refer to any religion or religious practice. Instead, we will attempt to understand it in terms of self-actualization. In 1943, the psychologist Abraham Maslow published a paper entitled *A Theory of Human Motivation* in which he proposed a hierarchy of needs, or motivations. The proposed theory paralleled other theories of developmental psychology and was derived from his study of what he defined as "exemplary people," such as Eleanor Roosevelt, Albert Einstein, and Abraham Lincoln. His research focused on what prompted healthy people to extend their efforts toward the "farthest reaches of human potential."

Maslow's hierarchy of needs is usually portrayed as a pyramid, with the most fundamental needs being the largest and supporting the base of the pyramid. The most fundamental and basic human needs are physiological, the literal requirements for human survival—food and shelter. Next is safety and security, followed in order by love and belonging and esteem. At the top of the pyramid we find self-actualization.

Maslow describes self-actualization as "What a man can be, he must be." This pertains to what a person's full potential is and the inspiration to realize one's complete capacity. You might say it is a drive to fulfill our destiny. Maslow describes this desire to be "more and more of what one is, to become everything that one is capable of being." This includes being an ideal parent, an excellent athlete, an outstanding teacher, or a great leader. It doesn't matter what the discipline. Whether we are defining self-actualization by quoting Maslow or looking at the meaning of the word through the lens of Emotional Intelligence, self-actualization comprises the evolution toward being the best human being you can be, no matter what you are doing as a human.

The motivation for self-actualization is propelled by our innate desire for self-direction, mastery, and living from our purpose. Self-direction involves the recognition of having choices in the direction in which one's life is unfolding. Mastery consists of the pursuit of personal development, accomplishment and lifelong learning. When we are participating in things we care deeply about, it inspires us to develop a level of skillfulness. This could include such pursuits such as writing, playing an instrument, gardening, photography, or any other endeavor in which one has a desire to advance their prowess. Finally, it seems that human beings, when asked to reflect deeply on the question of why we do the things we do, sense a gift of purpose that transcends ourselves. These intrinsic motivators are built on and connect to our values, purpose and vision and encompass a sense of wholeness. The innate yearning for wholeness is the essence of our spiritual energy and we engage it through our own individuality and unique quest for self-actualization.

As you have progressed along your CORE Journey, we have often discussed the meaning of those letters. Your CORE fuels your spiritual emergence—Courage, Openness, Reflection, and Energy. It takes courage to name and live by your deepest values. It takes an openness to embrace new vistas and ways of seeing the landscape. We enlist openness when we are willing to forge a different path than we normally would—to push our limits. Reflection is four-fold. The first skill of reflection means to be aware in the moment of what you are thinking, feeling, and wanting, to ensure that your response is aligned with your values. Second, reflection entails being willing to notice what you are seeing in the external world as a reflection of your internal condition. What's going on inside of me that is giving me what I perceive in the external environment? This awareness affords choice, rather than a triggered reaction. With this awareness, you are better able to craft a healthy, skilled response to any given situation.

The second aspect of reflection is relative to the third aspect of reflection, which is the ability to review your past to ensure you are not bringing the past into your present or allowing your past to create your future. The past is behind you. It is over and nothing you do will change or eliminate what has gone before. The power you have is to acknowledge what happened, accept it, and move forward. Too many people allow their past to dictate their future. This keeps them stuck. This limits their possibilities in ways they cannot imagine. Reflection in the moment enhances our awareness of our choices in the present so we can apply value-based actions now.

Lastly, the fourth way of looking at reflection is taking time to sit quietly and let your mind chronicle how your day unfolded and how often you were able to remain present to the situation and fully engaged in the human experience in order to provide a considered approach to the activity or interaction. How did you engage mindful living? Anything that sparks our spirit engenders a fully engaged body, mind, and soul. It is the foundation for extraordinary performance at any level or endeavor. Energy from all other systems fuels and is fueled by spiritual energy. Our spiritual energy is indispensable within the continued willingness and attention to developing all energy systems to their full potential.

Fundamental to spiritual energy is living according to your values, which takes courage. Sometimes your decisions, choices and actions may not be the most popular, but when they are aligned with your values, it invites a sense of peace. The ongoing conviction to make decisions and choices that reflect value-based and on-purpose living on a moment-to-moment basis creates a certain culture of character. With intention and a consistent commitment, mindful responses become a sustainable way of being, your wakeful mode of fully engaging in the ebb and flow of your life. One of the outcomes of your CORE Journey is that, by having the willingness, discipline, and energy to mindfully engage your values, purpose, and vision each day, you create a standard that becomes a part of the culture of your character. It is this "culture of your character" that is the power source for your spiritual energy. Your spiritual energy is supported by continued growth in compassion, humility, and wisdom, all of which feed the inner drive for self-determination.

Another important aspect of courage, as you become the guide for your own journey, is that the responsibility for a successful summit is yours and yours alone. It takes a lot of energy and courage to accept the fact that you are responsible for your perceptions, judgments, behavior and ongoing evolution toward self-actualization. No longer can you place blame on anyone or anything external to your self for an unskilled reaction. The journey inward lifts the "protective shield of unawareness," as A Course in Miracles calls it, and offers you the power of choice. The path you choose is on your shoulders and no one can take your ability to choose a response connected to your values and purpose away from you. Your spiritual evolution and path to self-actualization is open for you to compose. Design and designer are within you. Spiritual growth, or growing whole, demands courage. It takes less energy and no willpower to hide within the protective shield of unawareness. It's much easier to lay blame on the circumstance and plead ignorance than it is to embrace integrity and value-based living. That is, until you become fully cognizant of the benefits of awareness, choice, and trust.

This leads right into the concept of openness within the context of spiritual energy. Having a mind and heart open to new ways of viewing things, new modes of learning, and new challenges to accept, is a large part of spiritual energy. Openness involves a certain component of trust. As you climb your mountain, you will encounter obstacles and hurdles that impede or oppose your progress. Openness assures that you can and will consider alternate routes and ways of moving around or through the barriers. Spiritual evolution as the journey of becoming the best you can be will call for an open approach to the many varying and difficult challenges you'll encounter.

Earlier I mentioned that your spiritual journey is reinforced by humility, compassion and wisdom. Reflection in terms of spiritual evolution can be a source of all three. Through humility, we realize that we house a tremendous energy within. The energy from both our heads and our hearts extends to our world and those in it. This energy not only affects the space surrounding us, but it also forms a connection with those who enter our space. Our way of being affects everyone and everything in our world. So, reflection in the moment on the person we are being for the world and others is part of spiritual energy. We create our legacy every day through the memories we leave behind. I once picked up a bookmark at an airport store that said "You never know when you are making a memory, and you always are."

Compassion germinates with and through the realization of connectedness. Everyone is on his or her own path and experiencing their own individual struggles and successes. Compassion helps us understand that there are many paths that lead to the same summit. Ours is not the only way and, in fact, ours may differ greatly from another's. We all have an innate desire to self-actualize; some realize it and have taken the reins, and others aren't quite there yet. We meet and relate to everyone with compassion no matter where they are on their particular journey.

Compassion for oneself is also a necessary and helpful tool. We may know our purpose. We may have named our values. Yet there will be times when our reactions don't reflect either our values or purpose. It doesn't mean we've failed. It is an opportunity to learn as opposed to judging ourselves harshly. Mistakes are to be corrected rather than judged as good or bad—or right or wrong. Mistakes can be a matter of choice to acknowledge, accept and choose again the next chance we get. It's all part of the journey. You might say that life can't be mastered, but it certainly can be about mastery—engaging in the process and embracing the unabridged experience of the journey. I guess you could say that keeps things exciting! As we heard in Desiderata, "Beyond a wholesome discipline, be gentle with yourself."

Energy is pulsing through us all day long. As we have mentioned, extraordinary performance requires a skilled way of managing and renewing all of your energy systems. As you'll realize as this section unfolds, managing and renewing your spiritual energy can be one in the same. As you renew and use your spiritual energy, it becomes sustenance for the other energy systems. Even though physical energy is basic to fuel a consistency in our daily tasks, spiritual energy is the thread that weaves through not only what we do, but also who we are and what we are becoming.

Throughout the journey, you have been creating balance and wellbeing in your life through a disciplined engagement of your values. Your purpose involves a commitment to others as well. Your purpose is largely a component of legacy, a gift you bring to yourself and others. It could be for your partner, your children, your business, your church, or your community. Whatever your purpose is, it is an extension of you and it is beyond you. Your purpose is your distinct contribution to your community, both large and small. Spiritual energy is preserved and perpetuated by a purpose not only related to our own lives but to the lives of those we touch.

During the discussion related to the other three energy systems, part of the focus was on expenditure and renewal. Most of the time when we expend physical, mental, and emotional energy, the most efficient method of renewal is to take a break from using that specific energy and rest. In many ways, spiritual energy is expended and renewed at the same time, within the same event. For example, when I teach my classes I expend a great deal of spiritual energy because my intention is that my thoughts, words, and actions are based on my values and my purpose. Because that touches the core of my being, my passion and compassion are evident and my undivided presence is apparent. It takes a lot of energy. At the end of the day, I am exhausted and exhilarated at the same time. Throughout the day I have attended to who I am being for the participants and have used my spiritual energy to fuel my motivation and direction with my students. Many times the day is a continuous "flow" experience for me. When the day is done and everyone has left the room, I sit down and reflect on the day. Sometimes I feel drained. And, most times I also feel a positive high. I have expended and renewed my spiritual energy at the same time. When you live by your values and are moved by your purpose, you are expending and renewing your spiritual energy.

There are many ways to renew your spiritual energy. They include reading inspirational literature, listening to and playing music, watching an uplifting movie, walking in nature, hearing a profound speaker, planting in your garden, or engaging in a heartfelt dialogue. There are other ways that require more of an effort such as meditation, yoga, running, cycling or prayer. Whatever is a source of motivation or inspiration and energizes at the same time is an application in renewing your spiritual energy.

Service to others is also something that requires spiritual energy and renews at the same time. Many times it calls for considerable effort and is not our favorite thing to do. It may even make you sad, for example visiting someone in the hospital or helping someone come to grips with a difficult decision or situation, working as a hospice volunteer, serving food at a homeless shelter or volunteering to pick up trash in local parks or river ways. These examples are ways we put others' needs above our own. It is interesting to note that many of the ways listed above also renew us physically, mentally, and emotionally. It's a good example of how spiritual energy underpins all that moves us.

Another way to serve others is to offer your experience or expertise in a particular area as a way for others to grow and expand their awareness and choices. Amidst a busy work schedule, my sister, Michelle devotes one or two nights a week to teaching A Course In Miracles with my father. This involves studying the material for discussion as well as writing course descriptions and developing flyers and brochures. Teaching the class requires expending a lot of energy in preparation and delivery. And this is over and above running her business during the day. Michelle has said that despite the work involved, this endeavor extends her purpose and presents an opportunity to touch people's lives in a positive way. The experience renews not only her spiritual energy, but her mental and emotional energy as well.

Participating in the service of others calls on your CORE. All the things mentioned above take courage, openness, reflection and energy. This is particularly true in the face of adversity. When we have chosen the conviction to live according to our values and purpose, we are operating from our core being. This center provides a touchstone for choices and a way to navigate the steep, scary, even dangerous paths along our Journey.

Victor Frankl, the psychologist who survived the Nazi concentration camp that we spoke of earlier, epitomizes the power of spiritual energy. In *Man's Search For Meaning*, Frankl chronicles his time in a World War II prison camp. While many were questioning the meaning of life, and giving up hope, he searched for a way to bring answers to their uncertainty. Frankl realized that the Nazis could take away their freedom, but could not take their values and purpose, which he believed was the basis for meaning for every individual. He wrote:

"Our answer must consist, not in talk and meditation, but in right action and in right conduct. Life ultimately means taking responsibility to find the right answers to its problems and to fulfill the tasks which it constantly sets for each individual."

Together with his fellow prisoners, Frankl began to help others choose to reconnect and embrace their values and create their own meaning for the unspeakable experience in the prison camp. This passage from his book is a fine example of expanding spiritual energy. "Mental health is based on a certain degree of tension," he wrote, "the tension between what one has already achieved and what one still ought to accomplish, or the gap between what one is and what one should become [...] What man actually needs is not a tensionless state but rather the striving and struggling for a worthwhile goal, a freely chosen task."

Frankl valued his fellow prisoners and worked with them to find meaning within themselves to sustain them through the worst environment they could have imagined. In the end, many who followed his lead survived and lived with gratitude for their internal values and purpose, which served as a source of meaning to sustain them in the midst of horrific challenges. Such a story is an inspiration and model for valuing others and a purpose beyond oneself.

Hopefully we will never be faced with circumstances like a World War II prison camp. Still, we will be challenged on many levels and in many ways along our journey. Values and purpose deliver a concrete point of reference from which to successfully navigate challenging times. Spiritual energy requires vigilance in awareness of our inner condition so that we can offer a considered response to challenges. A considered, or mindful, response is linked to the other energy systems. You might say that spiritual energy is a culmination of all of the energy systems. Spiritual energy is an integration of your values, purpose and vision, a recognition and engagement of your strengths and unique gifts, the willingness and discipline to practice and grow toward self-actualization.

Spiritual energy contributes to and honors your personal destiny. It is the unique expression of your true self. When you engage your strengths and gifts, it allows for a distinct expression that is uniquely your own. All of this contributes to your experience of a deepened sense of fulfillment and peace, a sense of contentment and joy, a comprehension of compassion and love, a sense that you are creating the life you want to live. As you fulfill your gifts, whether they are to family, community, work or leisure, you are developing and honoring your full potential and exceptional destiny. When you have a little willingness and commit your internal power to fully embrace the choice to live a life that is self-determined—a life you design that is full, rich and meaningful—you are truly engaging your spiritual energy toward self-actualization.

APPROACH

- Develop a mindful approach: nonjudging, present-moment, on purpose.
- Develop a system to mange and renew your spiritual energy.
- Be able to shift from a cause-and-effect reaction to a value-based response.

PRACTICE

The practice at this Cairn is a culmination integrating all of the others.

- Observe your thoughts, feelings, sensations and memories as passing, transitory events (Awareness)
- Choose to ACT from your CORE values and purpose (Choice)
- Trust yourself and the process (Trust)
- Sustain your progress (Sustain)
- Engage mindful living

To practice awareness, choice, and trust, I offer a meditation from *A Path With Heart* by Jack Kornfield, a clinical psychologist who is one of the first Buddhist monks to introduce Buddhist practices to the West in an accessible manner. This is a meditation that is popular in many spiritual traditions and a central practice offered for awakening. I thought it would fit nicely to culminate our exploration of spiritual energy, not because it is a spiritual meditation, but because to choose to awaken is to engage mindful living. We have to open our eyes to our own patterns and destiny, and our impact on others and the world we all inhabit. This practice helps put us in touch with our true self.

Without being aware of it, we have accepted many things as our identity, from our body and physical sensations to our thoughts and emotions and the belief system they form. These become the internal rules that can unconsciously govern our behavior. The approach presented here invites you to sit quietly and sense a deeper level of truth about who you really are. It opens the way from looking beyond your thoughts, emotions, and sensations as who you are, to seeing them as part of the natural human experience. It allows us to see our internal states simply for what they are, passing events, rather than absolute realities that we have to react to. This approach provides a doorway to a deeper and clearer understanding and awareness of our authentic self. This adjusted and deeper sense of your true self supports you in choosing valued living and staying the path toward your summit.

When your choices are skilled and effective and engender an experience of satisfaction and peace, stay on that path. If you are not experiencing a sense of peace, calm or happiness, choose a different path. Remember, you do not need to fix yourself. You just need to remove the interference that has built up over time, casting a shadow on your authentic self, who innately wants to realize self-actualization. You need to maintain an open mind so you can choose with clarity those actions that mirror your values. When this happens on a consistent basis, you will begin to experience peace of mind more and more. This is the beginning of an internal transformation.

Transformation is not a superficial change in behavior. This metamorphosis is a shift in perception, unfolding a whole new way of seeing your life and purpose for living and awakening a renewed motivation to become whole. It is a reawakening, a remembering of your true self and your inherent nature of wonder, openness, creativity and love—and then responding from that foundation. Your inner transformation is sustainable through value-based and purpose-driven actions.

What is changing is your awareness. The growth in awareness offers you freedom, the freedom to choose your response to others, your situation, and yourself. As your awareness evolves, you will trust yourself to bring clarity and purpose to any circumstance. If our external experience is a reflection of our internal condition, you are the creator of your experience—self-determined and self-fulfilling. Mindfulness offers solid footing for this journey. Engage mindful living graciously and with heartfelt appreciation for your unique contribution and how it manifests in your life.

You can do this practice on your own by asking the question, "Who am I?" and listening to your responses. While it is effective as a lone meditation, it can be done with a trusted partner. Sitting with another person and asking the question over and over can be an uplifting and profound experience and it is interesting how the answers deepen as you query. Here's how the process unfolds.

Sit comfortably facing a partner, prepared to sit together for 30 minutes. At first, it might be best to start with a 10-minute session. Then as you become more comfortable, extend the session to the full 30 minutes. Decide who will ask the question for the first half of the session and begin by asking, "Who are you?" Let the answers come naturally. Don't force your reply. Allow for as much pause as needed. Say whatever comes intuitively or naturally. Once an answer is given, ask the question again. After one person has asked the question for the designated amount of time, switch roles.

All kinds of answers come forth. "I am a girl." "I am old." "I am a parent." "I am a teacher." After a while, the answers begin to take on a different hue. They get a bit more interesting. "I am whole." "I am love." "I am complete." "I am a mirror unto myself." "I am love extending love." "I am fully alive." "I am an instrument of peace." These are just some of the expressions I have heard from participants in my classes.

But the significance goes beyond what is expressed. Whatever the person says, none of it matters. It is about the process of looking, answering and listening. It is the reflective, thoughtful journey inward of touching your innermost sense of who you are and why you're here. If no answer comes to you, stay with the silence. Listen for your own words—your own voice. Sometimes it is the silence that lets you know the answer. Let the answer come in its own time. If confusion arises, tears, laughter, whatever, accept them as the full human experience. Continue to ask the question. Let the process unfold without trying to control or change it. Allow yourself to enjoy the practice.

At any given time, you can use this process to discover more about who you really are as well as factors restricting the realization of your authentic self and impeding your expansion to wholeness. It can be an enlivened approach to reconnecting to and supporting the emergence of your true self. This practice can also be used to develop the skill of observing and describing. When thoughts and emotions are seen as passing events, not who we are, they no longer trigger a kneejerk reaction. Instead, we can observe and describe them as objective realities that we are experiencing. From this vantage point we can make a conscious choice to act from value-based principles.

As a culminating practice for all four energy systems, I'd like to offer a meditation that I've done many times. Every time I engage in this meditation I feel a tremendous energy. Sometimes it feels overwhelming. It's a combination of peace, joy and love. The meditation is called *Just Like Me.* The *Just Like Me* meditation is often used to grow one's empathy. I use it in my classes to teach humility, empathy and to foster a non-judgmental mindset.

When I use this mediation in my classes, I ask people to get into pairs, but you can do it as a meditation practice on your own. If you have a partner, spouse or close trusted friend, you could ask them if they'd like to do it with you. Or if you are doing a sitting meditation by yourself you can simply visualize that another person of your choice is sitting in front of you.

A way to use this meditation is to extend it to everyone without distinction. Simply extend the wishes to your community, your nation and the world.

I offer it here for your experience. Enjoy.

"Just Like Me" Meditation

Sit in your favorite meditation posture. Become aware of your breath and settle into yourself. Feel yourself become calm and centered. Simply watch your breath flow in and out. There's no need to force or change your breathing, just breathe. Whenever you find yourself pulled into a thought, gently bring yourself back to the breath.

Set the intention that you are practicing this meditation to open your heart and mind—your entire being—to develop compassion and empathy for yourself and others.

Bring to your mind a neutral person, someone you don't have any particularly strong feelings about.

If you are with someone, become aware that there is a person in front of you. A fellow human being, just like me.

With attention on the person silently repeat the meditation.

This person has a body and a mind, just like me.

This person has feelings and thoughts, just like me.

This person seeks happiness, just like me.

This person has at some point been sad, lonely, disappointed, angry, hurt or confused, just like me.

This person has in their life experienced physical and emotional pain and suffering, just like me.

This person wishes to be free from pain and suffering, just like me.

This person has known happiness and joy, just like me.

This person wishes to be safe, healthy and loved, just like me.

This person wishes to be fulfilled and whole, just like me.

Now let's extend some wishes to this person.

I wish for this person to have strength, resources and support to navigate the difficulties in life.

I wish for this person to be happy.

I wish for this person to be free from pain and suffering.

I wish for this person a meaningful and fulfilling life.

Because this person is a fellow human being, just like me.

Continue to sit in silence for a few minutes noticing thoughts, feelings or sensations that might be arising within from doing this meditation. After a few minutes return to your breath. When you are ready slowly and gently open your eyes and reorient yourself to the room.

If you have the courage and openness you can offer this meditation to someone you have a difficult relationship with. You can extend it to your community, your family, and out into the world. This develops three mental habits:

1. Instinctively see goodness and kindness in yourself and others.

2. Be confident in extending goodness and kindness.

3. Create an intention to offer goodness and kindness to the world.

Begin to recognize that every person is a fellow human being, just like me.

REFLECT AND ENGAGE

- What are your CORE learnings from this Cairn?
- How will you apply these things in your life?
- What have you learned about yourself at this Cairn?
- Based on the practices at this Cairn, what will you do to expand your capacity and ability to be the creative force in your life?
- How will you celebrate the completion of this Cairn?

Interlude

The Paths of Practice

Throughout the CORE Journey, I've talked a lot about practice. At each Cairn there has been at least one practice to give you an opportunity to enhance and integrate your learning on that part of your journey. The practices have been specific for the competency at that Cairn. All of these can be blended into one overarching theme: engaging mindful living through awareness, choice, trust and intention. Even though each practice is unique to the learning at that Cairn, there may be similarities among the practices. For example, in the areas of Energy State Management and Belief Systems, the practices are quite similar because mindfulness is at the core of both areas.

I call them "practices" for a reason. To me, when we use the word practice, as opposed to exercise, it connotes that you will improve whatever it is you are practicing. And, practice implies that it is something you will do over time, as a process. Practice also intimates a presence of mind. When you practice something, you are typically engaged in that activity. For example, when I practice my guitar, I can't think of anything else. I don't think about what I have to do, what I haven't done, or any other worrisome thoughts. I am present to the music, the notes, my hands and what I am experiencing and learning right then and there.

At some Cairns, it may seem like there are a lot of practices and it may be a bit confusing exactly when and where to use a specific practice. I want to take a time-out and clarify the essence of practicing when it comes to your CORE Journey. We can use the analogy of many paths that lead to the same summit on a mountain.

They may go up different sides of the mountain. They may take various twists and turns. But, the bottom line is that all of the paths lead to the summit.

On many mountains there are paths of varying levels of difficulty depending on their location on the mountain, their steepness, whether there is scrambling involved, whether ropes are necessary, and the amount of exposure. Every mountain offers increasingly challenging paths to the summit. When you set off to summit a mountain, there is usually a primary path, usually the least difficult. There are also other paths that more advanced climbers and hikers might pursue. They are usually a bit more challenging and require more advanced skill levels, more focus, and more clarity of intention. And, the more difficult paths may even intersect the primary path at times. It is the same in practicing awareness and mindfulness. The primary path is the primary practice. For example, let's look at the practice of relaxation. The intent is simply to get comfortable with the practice for relaxation through paying particular attention to your breathing. The strength of this practice is that it brings focus and stabilizes your energy. It is the basic practice for creating coherence between head and heart. It is used any time you want to feel relaxed, calm, and peaceful. And, it is also used prior to engaging in an energizing visualization practice. We talked specifically about this practice and the concept of coherence at Cairn X, Energy Management.

However, the strength of noticing our breath may also be a weakness. If we stay with the focus of our breath, we may have a heightened awareness of our internal condition, but we may lose touch with the external environment. In terms of our CORE, remember that the second letter stands for Openness: openness to life, to what we are experiencing, to what is happening in the present moment, to new ways of seeing. This openness extends to both inner and outer worlds. Focusing only on our internal condition might cause us to shut out life in our external world rather than letting the complete background and context of life in. Notwithstanding that, this essential practice is a staple.

As we move on to the next practice, we move to a more challenging path. This practice involves hearing and naming our thoughts, experiencing the sensations in our body, and an enhanced awareness of our internal environment. This is the practice we did in the sections on Mental and Emotional Energy. Within this practice, we want to develop an acute and accurate awareness of what we are thinking, feeling, and wanting. We also want to open our awareness to how we are being in the world. In this practice we don't "do" anything. We open our experience to simply noticing and being. This is an important process through which we can experience coherence and it also provides an opening for effective action.

As we progress in our ability to create coherence, to welcome openness to our internal and external experience, we are ready to take the most challenging path to the summit. On this path we become aware of our emotional reactivity. Our emotions intersect with our thoughts that we believe are true. If we are not cognizant of our emotions and how they can cause us to react out of old, unskilled habits, they can interfere with our intention and disturb our ability to maintain awareness of our intention. This emotional reactivity sneaks up on us, throws us off our chosen course, and can cause us to react in ineffective ways. Emotional reactivity is another way of saying that we are acting out of our old mechanical patterns of unwanted behavior.

The practice on the third path is to focus on our emotional activity. If we have practiced naming our thoughts and sensations accurately, we can see how they are directly related to our emotional reactivity. The challenge is to stay with the emotions and simply notice and reside in the experience of that emotion. That's challenging because emotional reactivity is uncomfortable and staying with it doesn't feel good. But if we can sit with the experience, after a while we will begin to recognize the deeply ingrained beliefs that cause the reactions, thoughts, the sensations. We realize that those conditioned beliefs are present in the body. They are not outside of us where we have no command of them. And, they are not who we are. They are "in-habit-ants" of our body and when we realize that they limit our freedom, we can choose another option. We can change the belief when it does not accurately represent reality and reframe it with a more appropriate belief—one that allows for freedom and peace of mind. This path is the path of transformation.

You can begin to see that all of the paths are interrelated. The third path lets us work on our reactions to our emotions through actively challenging unrealistic beliefs. On the second path we develop an awareness of our thoughts and sensations. We learn to notice and observe this emotional energy like a passing cloud as it moves across the sky, without reacting from our blind spots. The first path, simply breathing and noticing, is the foundation for the clarity and focus necessary to follow the other paths, in particular the third path where we must question and work on our belief systems. If we do not address limiting beliefs, no path will lead to the summit. Your journey to the summit will consistently be thwarted by restrictive, unworkable and limiting thoughts.

All of these practices are of practical use in our daily lives. They can also be used to begin to understand the underlying truth of our true nature. Our true nature is open, spacious, and free. Our heart and mind are inherently open, curious and playful, much like those of a child. As we get older, we develop our structure of perception to keep us comfortable and safe, at times limiting our horizons, as well as our freedom and peace. Through practices that enhance awareness and choice, we begin to trust that we can create and sustain peace of mind even in the most challenging situations through value-based actions. We regain our freedom and rediscover our openness and our capacity to embrace the full spectrum of life.

This leads us to see differently. We see our life as one of possibilities, rather than one of limited freedom and choices. We don't have to change to realize our inherent spaciousness. We are simply reconnecting to our openness, our true nature, our own internal power. We are able to view life through a different lens—to literally see differently. Marcel Proust said that the real voyage of discovery is not in seeking new landscapes, but in having new eyes.

Rarely does practice go smoothly, allowing us to stay on a direct path up the hill. There will be storms, mud, snow, detours, and so much more that could distract us or take us off the path completely. That is why we worked on establishing a compelling purpose from the very start of the journey. It is essential for perseverance, determination, and discipline to work with the practices.

On my journey to the summit of Kilimanjaro, when I experienced altitude sickness, I had a tremendous headache and stomach upset, and didn't feel like eating. I thought, "How will I ever make it to the top?! Maybe I can't do it!" My focus on the goal, my intention to persevere, and no doubt, my teammates, helped me to go forward. When challenges arise, we have to be aware of what specific practice to bring into play. Which one will be the most effective and helpful in these circumstances? I chose to "be" with how I felt, focus on my breathing, and intentionally put one foot in front of the other. I accepted how I was feeling instead of worrying about why it happened or whether I would be able to continue. I focused on the process of moving upward. Well, obviously I made it. I did feel better after a couple of days, but not without some doubt, fear and, ultimately, resolve to follow my vision.

It's the same when we encounter dis-ease in our everyday activity. We choose a practice and persevere. It really is the intention to persevere through doubt, fear, and limiting beliefs that will enable us to awaken to our inherent capacity to be self-governing. And, the more we do that, the greater our realization of our true nature will be. We can tap in to our motivation for mastery. We begin to trust that we are open, and that we can activate our freedom to choose a life of purpose and meaning. We can "breathe" in spaciousness around our heartspace and create coherence with our minds to engage all of our knowledge, experience, and expertise.

Through coherence we can learn to integrate the energy of an open heart with the energy of a discriminating mind. Using the most complete information we can gather from both of these resources will help us sort out which practice will benefit our situation the most. Then we can get back on the path that allows us to create what we want. One of the greatest realizations from this experience is the understanding that, when we trust the process of choosing actions that align with our values, no matter the outcome, we can have peace of mind. We can dwell in the light of "success beyond success."

The practices themselves are a process and you will use them throughout your journey. An additional benefit of working with the practices is they also provide an opening to look at our resistance. We could envision resistance as completely taking off your pack, sitting down on the trail, and saying, "I am not going any further. This doesn't work. It's a waste of time. And, it's scary!" And you are absolutely right. The CORE Journey doesn't work! You work! The CORE Journey is a tool that noticeably builds and refines your ability to navigate through any environment, successfully actualizing your goals at home and at work. But you have to know how and when to use the tools. As you become more familiar and comfortable with the tools presented, they are transformed into part of your inner resources and provide an organizing framework for a lifetime of learning and growth. Combined with existing strengths, experience and internal assets, these tools supply the necessary ingredients to realize your desired outcome. They become part of the culture of your character, and that is what is working. You are working and functioning at an optimal level. What dwells within you is what contributes to your success. Practice makes you skilled at using all of your inner resources, qualities and strengths to make your summit.

Resistance will intrude on our journey from time to time. Don't brush off the resistance. Practice noticing the resistance. Name it. Where's it coming from and why is it showing up now? When you bring honest awareness to the resistance instead of ignoring it, that gives you choices, which allow for freedom. Resistance restricts us. But once you can be with it, it loses control over you and you can move outside of the fear. That is typically what resistance signifies—some fear of losing a sense of identity and moving into a space that doesn't feel comfortable and is beyond our safety zone. Let it in. Then you can "see" it with new eyes, accept it and continue on your path.

As I said at the start of your journey, we all have an inherent desire to create—to be self-governing. The Journey is a way to rediscover that inner quality we all possess. The CORE Journey takes courage because it isn't easy. As I said at the very beginning, the CORE Journey is not for the faint of heart. It is for people who have the courage, openness, and energy to reconnect with their true values and purpose and create their own life. So, yes, you will experience resistance. And, yes, you will learn to simply observe the resistance. And when you allow yourself to notice and reflect without judgment, you will see that resistance is part of the journey. And when you stay with it, you will gain clarity, which can provide distance from what you are resisting. It will be an opening that, with courage, you can walk through with curiosity, gratitude and wonder. And, like all the other paths and practices, it will open the way to the summit. It will lead to choice, freedom, and peace.

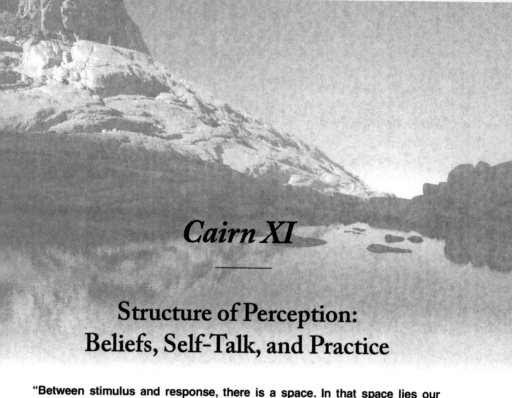

Cairn XI

Structure of Perception: Beliefs, Self-Talk, and Practice

"Between stimulus and response, there is a space. In that space lies our freedom and power to choose our response. In our response lies our growth and development."

—Victor Frankl

Shaping a vision that inspires you, tailoring a purpose that resonates with you, and actively engaging your core values establishes focus for your attention and creates a direction for your intention. Our next several Cairns make a special point of solidifying your commitment and ability to reach your summit. We want to blend your values, purpose, and goals into a single intention: to be the creative power behind a rich, full and meaningful life. Your willingness to practice the skills necessary for this is strongly based on your perception and the story you tell about others, the world, and yourself.

This Cairn is geared specifically toward addressing the cognitive blocks that limit your perception of what is possible. The more you widen the horizons of your perception and intentionally choose purposeful actions, the more you will experience a sense of freedom to choose your destiny and a corresponding sense of peace. Sometimes freedom and peace of mind come from giving up tight control of any perceptions that might seem to intrude

237

on your intentions and limit your vision. The concept that our intention has an impact on what we create in our lives has been around for years. The energy that is set in motion and the results you achieve are impacted by your perception, your focus, and your intention—what you choose to do. Your perception and intentions prompt your actions and intensify the energy you bring to your aspirations.

How you see reality is directly related to your Structure of Perception. Our Structure of Perception provides a framework through which we view others, our world, and ourselves. It is primarily composed of the beliefs that we have integrated into our identity over our lifetime. Perception has a focus. It can be projected into the future and sometimes appear as anticipation, worry or hope. Projection can also be cast back to the past, creating feelings and thoughts such as foreshadowing and distress. You might be involved in a situation that reminds you of a past experience and you might let that occurrence impact how you see the current situation as well as what you anticipate, or foresee that the outcome might be. For example, in golf many players have a particular hole that they dread, often with some sort of water hazard. If they have hit the ball in the water on several past occasions, they may let that past experience cause them distress. Their distress causes them to be tense and to lose their focus on what they need to do in the present to create the shot they want. The next thing they know, they have hit the ball in the water again, probably right after they told themselves, "Don't hit the ball in the water." When you change your focus to the present moment and what it is you want to create now, rather than letting your past influence your present and ultimately impact the future, what you see as possible will change accordingly. Your focus is to govern your life from a foundation of values and purpose. Focus intensifies intention. Your intention is to design a rich, full and meaningful life.

Sometimes we encounter obstacles that exist in the form of a belief system and, for many of us, appear to be the truth about who we are and what we can, or can't, accomplish. Unknowingly, your belief system itself may be the biggest hindrance to the realization of your goal. Many times our belief system is a formidable opponent that, if not brought to our awareness, can interfere with our focus, limit our perception, and derail our intentions. At this Cairn, we want to ensure that your belief system supports your intentions, your values and your purpose; if we discover otherwise, we will commit to reframing your belief system to one that works within the framework of your values and purpose.

Intention becomes more and more clear once you make specific choices about the life you want to create. It clarifies your focus, prioritizes your attention, and leads you to initiate actions that resonate with your purpose and values. A factor equal in potency to your intention is a belief that you possess the commitment and discipline to stay focused on your priorities and persevere toward the results you want. This belief originates from an underlying system that permeates everything you do, whether you are aware of it or not. Your belief system will play a large part in your success. This can be summed up in a quote attributed to Henry Ford: "Whether you believe you can or you believe you can't, you're right." Or, put another way, if you believe like the Little Engine that Could—"I think I can. I think I can."— you will make it up the hill! Given the influence of our belief system, it behooves us to assess our beliefs about others, the world, and ourselves. As we uncover our beliefs, we enlarge our capacity to effect them in the cause of our vision rather than letting the beliefs unknowingly cause unskilled and off-purpose actions.

Your belief system is fundamental to your purpose and vision. It guides the core values you select. It informs your thoughts and emotions about the world you live in. It influences your actions. Your beliefs form the platform for who you are for others and yourself. Their imprint dominates your perception of the world. While I was writing this section, I was looking through my dissertation on the relationship between moral development and epistemology, or the way we come to know our world and ourselves. This was in the chapter on "Ways of Knowing": "Each one of us has a unique perception of reality proceeding primarily from our belief system, and from this way of viewing the world we organize our thoughts and feelings about the world we live in, our interactions with that world, and the people we relate to. Our perceptions, thoughts, and feelings are our way of knowing about certain things and judging them to be true or not true." In many ways, we are the manifestation of our belief system.

Over the past 20 years, there have been significant findings from various disciplines showing an undeniable link between what we believe and our correspondence with others, the world, and ourselves. As you know by now, I believe it is helpful to be aware of research that authenticates the ideas and concepts presented. Therefore, I feel it is advantageous to be informed about what some of the experts who study the notion of belief and its repercussions on our overall existence have to say. Let's take a brief look at some empirical findings from disciplines including quantum physics, the positive psychology movement, and Eastern philosophy surrounding the understanding of the overall impact of our beliefs and their significance for a journey toward self-actualization.

As early as 1987, scientific findings were hinting that our beliefs were the organizational unit for our thoughts, emotions, and behavior. Over the next two decades our ability to study the workings of the brain through research in neurophysiology, psychology, and neurobiology increased our understanding of how the brain works. We began to get a much clearer view of the origins and influence of our thoughts and emotions. As we saw earlier, scientists, clinicians, and practitioners in these areas acknowledge the significant influence that our emotions have on our thoughts and how both thought and emotion impact our behavior. The depth of research over the past two decades has not only given us a better understanding about how thoughts and emotions are generated, but also how we can begin to tune in to and regulate them.

Since research substantiates the findings that emotions and thoughts affect behavior, the significant question that arises from that research is, what then governs our emotions and thoughts aside from our physiology? Researchers and theorists considering that question come from such diverse disciplines as psychology, sociology, sport sciences, neurobiology, cell biology, and quantum physics. The findings continue to expand our awareness of our self-determination for who we are and who we become. Ongoing scientific investigations lend support to what Eastern philosophies have illuminated for centuries—that we are the authors of our happiness, peace of mind, and overall well being.

To magnify our understanding, knowledge, and experience of our part in the governance of the character of our lives, I offer a bit of information about a major scientific revolution, as it informs a paradigm shift of our understanding of our own import in how our lives unfold and evolve. My shelves are full of books by writers, both notable and obscure, whose research resides at the forefront of a major shift in our understanding of the connection between our mind, our consciousness, and the emergence of our lives. They are discovering, experiencing and scribing what the ancient spiritual traditions have been saying for thousands of years: our minds are powerful; they are creating the world. If we are to live a life by design, our mind is a kingdom we must rule. Few of us appreciate the potential of our mind. None of us are consistently aware of the mind's power all the time. On my own spiritual path I have tried to burn this quote in my memory:

"The mind is very powerful, and never loses its creative force. It never sleeps. Every instant it is creating. It is hard to recognize that thought and belief combine into a power surge that can literally move mountains [...] There are no idle thoughts. All thinking produces form at some level." The quote comes from the *Course in Miracles*, a pure, non-dualistic spiritual path that combines metaphysics and a sophisticated psychology depicting the ego's thought system to present a self-contained curriculum for spiritual growth. One of the Course's primary principles is that there is nothing outside the mind. The world is an illusion. Therefore, yes, our mind can "literally" move mountains because they only exist in our mind. Whatever is happening in the mind, our belief system is projected outward, making the external world a reflection of our inner condition. With a willingness to develop mindful awareness and a commitment to conscious choice, we can unveil the form of our potential as human beings—to create our reality by choosing our perception.

The archetypal shift originated from groundbreaking scientific discoveries about the makeup of our brain. Scientists have discovered that the brain is much more than a computer processor. Upon further examination, scientists broadened their concept of the brain as a network of synapses to one that recognizes the brain as a complex organizational unit that assimilates the concepts of mind into consciousness and then into perception. Their findings fueled questions relating to the evolution of consciousness, the location of the mind, and the correlation between perception and our "thinking" and our "seeing."

We are in the midst of a paradigm shift that is transforming our ideas regarding consciousness, mind, perception, our understanding of reality, and ultimately our participation in the creation of our existence. Professionals from a wide array of disciplines are contributing to this metamorphosis. One of the most comprehensive philosophical thinkers of our time is Ken Wilbur. In his book *A Brief History of Everything*, Wilbur examines the evolution of consciousness. He suggests that human beings evolve along both horizontal and vertical lines of consciousness. His view celebrates the ongoing endeavor of one's continuous search for the authentic life. As our development proceeds, this evolutionary process expands our concept of ourselves and provides an opening to the idea that we are more than our bodies. We have a mind that is constantly active and creating and is integral to our advancement. As our consciousness grows and the awareness of the power of our minds becomes apparent, we acknowledge the impact we hold on the very mode of our existence. As the pages unfold, the reader realizes Wilbur is holding up a mirror for us to look in and see the "who" that process creates. He offers, "a universal smorgasbord of human possibilities, all arrayed as a shimmering rainbow, an extraordinary spectrum of your own deeper and higher potentials. This metaphorical map is simply an invitation to explore the vast terrain of your own consciousness, the almost unlimited potentials of your own being and becoming..." Wilbur lays out the complex association we have with our personal evolution into our deepest nature and most authentic self.

Another voice for the expansion of our awareness of our minds' dominion in the pursuit of our human potential is quantum physicist Amit Goswami, whose name you may recognize from his participation in the movie *What the Bleep Do We Know!?* Part documentary and part fictional journey, the movie redefines the way in which we view life and the way in which we live it. The 2004 film included commentary from many of the world's renowned neurologists, biologists, physicists, religious scholars, and physicians, who delved into questions about quantum physics, spirituality, and the meaning of life, as well as the parallel between our perceptions, beliefs, thoughts, and the mind itself. The movie depicts the correlation between our self-perception and our reality. Much of Goswami's comments were directly related to his book *The Self-Aware Universe*, in which he says outright that we are the creators of our universe, both internally and externally. Consciousness didn't arise from matter. Goswami purports that it is just the opposite: consciousness manifests matter—be it organic or inorganic. Consciousness is reflected in the world as material substances including our body and everything around us. He postulates that consciousness constructs our being in the world; the material universe only exists as a product of human consciousness. This concept has implications beyond the scope of this book, but it's somthing to ponder now.

Theoretical physicist David Bohm, in *Wholeness and the Implicate Order*, talks about an "implicate order," a microcosm within each individual. From this implicate order emerges an "explicate order," the macrocosm which is the universe we live in. We create and participate in both the micro and macrocosms of our world. Bohm advances a theory of quantum physics which presents the sum total of existence, including matter and consciousness, as an unbroken whole. Both micro and macrocosm interweave and extend in and through one another. Many scholars familiar with the depth and extent of Bohm's research and writing consider his major contribution to modern physics to be his refinement of the concept of wholeness and an ideal of the unification of all things. The confederation of all things organic and inorganic accentuates Bohm's belief that we are all connected and each whole within ourselves. We have within each and every one of us all that is necessary to evolve to our highest potential. The implicate world encapsulates our inner world and it is precisely what manifests into the explicate, or outer world. Conscious awareness of our implicate world provides us with the key to open the door to how we want our explicate world to appear and evolve.

This growing awareness of our import in the unfolding of our lives is not new.

The 20th Century heralded changes in the scientific assumption that we are simply an effect of Newton's mechanical universe. The Newtonian view held that we have little, or no control of our destiny, being continuously impacted by external circumstances. We are inert victims of the hand dealt to us by our genes and environment. Enter Einstein with his classic experiments demonstrating that we are active participants—that the very act of observation impacts what we see as well as the outcome of our experience. Now decades later, further investigation of quantum mechanics affirms that we are not passive observers, but rather active participants in the unfolding of our world and our lives.

As I said earlier, traditional writings such as Buddhism have conveyed how consciousness plays a vital role in the life we experience and the life we create. The 11th-Century Sufi poet Rumi spoke about how we are continually creating our world and are doing so while we are experiencing our creations, either consciously or unconsciously. Gregg Braden, author of *The Spontaneous Healing of Belief*, put it this way: "…we are the artists as well as the art, suggesting that we have the power to modify and change our lives today, while also choosing how we fashion them anew tomorrow."

The interconnection between consciousness, belief and the unfolding of our lives has far-reaching ramifications. At the very least they include our emotional well being and physical vitality, our capacity for positive, effective behavior, and our ability to generate happiness and joy in our lives, and the lives of those we care about. On a larger note, what we create through our thoughts, feelings, and beliefs impacts not only the environment we live in, but also all those we are connected to and relate with on an on going basis. The list of professionals contributing to our changing views is impressive. I couldn't begin to enumerate the entire roster of people instrumental to this research. I've already mentioned a few earlier in this Cairn, and the list might also include Margaret Wheatley, a writer and management consultant who studies organizational behavior. Her writings investigate the relationship between our thoughts and the impact we have on others and the environment we live and work in. *The Tao of Physics* by Austrian-born physicist Fritjof Capra is built on the assertion that physics and metaphysics are inexorably connected to the same knowledge—we live in a world of our own design and must become aware of our higher consciousness so we can create toward our highest potentials.

The list would also include such outstanding investigators and writers as Peter Senge, an aerospace engineer and Director of the Center for Organizational Learning at MIT Sloan School of Management. His work in organizational learning has contributed to our understanding of interconnectedness. He is a proponent of the school of thought that organizations, like the people who work in them, are self-organizing and completely capable of creating what they truly want. *The Harvard Business Review* identified Senge as one of the seminal leaders in organizational thought today. Another of his books, *Presence,* extends his thoughts to individuals and groups—that we are all interconnected and create our reality and contribute to the realities of others. He is adamant about the importance of realizing how our beliefs affect our environment, others and ourselves.

A section addressing the human potential would be remiss if it didn't include Gary Zukav, a spiritual teacher who was made popular to lay audiences when Oprah Winfrey introduced him as her spiritual guide. His book *Seat of the Soul* was one of the first introductions to Western audiences of the concepts of karma, reincarnation, and the Eastern concepts of the soul. In it, he elaborates on the importance of spiritual growth in the evolution and transformation of our species and our planet. He writes that we are evolving from a five-sensory human experience to a multisensory maturity, to involve the whole human from physical to spiritual. "The human experience is an experience in movement and thought and form, and, in some cases, an experiment in movement and thought and form. The most that we can do is comment on the movement, the thought and the form, but those comments are of great value if they can help people to learn to move gracefully, to think clearly, to form—like artists—the matter of their lives."

The major take-away from these authors is that we are designing and bringing our worlds to fruition during every day. As we interact with the environment, others, and ourselves, our beliefs affect our perceptions, interpretations and interactions. We must bring to consciousness the ways in which we are being in the world because it has ramifications on many levels—both internal and external to us. And, we can determine how we see the world and others, and how we want to relate. We can choose to impart value-based and purposeful actions. The outer world is a representation of an inward condition. What we want to see, is what we get. As said before, the mind is a kingdom we must rule if we are to realize our true potential.

A fairly recent advance in the power of our minds to generate a healthy mental and emotional environment is the formation of the positive psychology movement, which has made major contributions to the notion that our inner condition is highly influential in determining how we perceive and interface with the world. It, too, is brimming with distinguished scholars including Martin Seligman, Barbara Fredrickson, Daniel Goleman, John Haidt, and Peter Salovey. The body of their research indicates the power of our minds to shape our physical, mental, emotional, and spiritual well being, leading to more fulfilling and happier lives.

The other notable outcome from this research is the notion that our brains are pliable. Our patterns of behavior may have created well-worn pathways in our brain, but through awareness of these habits and a willingness to alter them, we can redirect the pathways. We can rewire the way our brain processes information. By so doing, we reframe our perception of events, people, and ourselves.

With discipline and practice, we can refashion the inner workings of our brains to enhance our ability to fashion our outer lives. As our awareness evolves, we mindfully construct an inner condition, a support system that maximizes our prowess for creating a life of our choosing.

The cellular biologist mentioned previously, Candace Pert, author of *Molecules of Emotion*, has written extensively about how our thoughts and emotions affect our physical and emotional wellbeing. She has compiled a body of research demonstrating that our cells are in constant communication throughout our body and that this has an overall effect on the body's health. What we communicate through our thoughts and self-talk influences our internal functioning. You might say that our cells absorb our thoughts and emotions and then communicate that information to the rest of our body. We must bring a mindful attention to what we are thinking, wanting, and feeling, otherwise we are victims to mechanical actions that do not support our wellbeing. The bottom line of the knowledge discovered through these investigations is that what we think, what we feel, and what we say to both ourselves and others is acutely tied to and has a tremendous effect on our energy, our mental and emotional security and our overall constitution.

The paradigm shift supported and influenced by the aforementioned disciplines and practitioners within those fields purports that we are no longer victims of our genes, environment, or past experiences, but rather hold the capacity to live a life of our choosing in which we can sustain peace, happiness, and an expanded sense of freedom. But to have that kind of self-determination, we must become aware of what our belief system is, what it is telling us, and how it serves us. There are some beliefs developed over our lifetimes and still held on to that supported us at the time they were conceived, but now may be a limiting factor to our freedom and wellbeing. Transformation can be sustained only when we reframe any belief that is limiting our self-expression and our ability for self-determination. You might say this shift is "changing our mind about our mind."

The concept of "belief system" is a challenging one to get a handle on because it doesn't just refer to our moral and ethical standards or a religious or political conviction. It is much broader than that. Let's take a look at what we mean when we talk about beliefs. Our belief system is composed of past experiences and preconceived ideas and notions influenced by parents, teachers, peers, and society at large. These ideas and experiences become our way of thinking and feeling about our world, other people, and ourselves. Beliefs congeal into a mental model that we use to make sense of the world and our place in and experiences in that world. They form the identities, strategies, judgments, expectations, and opinions that we use to make sense of and to navigate through our experiences and activities. Our identities, strategies and opinions stem from a belief system that seems to exist at a subterranean level, well below our awareness. They are already and always present within us and impart a powerful influence on our daily activity. Our beliefs begin to configure a foundation for how we engage and conduct our interactions within in our world. Beliefs comprise an infrastructure that substantiates our routines, habits, and patterns of behavior. They embody our structure of perception. As we travel through our day, the familiarity and comfort of our structure of perception can become involuntary, acting at a subconscious level. Our actions become mechanical, automatic, such that you might say we could do them in our sleep. And, that is what many do, sleep walk through their day without considered awareness of why they act the way they do. Waking up to what constitutes our structure of perception affords freedom of choice and more consciousness in our actions, thereby contributing to self-determined behavior.

Our structure of perception is present within us and forms a filter through which we view the world and our place in it. It also brings such baggage as "should"s and "ought"s, which we will discuss shortly. Upon this structure, we build identities for who we are and who we think we should be. We construct strategies to cope with our environment and all those in it. It gives us instant access to assumptions, opinions, and judgments about how the world, and ourselves, should be. It houses our wanting, thinking, obsessing, and needing. You could say it gives us a "self-centered" view of reality; it helps us organize our world so we can navigate through it in comfort and safety. Many times our structure of perception supplies a hub from which we see things the way we are rather than the way things really are.

We see the world and those in it through a lens that is overlaid with our thoughts, emotions, and needs. As we begin to bring awareness to our structure of perception and understand the construction of our beliefs, thoughts, and emotions, we can begin to deconstruct those aspects that intrude on our freedom and curb our enrichment. But bringing a keen awareness to our structure of perception is no easy task, as it permeates every fiber of our being. It is our self-centered safety zone, and to explore and question the reality of our perception is scary because it will disrupt our mechanical ways of acting. It will unravel our very sense of who we are (and sometimes who we can become). We need to understand that our structure of perception has helped us synthesize and organize our lives for a long time. To begin, we must bring our beliefs to the surface.

Beliefs are the organizational unit of our lives. They impose a powerful influence on our emotions, thoughts, and perceptions, and the meaning we afford to others, our circumstances, the world, and ourselves. They form a potent system that either supports or thwarts our growth and development. They convert to patterns of behavior that often operate outside of our awareness and become default reactions, or blind spots. That is the primary reason efforts to change ineffective behavior don't last unless we address the underlying beliefs. Without confronting the underlying belief that causes our mechanical behavior, we will automatically react and default to old habits of behavior in difficult situations. To address unwanted beliefs is sometimes uncomfortable and takes courage because we are moving into unfamiliar, and what might seem unsafe, territory. We have assumed our beliefs to be the truth about who we are and what the world is. To question our beliefs is to question our identity. It is scary, and once again calls for courage and openness.

Many times our beliefs are judgments about how the world should be, how other people should be, and how we should be. "I'm a bad person." "I'm irresponsible." "After all this time I should be farther along than this." "I should know this by now." "People should not drive so fast." "The world owes me a living." You can fill in the blanks for yourself. "I should…" "People should…" "The world should…" These filters become the basis for how we act and decide. Many times we take these tenets as the truth and they shape our reality, even though they don't support an objective reality. Over time we are not aware of the influence these convictions have on our ability to be effective and successful. We are blind to them. We are asleep, so we take the path of least resistance, which is comfortable and secure. We act in a mechanical, default mode based on "what should be" rather than what is.

Humans often gravitate to the familiar, the way that holds minimum opposition. The familiar becomes our default, our comfort zone. Because it is part of our past experience, and probably has worked for us in the past, we trust what we are accustomed to. Things that have worked in the past are trusted to give similar benefits in the present. We have a propensity to establish routines and patterns and these become hardwired action steps to maintain safety and comfort. They become the road of least resistance. This isn't inherently good or bad. Many of our routines and habits serve us quite well. For example, if you were to walk into your house and find the electricity off, you would probably be able to navigate through the rooms in the dark because you know where things are. Certain reactions when you are driving in traffic or walking in the dark warn us of trouble and cause specific actions. These default modes of operation serve as a protective mechanism.

However, some reactions, although they may be a safe response, they do not serve our purpose and vision. Our proclivity to respond in a given way may have worked for us in the past, but may now be holding us back and restraining our progress toward realizing our potential. Becoming aware of what beliefs favor our evolution and growth and which ones may be a limitation to our fulfillment is an undertaking that takes energy and ongoing practice.

We cannot move away from ingrained habits until we are aware of the impact they have on us and the significance they have on how we think, feel, and behave. Once we are conscious of limiting beliefs, we can begin to loosen their grip on us and choose different options. We don't have to be prisoners of our past. Moving from awareness to the point of choice, the present expands our freedom of experience, influence, and participation. We are no longer simple effects of our belief system, but rather occupy a position to participate as a cause in our life.

We'll explore your beliefs through a couple exercises at this Cairn to tease out those that support your vision and purpose and those limiting your freedom to choose and self-govern. As you evolve throughout your journey there may be specific behaviors you want to move beyond—ones that undermine your internal power. An efficacious way to implement sustainable behavioral change is to develop an awareness of and address the belief underlying the behavior. This isn't psychotherapy. Although counseling is a necessary and beneficial pursuit for some, it is not essential for our purposes. We do not need to delve into our past. What we want to ensure, however, is that our past does not create our future. We can start where we are, in this moment, by observing our habits and patterns of behavior and observing whether we are as effective as we would like to be. We slowly wake up to limiting factors and, with that awareness, begin to choose and verify more effective options. We transition from a state of sleeping mindlessness to a state where we are able to "see" what is and act in a more efficacious way. We become mindful—awake.

Engaging Mindful Living

A worthwhile endeavor for recognizing a limiting belief and ascertaining its effectiveness or lack thereof is developing the faculty of mindfulness: intentionally cultivating awareness of and attention to our inner and outer conditions—a moment-to-moment presence. Mindfulness gives us the space to observe the beliefs behind our perceptions, interpretations and assumptions. It opens a window into our structure of interpretation. Mindfulness allows us to be in the space beyond stimulus-response that Frankl spoke of. It provides the opening to act freely from our values. As we become capable of pausing and reflecting on how we approach and act in various circumstances, we gain insights into what is driving our assumptions, perceptions, interpretations, and opinions. We begin to simply notice our patterns of behavior and habits of mind. Noticing, being mindful of ourselves, opens the door for understanding and insight.

Mindfulness is probably not a new concept to you. In fact, today it is used so liberally in certain circles that it could bring up some negative connotations. To dispel any unworthy undertones, let's take a brief look at its origins and true meaning. I think you'll realize that it is a competency, a skill that allows for an enhanced openness to freedom, growth, and creativity.

Mindfulness is an Eastern practice that has gained a foothold in the West. In many Eastern texts, mindfulness is defined as the awareness of our body's sensations, what we are feeling, what we are thinking, and the moment-to-moment awareness of events. Mindfulness ia a key component of Buddhism and the Eight-Fold Path, a quest for enlightenment, learned and expanded through meditation. Right Mindfulness, the seventh step on the Path, uses meditation as a means to awaken to an open state of mind and live in the present moment. The Buddha focused on four foundations for mindfulness: the body, emotions, mind states, and what we say and do. Fortunately, mindfulness has been tailored for our fast-paced culture. It has become part of our culture due primarily to New Age philosophy. Just visit the shelves of self-help books that include many pages on personal-growth techniques that teach us how to let go of our attachment to the past or future and simply be present to the now. Many have benefited from the practice of mindfulness without realizing it. If you've ever been told and tried to "live in the present" or "slow down and get in touch with your feelings," you've been in contact with basic mindfulness techniques. We can all benefit from conscious awareness, which is the foundation of mindfulness.

Coming home to the "now" is the practice of being aware of physical sensations, emotions, and thoughts, as well as conditions in your immediate external environment. Those pursuing the path to enlightenment were encouraged to practice meditation on these subjects to develop mindfulness and insight. Many people get hung up on how to "do" meditation correctly. "Am I holding my hands in the right position?" "Am I sitting right?" "Is my back straight enough?" "Do I close my eyes or can I have my eyes open?" "When do I have the time to do all this?" With all the questions as to what, when and how to do meditation correctly, many people shelved the idea completely as too complicated or time-intensive. In many ways we missed the point of meditation for developing mindful attention in our lives. Rather than being a complex specific technique, meditation is possible during any activity, anywhere and any time. The Buddha said there were four ways to meditate: sitting, standing, walking, and lying down. So basically you can practice meditation no matter "what, when or how" you are doing or being.

The goal isn't to "do" it right. Meditation is the way we train ourselves to be mindful and aware. In sanskrit, the primary liturgical language of Hinduism and a literary and scholarly language in Buddhism and Jainism, meditation means "familiarization". Meditation is about becoming familiar with the processes of our mind. The practice of meditation helps to improve our capacity for engaging mindful living. Pure mindfulness is relaxed and open. It is non-judgmental, non-clinging, and doesn't require that we do anything. However, in the state of pure mindfulness, a clear, present aware-ness in the moment, we can choose value-based, thoughtful action with a sense of freedom and clarity. Through mindful action we are gaining con-trol over that kingdom we must rule for complete freedom—our mind. In *Journey To Enlightenment*, Khyentse Rinpoche wrote "The whole thrust of Buddha's teaching is to master the mind. If you master the mind, you will have mastery over the body and speech...mastery of the mind is achieved through constant awareness of all your thoughts and actions. Maintaining this constant mindfulness in the practice of tranquility and insight, you will eventually be able to sustain the recognition of wisdom even in the midst of ordinary activities and distractions."

Meditation helps us explore, investigate, and recognize what is within us and around us. This is deeper than simply being alive. This is about being itself. It involves the ability to see things just as they are without grasping, averting or judging what we're feeling, thinking or wanting. For example, you've probably heard the saying, "Let go of your thoughts." And, you ask "What am I supposed to do with my thoughts?" Nothing. Just look at them. Bring awareness to them and observe the process of thinking. See your thoughts, physical sensations and emotions as passing events, much like you would watch a parade pass by on the street. This is how we begin to be the governor of our mind. It's like seeing your thoughts and emotions as leaves floating downstream. You just watch them go by. Or as my eight-year-old nephew says when asked what he does with his thoughts when he wants to go to sleep, "Oh, I just put them in a box."

To reiterate, we begin to label our thoughts as transient phenomena. We don't have to act on them or identify with them. We have our thoughts, but we don't have to be controlled by them. Our mind is like the ocean, constantly churning out wave after wave of thoughts. Being mindful gives us space to name them as "thinking" without judgment or feeling like we have to act on them. For example, you might have an angry thought about a co-worker. "I hope they get fired." There's no need to do anything with that thought or judge yourself as a bad person for having that thought. Just tag it as a thought. Or you might have a thought like "I was such a kind person for helping that woman with her groceries." No need to follow up with more self-indulging thoughts. See it as a thought passing by. In this way, we are not manipulated by our thinking or feeling. We can, then, in the moment, choose our actions based on our values and purpose. Which, by the way, could mean taking no action at all. Some situations call for silence. I often tell my classes that sometimes it's the silence that lets us know what the conversation is supposed to be about or what the appropriate action might be.

Recognizing thoughts for what they are amplifies our ability for self-governance. Awareness is curative. It expands our mental clarity as well as the possibilities. Mindfulness is an effective means for expanding our emotional intelligence, as we spoke of earlier. We recognize thoughts and emotions as transitory events, without judging, suppressing or acting on them. They no longer drive us and we can act from our values and purpose. Engaging mindful living is the ever-expanding process of being present to your "now" existence, right here, right now, moment-to-moment. As American poet Emily Dickinson wrote, "Forever—is composed of Nows."

So, meditation is an intentional enrichment of mindfulness in the present moment—an alert, awake presence. Meditation is a practice that helps us develop the presence of mindfulness. And, we can meditate any time, anywhere. We can be in the process of developing our mindfulness anytime, anywhere. There are no special tools or postures necessary. Simply breathe and be aware. You have your breath with you all the time. A way of meditating is increasing your awareness of your breaths as they go in and out. You can say, "I'm inhaling now." "I'm exhaling now." Be conscious of your breath flowing in and passing out through your nose. As you're doing this, be aware of the thoughts, emotions, sensations and external happenings around you. Again, without judging, grasping, suppressing any of the sensations, thoughts or feelings passing along, simply by noticing them you can redirect your attention to the task at hand so you can engage actions aligned with your values. I recognize that it is not as easy as all that or we would all be enlightened beings. It is a process in which we must intentionally engage. With deliberateness, anyone can expand their skill in mindfulness. Let's look at a number of ways mindfulness has been used and how it can be beneficial. We'll also look at why it is a challenge to all of us.

Since the 1970s, psychology has developed various applications based on the concept of mindfulness. Some of these include Gestalt Therapy,

Mindfulness-based Stress Reduction, Mindfulness-based Behavioral Therapy, and Acceptance and Commitment Therapy. As you'll recall, the Heart-Math Institute uses mindfulness-based practices to create coherence and reduce stress. According to various noted psychological definitions, mindfulness refers to a quality of the mind that involves "bringing one's complete attention to the present experience on a moment-to-moment basis." Jon Kabat-Zinn offers other definitions such as "paying attention in a particular way; on purpose, in the present moment, and nonjudgmentally" and "seeing things just as the are." About 2,500 years ago the Buddha described someone who is mindful as one that "acts with clear comprehension in going and coming [...] acts with clear comprehension in looking forward and backward [...] acts with clear comprehension in eating, drinking, chewing, and tasting [...] acts with clear comprehension in walking, standing, sitting, falling, asleep, awakening; acts with clear comprehension in speaking and keeping silent." In 2004, Bishop Lau, and colleagues wrote an article for Clinical Psychology: Science and Practice entitled *Mindfulness: A Proposed Operational Definition*, which offers an excellent working definition of and sheds light on the concept of mindfulness as a skill that, when well-developed, can aid in decision-making, problem-solving, and the ability to successfully cope with a dynamic environment.

The definition presents a two-component model of mindfulness:

> "The first component involves the self-regulation of attention so that it is maintained on immediate experience, thereby allowing for increased recognition of mental events in the present moment. The second component involves adopting a particular orientation toward one's experiences in the present moment, an orientation that is characterized by curiosity, openness, and acceptance."

This definition is significant to our earlier discussion about our innate drive for self-direction, mastery and purpose, as well as the learning point at this Cairn, which is that, in order to lead a life of our design, it becomes necessary to investigate our belief system for consideration of how it is either encouraging or restricting our capacity for valued living. Self-regulation, in this two-component model, involves a conscious awareness of one's thoughts, emotions, and circumstances. This can result in generating meta-cognitive skills, or "knowing about knowing," a competency used to control concentration. The second component, orientation to experience, implies accepting whatever is streaming through the mind, conserving an open and curious attitude, and being able to adopt alternative ways of thinking in the moment, rather than falling back on our default modus operandi. Training in mindfulness can impact the expansion of these skills, as well as being able to look at experiences as if for the first time, or being able to have a beginner's mind, free from preconceptions, assumptions and judgments.

You can see how mindfulness can furnish us with an insight into our internal condition interacting with the external environment. Beyond awareness of our own inner condition, mindfulness aids in successfully coping with our environment by expanding our ability to comprehend the impact we are having on others. When we develop a conscious awareness of our internal territory, we can self-regulate our attention and concentration in order to address the external environment through a considered choice that aligns with our purpose and values.

The body of research published over the past 30 years has shown that mindfulness has promising effects for the treatment of pain, stress, anxiety, depression, disordered eating, and addiction. It has also been shown to improve the immune system and enables faster recovery from negative experiences. As you'll recall, a large body of research from Fredrickson and Seligman examined mindfulness as a tool to elevate and sustain positive feeling states. Mindfulness is a valuable skill to refine in order to enhance our passage toward more effective action within valued living. It takes intentional practice for mindfulness to become a reliable state of mind under any circumstance.

Choosing to enact more effective behavior, to redesign ingrained habits, to act in alignment with values and purpose, is not an easy task in the best of circumstances, much less in difficult situations. Over a long period of time we have established a "hard-wiring" in our brains for certain actions in certain situations that keep us comfortable and safe, but not necessarily fulfilled and happy. Bringing this hard-wiring into our awareness so we do have the freedom to choose an effective response is most definitely a worthwhile endeavor, and it will require practice. It may seem like I am repeating myself, but I do this to give a clear sense of the discipline and commitment involved in choosing to live a life of freedom, rather than blindly acting out of a default mode.

Let me reiterate why it is such a challenge. Our structure of interpretation has been built over a lifetime and provides us with a framework for an understanding and explanation of how we see our relationship to others, the world, and ourselves. It has kept us comfortable and safe for much of our lives and therefore has become our modus operandi, or path of least resistance, because it is so comfortable and easy. It is the substructure that supports us and fashions our identity.

The foundation for this framework is our belief system composed of input from parents, peers, society, culture, and our genetic makeup. Our values, purpose, and vision are byproducts of our beliefs, giving rise to our emotions, thoughts, desires, and behavior. You have chosen to embark on a journey to evolve your capacity to design the life of your choosing, free from the past. You may not have many limiting behaviors, but chances are that, to successfully continue your journey, you will have to address an unwanted belief from time to time. And, you will be successful with practice!

At this junction, we will look at your structure of interpretation in order to understand what habits of mind might be limiting your ability to be mindful, as well as your ability to effectively engage your values and purpose in the service of your vision. Habits of mind are primarily outcomes of your belief system. They have been learned and integrated over a lifetime. They truly are mindless routines that we have developed to understand and explain our world. They are part of an internal structure directing our perceptions of and interactions with reality without us knowing their true import or impact. Some habits of mind stem from memories of similar situations and we employ them to keep us safe and comfortable, but sometimes we realize they are barriers to forward momentum.

Mindfulness enhances our awareness in the moment of habits of mind and furnishes an opening for us to discern whether they are effective or ineffective. Once we are aware of limiting behaviors, we can begin to uncover their belief sources and confirm whether or not they are a deterrent to our success. Then we can begin the process of reframing an irrational or ineffective belief into one that nurtures and advances our purpose and vision. It is similar to the process you used in engaging and renewing your spiritual energy.

This shift away from an ineffective belief opens us to different options to play with to see which ones might be more effective. Continued mindfulness lets us verify whether or not our choice is working. If not, without judgment, we can choose again. It is an ongoing process. The outcome, however, is that we have moved from habitual, default behavior to freedom—freedom to choose and freedom to enact behavior that is purposeful. We are engaging mindful living.

Let's take a moment and revisit the meaning of success. Every action potentially has two purposes. The first is to attain an outcome that moves us toward our goal. It is enacted to accomplish a desired result. The second purpose of our actions is to articulate our values. Sometimes this second purpose of our actions has a less obvious purpose and an outcome. This provides us with two ways of evaluating our actions and two ways of perceiving our success. Success in reaching desired outcomes is important. I suggest that another way to evaluate success is by measuring the alignment of behavior and values. Your actions are a measure of integrity. Every behavior is a value in action. Integrity is when actions and values have a common cause. Whether you reach a goal or not, if your actions were in alignment with your values, you have achieved success—you have acted with integrity. In his book *Conscious Business,* this is what Fred Kofman called "success beyond success."

Mindful awareness is essential in order to ensure value-based actions because our structure of perception is such a strong force. If we have not taken a hard look at why we do the things we do habitually, the structure that funds how and what we perceive will continue to manipulate our actions, especially under stress. It takes willingness and constant vigilance to alter a belief system to trust that, even under duress, our behavior will be contingent upon our values. When you combine a belief system with values, you have a force that can move mountains. In order to engage values such as self-direction, mastery and purpose, we must rule the kingdom of our minds, otherwise we will continue to be held prisoner to an unexamined structure of perception. That's why this Cairn is so important to the unfolding process of autonomy, mastery and purpose. It is about us governing our mind instead of our mind holding us under its dominion. Let's continue exploring mindful living.

Engaging mindful living is a way of being that takes energy, practice, and intention. During the initial practice periods, this is an arduous undertaking, but well worth the effort and perseverance. Mindfulness raises our level of consciousness and opens our minds and hearts so we can respond in accordance with our values. Surya Das described mindfulness as a process that takes years to develop. Take heart! What I have found in my coaching and teaching is that a shift begins to take place fairly quickly when we begin to develop a simple awareness and have the willingness to notice our inner condition. The ability no doubt becomes a more reliable, consistent skill with practice and intention, but we can begin to feel and see the effects in a short amount of time. And, like was said before, you can practice anywhere, anytime. It doesn't take a lifetime to be able to bring mindfulness into the culture of your character. It involves a process of simply noticing, actively choosing, and consistently engaging in the practice.

As you practice and develop your capacity to notice, you will experience an increased sense of command in everyday situations. For many, life is something that just happens to them. They see themselves as helpless victims of forces existing outside their control. Some people surrender to what they see as imposed constraints from peers, society, bosses, government, or partners. Still others perceive themselves as a casualty of the past, or feel they are innocent prey to an unsuspecting and fearful future. They have allowed outside influences to rob them of their freedom. The sad story is that there are too many people subsisting in a discontented life as frail and powerless human beings in a world in which they see themselves as having no, or at best, limited, choices. They feel powerless and live their lives as if they have restricted freedom to choose the direction of their life.

In Tibet there is no word for Buddhism. Those who practice Buddhism are called nangbo, meaning "insider." Insider in this instance does not mean anything reserved or anything that excludes certain people. Insiders are the ones dedicated to looking within. Upon looking within they become aware of information that others may or may not be privy to. As an aside, the Western definition of insider is "one who has privileged information." Considered that way, the Eastern and Western definitions aren't so different. However, in the context of Buddhist philosophy, insiders are devoted to doing honest and authentic inner work. Socrates said, "The unexamined life is not worth living." Peter Drucker, a guru of management science, said that one's "first and foremost job as a leader is to take charge of your own energy." And, Plato said, "Know thyself." Sayings like these for those who embrace their validity and wisdom have a profound impact. To do genuine inner work means we are willing to apply the effort, courage and perseverance necessary to examine our lives. Insiders are cultivating mindfulness and raising their levels of consciousness. If we are willing to truly look at ourselves and how we are being for ourselves and others, we will grow in all dimensions of our life and we will bring meaning to our existence.

It is beyond the scope of this book to go into the depths of research indicating the power and freedom we give up by playing the role of the victim and sleepwalking through our lives. It creates dissatisfaction, unhappiness, and, at worst, feelings of desperation. The self-help section in the bookstore is an indication of the breadth of feelings of unease and dissatisfaction we have with our quality of life. In order to create an environment for openness, I have attempted to offer empirical evidence corroborating the copious research showing that thoughts, feelings, and beliefs shape interpretation, perception and experience. Empirical studies testify that an increase in awareness of our mind's processes provides choices through which we can liberate ourselves from falling prey to ineffective and valueless actions. We are not meant to be passive creatures. Research also provides solid evidence that we are participating members of an interactive universe. In fact, we are creating our universe through the energy emitted by our emotions, thoughts, and actions every moment of the day. We can sleepwalk through our lives and be mindless victims of our habits, or we can choose to wake up to our freedom and design a meaningful and satisfying life through engaging mindful living.

Approach

To increase awareness of your belief system, we will begin with tuning in to your self-talk. Our internal dialogue is ongoing. Sometimes we are aware of it and sometimes we chatter away unconsciously. Our self-talk gives us clues about our beliefs and many times the inner chatter is responsible for the way we feel and behave. When you begin to notice your internal voice, you can begin to identify the beliefs that are underlying the self-talk.

Once you have done that, you can begin to sort out the beliefs that are limiting your potential and those that support you on your journey. You'll work through a process to determine whether your beliefs are rational or irrational, harmful or productive, negative or positive. You will learn to identify the source and then dispute the negative, irrational thinking. Challenging a limiting belief offers the opportunity to reframe the belief so it is more aligned with your purpose, and one that supports your values and lends itself to fulfillment and happiness.

Practice I

When I woke up, I instantly felt anxious about the day. I had so much to do and I was already chasing a deadline I knew was unrealistic. It seemed like I was behind and the day had just begun. I ate breakfast while I walked around straightening up the living room, and before I could sit down at my desk to begin to write, I had to complete some paperwork for a meeting later this week. When I finally sat down to delve into my unfinished book, my mind was racing and I could not focus. I forced myself to begin, only to realize I had already written about that particular idea. I had to tear up the pages (well, delete them at least). How am I going to finish this book by the end of the month? I've completely missed the deadline I had set for myself. That's so typical. I'm always behind. There is no way I'll finish on time and if I don't I'll get further and further behind in my business plan and my own study. I set a goal to be finished with this book by the end of October and now we are in the first week of November. I wanted to write three pages a day to meet that goal. Yesterday I barely got through one page because of constant interruptions. It seems apparent that I'll have to carry it over to the next year. More time wasted during which I could have been expanding my business! I'll never finish it now. I should have never started a book. I'm not a good writer anyway. I should have never told people I was writing. Now they'll think I was full of myself. My business is never going to grow if I don't have a book. I'll have to get a real job. I never finish any project I start. I really am irresponsible. Okay. Now I'm really depressed. I certainly can't write anymore today!

Sound familiar? Maybe not the specifics, but I'm sure you have experienced that downward spiral created by negative self-talk, which exacerbates the situation and leads to more self-defeating behavior. Maybe your downward spiral was about work. Maybe it was a goal you had in your personal life. Perhaps it surrounded completing or starting a particular project. You experienced an event that started you down that negative self-talk path. It almost seems that nothing can stop that runaway train once it starts down those tracks.

This is an example of a type of negative self-talk that we all engage in from time to time. If we don't put an end to the negative energy created by our inner discussion, it can lead to less perseverance in the future and negative moods whenever we encounter setbacks, which we all do. Negative internal dialogues make it worse, and it can become habitual. The skill at this Cairn is three-fold. The first skill we want to develop is to be mindful of when the negative thoughts occur so we can stop identifying with them and thinking that all mind chatter requires action.

The second skill is to accept the thought or emotion as nothing more than what it really is—a thought or emotion, neither of which determines our identity. Then engage the resolve to act according to our values despite the ongoing chatter. We've discussed methods for accomplishing this in previous activities. As I said, this is an ongoing practice and one that must also be applied in the practice of becoming more skillful in our ability restructure our belief system.

The third skill in this area is to become cognizant of the underlying belief that is attached to the event that started the negative chatter. We also want to start recognizing the consequences of the negativity. What is it costing us emotionally and cognitively? Once we acknowledge the limiting belief that underlies the negativity, we can examine the factual or nonfactual evidence around the belief and dispute it. We do this by bringing to the forefront the specifics about the event and yourself and testing them out within reality: are they based on fact or are they based on assumption and inference? Let's look at the process.

Negative self-talk is life-draining. It can take us into a freefall faster than we realize. A scientifically proven way to stop this downward spiral thinking is to dispute negative thinking. Dispute your negative thoughts just like a good attorney. Then, acting in the same vein as a good lawyer, examine the facts. What was the activating event? What set you off? What were your negative thoughts and emotions and what triggered them? How did they make you feel? How did they compare to the facts? Did they have any bearing on reality? What are the true facts of the situation? When you think about the facts and truly own them, how do they make you feel?

An effective process to observe, name, and challenge our beliefs is called the ABCs. It stands for:

- A=Activating Event (What was the event that started the negative self-talk or unwanted behavior?)

- B=Belief (What are your beliefs underlying the negative talk or unwanted behavior?)

- C=Consequences (What were the consequences of the negative self-talk or unwanted behavior? What did you have to give up?)

- D=Dispute and Debate (Dispute and Debate the belief just like a good lawyer. What are the facts? What would you tell a friend who was experiencing a similar event? Is this a limiting or unfounded belief?)

- E=Effective Emotion (What emotion or self-talk would create a more realistic and positive way of coping with the event?)

Example of the ABC activity.

- A=Activating Event – During a presentation, you notice someone on their Blackberry for a considerable amount of time.

- B=Belief – They aren't interested in my presentation. They are bored. They think they know this stuff already. They don't agree with me. Even worse-they don't like me. I'm just not very good at connecting with people. I'm not a good trainer.

- C=Consequences – I became tentative in my delivery. I second-guessed the validity of what I was presenting and therefore did not sound like an authority on the subject. I said something sarcastic about Blackberry's.

- D=Dispute – I am an authority. What I have to present will help people in their work. During a break I need to go check to see what she's working on. She may have a sick child at home or an emergency at the office.

- E=Effective Emotion – Stay confident in my own understanding of the subject. Present with understanding and authority. Understand I am not going to capture everyone's attention or agreement. Act with focus and poise.

What do I need to do to engage this positive self-talk? Can I let the limiting thoughts and emotions go and focus on the task of teaching? Can I let go of an expectation that I must appeal to everyone and have everyone learn what I am teaching, and move to my intention-to provide a safe space for people to explore and discover their Internal Power? Which one do I have control over? My intention. Expectations drive outcomes in perception. If I have an expectation and it doesn't happen, I have failed. If I engage my intention, which I have complete control over, the outcome is a safe space and therefore a success.

Once you understand how an unfounded belief is limiting your potential or even just limiting you from breaking out and giving something you want a try, you can begin to restructure the belief. It doesn't happen overnight. You have to be vigilant about your self-talk and the language you use around the idea. It is not just positive thinking. The whole self-help movement behind affirmations doesn't do a bit of good until you understand the reason precipitating the behavior. Our positive thinking has to be founded in our values and we have to believe in it at some level. Thinking that is not intentional, just simply words on a page that we read aloud to ourselves, won't produce new, consistent and sustainable behavior. Our gremlin is much too smart to be tricked by smoke and mirrors. We have to mindfully attend to the thoughts, emotions, and words that we wish to incorporate into our being. It is a system, a process, based on strengths, passion and facts. You can develop a positive and supportive way of talking about yourself that is realistic, believable, and attainable without arrogance.

A reminder: once you become aware of your self-talk, it doesn't go away. That little voice, your internal gremlin, will always be there. In fact, the gremlin wants to control our lives and keep us in old familiar patterns. It is quite loud and active. It wants to maintain its own sense of comfort and its familiar identity, as well as its own survival. It does not want us to recognize our true nature, but instead wants to keep us prisoners of our old patterns. The gremlin is like a familiar path to work. We're accustomed to taking it. We know it well and it is part of our routine. We can walk it without much thinking or much need to pay attention to where we are going. It is the path of least resistance we spoke of earlier.

Breaking the routine of taking the path most traveled will take diligent observation and practice. Recognizing that the negative chatter will persist over time, we have to engage the skill of "feeling the pain and doing it anyway." We have to be able to hear the unwanted thoughts and feel the uncomfortable emotions, accept them for what they are by not identifying with them, and commit ourselves to behavior that expresses our values.

The voice that is central to our true nature is typically quiet. It is always there for us to hear, but we have to ask, be open and listen, and then intentionally bring that voice into play. The voice of our true nature speaks to an experience of compassion, connectedness, kindness and love. By noticing the difference between these two voices, the gremlin and our authentic voice, we then have a choice of which one we will attend to and to which self-talk we will give our energy.

There is an old Cherokee proverb that perfectly describes choice and its rewards.

One evening a wise old Cherokee chief told his grandson about a battle that goes on inside people. He said, "My son, the battle is between two wolves inside us all. One is Evil. It is anger, envy, jealousy, sorrow, regret, greed, arrogance, self-pity, resentment, inferiority, lies, false pride, superiority, and ego.

"The other is Good. It is joy, peace, love, serenity, hope, humility, kindness, benevolence, empathy, generosity, truth, compassion, and faith."

The grandson thought about it for a minute and then asked his grandfather, "Which wolf wins?"

The old Cherokee simply replied, "The one you feed."

Many times our self-talk is an outcome of difficult emotions and thoughts. Overwhelming emotions like anger, jealousy, grief, worry, insecurity or despair, along with the thoughts that accompany them, can feel like monsters that are much larger than we are and they can seem to threaten our very existence. Sometimes we try to resist them, run away from them, or shove them out of our mind. Other times, we hold tightly to them, wrestling with them as if we were at war with them. The skillful approach is not grasping or avoiding the intolerable emotions or damaging thoughts, but instead substituting a mindful approach to understand our relationship to the thoughts and emotions that trouble us, recognizing that grasping or avoiding these inner struggles gives them power. Seeing them as passing events changes our relationship to them. First, when we view thoughts, emotions, or sensations as passing events we are more apt to be able to compartmentalize them for the time being and apply our values to our actions. Second, accepting that they are there and do not need to be acted on, believed or identified with, we can look closer to see what belief underlies them and whether that belief is supporting our efforts for growth and development or is keeping us stuck.

It's much like the skill of Aikido, where you learn to move with your opponent in a give-and-take fashion. In Aikido, when you struggle against your opponent, you are using valuable energy in the process and probably not getting any closer to your desired result. But when you relax, your head and your heart are more open to opportunities that present themselves so you can then take advantage of a move that will advance you toward your goal. Being open and relaxed under pressure is like learning to dance on a shifting carpet. Instead of feeling like the proverbial rug is being pulled out from under you, your movements are balanced. Through acceptance you are learning to dance and move in balance in the midst of conflict and challenge. This valuable skill gives you a space for more clarity and openness to the expression of your core values.

Through the process of nonjudgmentally looking at our thoughts, emotions, and sensations, we can begin to feel some freedom from the constricting ties these thoughts and feelings have on us. We can, in a sense, lay them down and notice that we are not those feelings and thoughts. When we don't identify with them, we are not grasping them, nor are we avoiding them. We learn to label them for what they are, our "monkey mind," self-talk, part of our mind jabbering on and on about what it wants us to believe and how it wants us to behave. Once again, the gremlin wants to dictate our self-concept and control our actions. The gremlin doesn't live in a world of possibility. It lives in a world of "should"s and "ought"s, guilt and denial, a world of scarcity and lack of freedom.

Mindfulness, that wonderful power tool that we can use any time to keep us from getting lost in the swirl of mindless, limiting chatter, is always a possibility. It's like our breath. It is always with us. All we have to do is remember that we have the tool. Sometimes when we're lost in the chatter and confusion that often accompanies difficult circumstances, we forget to even look in our tool chest, much less remember that we have tools we could use to tackle the situation. Under stress, even the most advanced person can make ineffective choices. Being present to what we are feeling and thinking gives us space to remember. It can help us be aware that we are not the monsters in our mind. It can help us wake up from the horror film running in our heads. And with practice, we can engage mindfulness even in the worst of nightmares and bad movies. Let's look at another practice that can help.

PRACTICE II

The practice is called RAIN and it is a mindful approach to working with difficult thoughts, emotions, sensations and memories. It is an acronym for Recognize, Accept, Investigate, and Non-identity.

Recognize

The Brain Mapping Center at the UCLA School of Medicine found that when subjects in an experiment were shown pictures displaying faces of anger or fear, the fear centers in their brain had an increase in blood flow. This was a sign that the amygdala was being stimulated and the fight-or-flight response was being triggered. The subjects were then asked to choose a word to name the feeling they were experiencing as they viewed the faces. As they were able to describe or name the emotion they were experiencing, the blood flow to the amygdala decreased. The researchers discovered that naming, or describing, both of which are activities that require activity from the cortex, could regulate the emotional reaction, leading to less agitation and a more calm approach.

In the R for Recognize, the first step is to be aware that you are experiencing a situation that is causing a sense of discomfort. The next step is to name the emotion, thought or physical sensation. For instance, during a conversation in which you are being confronted, you might recognize, "I am feeling defensive." Naming the emotion, without censoring, resisting, or opposing the feeling, keeps you from getting hooked or drawn into it. Or you might feel lethargic and recognize the feeling of sadness and simply name it and say, "I am feeling sad." Even if you can't quite name the feeling, you can just say, "I don't know, I just feel a bit out of sorts." At least this keeps you from going down the negative spiral that our negative self-talk can take us if we are not aware of it.

Accept

Accepting a painful emotion or distressing thought can be taxing. Most of the time, we try to distract ourselves by thinking about other things, planning supper, what we're going to do after work, who we'll call for a movie date. Or we ruminate about why we are having this particular thought or feeling. "I always get this feeling right before…" "When will this feeling go away and not come back?" Whether we grasp or resist what we feel or think, it gives the pain and discomfort power. It has hooked us because now we want to do something with it. When we can simply accept the emotion or thought, we let go of our agenda around it.

Accepting means you stay with the thought or feeling, remaining aware of it without pushing it away or getting tied up in it. We have allowed the energy of the feeling or thought to dissipate because we are no longer pushing it or grabbing at it, giving it energy. Because we have let it go for the time being, we can now engage in the present situation with more clarity and energy.

Investigate

Investigating is like doing a body scan to discover more about the thought or feeling you have accepted. Without trying to figure it out, notice how your body is manifesting defensiveness. How is your body expressing it? What does being defensive feel like? Restricting? Heavy? Cold? Hot? Tingly? Where is defensiveness in your body? Your throat? Neck? Shoulders? Stomach? What color is it? Gray? Black? Red? How big is it? The size of a watermelon? A softball? A grape? A grapefruit? Notice if the sensations remain consistent. They might get stronger or they might become less intense. It is not your job to judge, but only to ascertain the qualities of the thought or emotion in a non-judgmental way.

Investigating allows us to bring a curiosity and interest to the thought or emotion without attaching ourselves to it. It's very much like approaching it with a beginner's mind, as if we were experiencing it for the first time. We are open to learning from it. What is this thing I am seeing, feeling, thinking? It allows us to look at it in an objective way, almost like our self-coach is outside of us looking in. We begin to realize that having anxiety, for example, doesn't mean we have to be anxious. We can actually have anxious thoughts and feelings of anxiety without being anxious or being anxious about having anxiety.

Non-identification

Non-identification is saying, "I am not this defensiveness that I am experiencing." No thought or emotion is you. Nor is it unique to you. Emotions and thoughts are constantly coming and going. They are passing occurrences. Everyone has them. Understanding that we all have these emotions and thoughts creates a sense of compassion and recognition that we are not so distant from one another. There is a commonality, an interconnectedness. Although we can bring our own story about the thinking or emoting, it is an it, not who we are. It is helpful when facing an emotion or thought that is disquieting to say, "This mind is being defensive." Or, "My mind is having a defensive thought." Instead of thinking "I'm defensive," you can begin to realize that the defensiveness does not define who you are. It is a thing you are experiencing. It isn't your identity. It does not define you. Therefore, it doesn't have a restrictive power over you. It is not limiting you; your relationship to it is what is holding you tight. RAIN will help change the relationship. This is a freeing recognition and allows for a considered response from your values and purpose.

To recap: when you find yourself experiencing a strong emotion or distracting thought, take a moment to walk through the process:

RAIN

When you find yourself experiencing a strong emotion or distracting thought, take a moment to walk through this process:

Recognize what you are thinking and feeling and name it. Frustration, anger, irritation, sadness.

Accept the thought or feeling and let it be without pushing it away or struggling with it.

Investigate the sensations in your body. Probe the experience with curiosity and interest. Where are you feeling it? How does it feel?

Non-identification is the freeing experience you have when you realize you can have an emotion or thought without being it. You don't have to take it personally. It does not define you.

RAIN is a skill that can help clarify emotions and thoughts and offers a sense of freedom from entanglement in the attached storyline. Like the story about the two wolves, our emotions and thoughts gain energy when we feed them. It can be negative or positive energy. And, those emotions and thoughts we feed the most will be the ones that grow and gain a hold on us. RAIN gives us a choice of which ones we will nurture and fortify. The process of RAIN provides us with an opportunity to continue to expand our awareness about how emotions and thoughts are affecting our beliefs and enlighten us that we may be feeding those that are limiting our ability to create a rich, full and meaningful life.

Awareness provides us with options. Mindfulness is key to the process and is the skill that, with practice, provides us with a present-moment metric on our thoughts, emotions, and actions, as well as how we experience all of that in our body. It gives us the power of choice to release the beliefs holding us back. Mindfulness opens the door to revise what you identify with. It is about shifting the correlation with our beliefs and our selfhood. Are we the designer, or the victim? Either way, it's our choice and our power to choose. Appreciating that we are not victims of external circumstances supplies the courage to sever our attachment to old patterns and create new, positive designs. RAIN can help us with that process.

This is a process, a journey. Practice will bring trust in yourself that, even in the most challenging situations, you have a choice of how you will respond and the relationship you will have with the thought, sensation or emotion. You put yourself in the architect's seat and become the designer, the creator of your life.

You are far along your journey. At this juncture most people I work with are applying their individual understanding and practice of Courage, Openness, Reflection, and Energy to their daily lives. The questions that have followed previous Cairns are no longer necessary to prompt reflection and assimilation. A foundational piece of your journey is perseverance. The following Interlude provides questions and reflections for you to consider.

REFLECT AND ENGAGE

- What are your CORE learnings from this Cairn?

- How will you apply these things in your life?

- What have you learned about yourself at this Cairn?

- Based on the practices at this Cairn, what will you do to expand your capacity and ability to be the creative force in your life?

- How will you celebrate the completion of this Cairn?

Interlude

Don't Let Up—Strengthen and Sustain Commitment

"Personal transformation can and does have global effects. As we go, so goes the world, for the world is in us. The revolution that will save the world is ultimately a personal one."

—Marianne Williamson

The Approach at the end of this section is critical to ensure that you continue to persevere toward your summit. The last few Cairns may have been intense for you, and the work that you began during those Cairns will be an ongoing process. It is vital that you designate specific accomplishments as mile markers and make sure that you recognize short-term wins to celebrate progress toward and achievement of important goals. Short-term wins honor the headway that you are making and can propel your transformation forward, and give you visible evidence that you are progressing. However, sometimes there is a tendency to let down following a short-term celebration. Resistance is always waiting behind the scenes to seize a moment of doubt or, even more detrimentally, allow you to think that you can let down or decrease your effort and commitment.

From the beginning of your journey, we've distinguished between making a change and going through a transformation. Let's revisit the distinction between change and transformation, or transition. Our society usually defines change as adapting, altering, modifying or replacing. It is relegated to things like moving to a new city, starting a new job, getting used to a new manager at work, or altering your workout routine. Change seems to constitute something that is situational.

Remember that transformation, however, is about bringing something new into existence that didn't exist before. It's about creating. Transformation is defined as a thorough or dramatic shift in form or appearance. From the standpoint of the CORE Journey, transformation is a shift in your inner condition. It's not about situations or circumstances. It's about redefining yourself and integrating that distinction into your way of being. This type of transition is difficult and requires ongoing awareness and support. If you're this far along in the book and you've been following the Practices, you are grounded in transformation. But, since you're reaching the end of this book and maybe the completion of a coaching program or a self-guided tour through the CORE Journey, you might think your transformation is coming to a close.

Sometimes when we come to what we perceive as completion or an ending, it is really a beginning. This can be overwhelming and a bit frightening. "What do I do now?" "Which path do I follow now?" "Is it the right one?" "Do I even need to be on a path?" All kinds of questions and possibly a little self-doubt can pop up. The question arises: "Now what?" You've come to a stopping point, which seems like the end of something, but it seems like there's more.

I appreciate the challenge because I've struggled with it as well. I made substantial shifts in my life, thinking afterward that I was done and could settle into a normal pace, a normal way of being. What I realized, though, was that the transformation wasn't over. Transformation involves a consistent renewing and realigning of our energy. It is an ongoing process of recognizing and engaging our internal power to create our life. That's one reason why energy management is a foundation of any transformative effort. It takes a certain vitality to continue to grow, to make that growth meaningful and to integrate the learning into who you are becoming.

We discussed managing energy in a previous Cairn, but maybe what I should have said is that it isn't just a cairn along the path. Managing energy is a steady strategy and a sustained effort. As you continue to work through your transformation, you are defining yourself anew and gaining momentum. So, even though there may have been key shifts in your external world, the major amendment has been internal. You are not the same person as you were at the beginning of your journey. Through the simple act of increasing awareness, you are different. Not that you were worse or less than you are now, but, through the process of the CORE Journey you've taken more control of your life. Your responsibility has increased because now the only person in charge of you is you. That may seem like a daunting proposition. That's why I've stressed the need for a little willingness, perseverance, discipline and a team for support. Along your journey, you no doubt ran into some times where you felt lost, alone, and maybe like quitting. I understand. I've been there. Sometimes in transformations there's a feeling of emptiness. It would be easy to just go back to the old ways, to not employ the necessary energy to stay the course. But I hope that what you've discovered as you've made significant strides toward your summit is that staying the path generates a swell of enthusiasm and vitality, as well as renewed energy and commitment.

So, what's germinated, or become increasingly more explicit, over the course of your journey is a rekindled sense of self and recognition that inside you lies the power to create a joyful and fulfilling experience of living. You must ensure that your stamina to stay the path continues to evolve. You must be aware of resistance and be vigilant about continued transformation. You must make the transformation a part of who you are—a part of the culture of your character.

You've been doing all the right things up until now. Previously, you celebrated some of your wins. That's a good thing. But sometimes the celebration can lead to a loss of urgency—a loss of your compelling reason for the transformation. If you let yourself settle into complacency at this point, the old ways can swarm in with astounding weight and momentum. Let's not let that happen. With renewed enthusiasm and dedication, now is the time to ramp up your energy.

Here are several things to consider:

APPROACH

- Leverage your momentum. Take a serious look at what's working in your plan. If anything needs to be readjusted, refocused or simply changed, now is the time to do that.

- Revisit your compelling energy. What might you do to reinforce your commitment to grow and transform? Are your current goals taking you in the direction you want to go—toward your summit? Are you using your short-term wins to solidify your progress?

- Continue to enhance mindfulness of your choices and actions. Are your actions aligned with your purpose and vision? Is your behavior aligned with your values? Are you operating from your source?

- Communicate to your "teams" about how the CORE Journey is going. Inform them of significant transitions in your life as well as within you. Hold a conversation with those stakeholders that you want to support you.

PRACTICE

Here is a list of questions to sustain momentum and commitment.

- What is different now that you have begun to implement action toward your goals and achievement of success?

- How have the changes affected you? How do you feel about them? What are you thinking differently? How are you seeing things differently?

- Do you believe you have enough momentum to achieve your transformation? If not, what do you need to do to refocus your commitment?

- Are there new yardsticks you might design to measure progress?

- How are you challenging yourself to be the best you can be?

- How do you continue to encourage yourself to take risks?

- What additional actions can you take to remove any slack in your commitment?

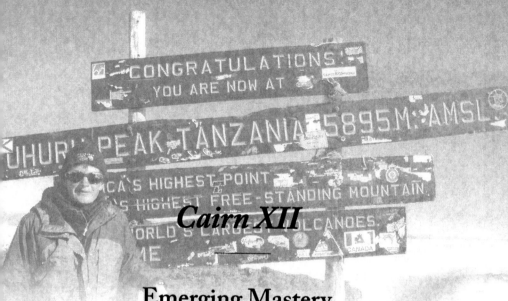

Cairn XII

Emerging Mastery
The Culture of Your Character

"What we call the beginning is often the end and to make an end is to make a beginning. The end is where we start from."

—T. S. Eliot

The CORE Journey is a lifelong trek—a process and practice you will continue to expand. You might think that Cairn XII is the end of your journey. It is the beginning. Your MAP is a living document that will continue to evolve throughout your lifetime. You have developed skills that enable you to be the cartographer of your life map—to envision possibilities and create results.

Let's recap your travels. To begin the journey, you uncovered a compelling energy primarily from the recognition that there must be a more fulfilling way to live your life. You had a sense that your life was not as satisfying and meaningful as it could be. A sense of inner motivation was established. We teamed up and began to look at who you were, where you were starting from, and where you wanted to go. You completed your CORE Compass for a clear picture of where your life might not be progressing in the direction you truly desired.

The next step was to take a look at your strengths, passions, values, and commitments. From there you began to create a vision that represented an image of the future you wanted to live into. Then, using your Compasses, you listed ways to bring your life onto the path to your chosen summit. You prioritized the compasses, or areas of your life that you wanted to focus on first. It was time to design your MAP.

Developing your Mindful Action Plan (MAP) began the process of closing the gaps between reality and your vision. From there to now, you have learned how to practice and implement specific competencies to overcome obstacles and set attainable milestones along your CORE Journey. You can now apply those practices whenever you need them. Whether you are facing a transition, making a difficult choice, or reaching for another summit, you have the "knowing" to direct and create the life you want.

I encourage my clients to use their MAP as a lifelong tool to revisit and recreate. The skills you have learned are an invaluable addition and will be useful in your life's endeavors from this point forward.

Look back at your CORE Journey and your MAP. The Cairns have guided you along the path to accomplishing your goals. Are there goals you want to add, change, or remove? Have you reached a summit that you've celebrated and now it's time to set another? Are your actions aligned with your values, purpose, and vision? Are you mindful of your beliefs so you can effect the ones that support your evolution? Do you keep a mindful awareness of your true nature?

Take a look at your Compass from time to time. Are there any that are not pointing toward true north or are out of alignment or balance? Maybe you've had a career change or are involved in a significant relationship. If so, your priorities may have changed. Revisit them to make sure your life stays balanced, fulfilled, and heading in the direction you care about.

We also created teams. You have communicated with the people in your life that in some way may have participated in your journey, even if it was simply to enjoy the benefits of engaging with an exceptional person who really wanted to make life better for themselves and others. It is encouraging to have the support of those you care about. People in our lives can be a touchstone of motivation. Continue to check in with them. If you want to, get feedback from those closest to you. Are you communicating and sharing in an authentic and mindful way?

When you review your MAP, it helps you stay focused and committed to creating the life you desire. Congratulations! You have made tremendous strides toward enhancing your life and making it what you want. And, the journey continues.

You are the designer and architect of your reality from this day forth. You've recognized your internal motivations of autonomy, mastery and purpose. They provide you with the skills, commitment, energy and the desire. You will have breakdowns and run into barriers at times. The biggest difference now is that you have the mindful awareness and skillset to deal with them through openness. You have created spaciousness within your heartspace that exposes your true nature. You can catch yourself if you fall below the line into feeling and thinking like a victim and use your skills to get back on the path you have chosen; an extraordinary path: an extraordinary life.

APPROACH

To make sure your transformation continues and is sustainable by ensuring that the changes you have made are part of the culture of your character.

PRACTICE

Use the tools you have developed and engaged throughout your CORE Journey to monitor whether you are engaging value-based actions.

- Use your CORE Journey as a guide.
- Revisit, refocus, redesign your MAP.
- Reflect on your priorities and adjust when necessary.
- Set SMART goals.
- Celebrate short-term wins.
- Communicate. Be present to your team members.
- Expand your awareness. Notice. Notice. Notice.
- Practice.
- Expand your courage. Challenge yourself to step beyond your edge.
- Trust yourself.
- Open yourself to the whole experience of life. Be a player. Participate in the texture and constellation of your thoughts and emotions.

- Breathe in a spacious awareness of your true nature.
- Extend your true nature to the world.
- Reflect. Are your actions in alignment with your vision? How is the outside world a reflection of your inner condition?
- Regulate and renew all energy systems. Stay well.
- Engage in mindful living.

As your future continues to emerge and you progress along your CORE Journey, continue to engage yourself with these fundamental questions. This is the conversation that will keep you in the game of self-determination, mastery and purpose!

- What is my source—my true nature—the voice that sustains me?
- How am I engaging in mindful living?
- What belief system is supporting or limiting my emerging future?
- How do my actions align with my values and purpose?
- How am I engaging my strengths?
- How am I sustaining and growing my wellbeing and balance?
- Where do I want to go?
- How will I get there?
- What is my current reality?
- Who is going with me?
- How will I know when I am there?

REFLECT AND ENGAGE

- What are your CORE learnings from this Cairn?
- How will you apply these things in your life?
- What have you learned about yourself at this Cairn?
- Based on the practices at this Cairn, what will you do to expand your capacity and ability to be the creative force in your life?
- How will you celebrate the completion of this Cairn?

Epilogue

"A fish cannot drown in water. A bird does not fall in air. Each creature God made must live in its own true nature."

—Mechthild of Magdeburg

We have come full circle, arriving where we started—at the beginning. The beginning because your CORE Journey is a lifelong quest for fulfillment and well-being. T. S. Eliot wrote, "to arrive at the place you started is to know the place for the first time." You may know yourself differently now even though you've always been you—you've always been your true nature—you just needed to recognize and engage your essence. You have arrived at your summit, traveling along difficult paths, across wide gaps, and up steep inclines. It has not been easy, but you not only survived, you transformed.

The dictionary defines transformation as "a process by which one form, expression, or function is converted into another that is equivalent in some important respect but is differently expressed or represented." Yet another definition is "to make a thorough or dramatic change in the form, appearance, or character of." The CORE Journey is your creative engagement through a transformation of who you were and how you were being for yourself and others to a renewed expression of your true nature, your values and your purpose.

You may have undergone a dramatic change where who you are now has totally transformed your experience of your life compared to when you set forth on the journey. Or you may have experienced a subtle shift, for example, in your perception, which created a transformation in your capacity to create the future to which you aspire. You learned that perception has a focus. Change the focus and what you see will change as well. The power is internal to you. Whatever you experienced on your journey, it is now part of you. You operate from your source—your true nature. You now hold the skills and abilities to sustain your own evolution and create your own future no matter what your endeavor.

You have taken full responsibility for the creation of a transformative life through the evolution of a CORE set of skills. The path you have chosen is a path of lifelong growth and enrichment. The journey to live with purpose and intention, to meet your world within valued living, is ever unfolding and requires engaging and sustaining a mindful approach day-to-day, moment-to-moment.

In reality, your MAP will continue to be your guide as you create it over time. This little book is a chronicle of your Journey. A keepsake of a path well traveled. Use it as a refresher, a reminder, and a practical tool to utilize for any journey where you want guidance. The Journey never really ends. The process continues, sometimes along the same path and sometimes to a completely different summit. Consistently review the Cairns and tools you have learned through the Journey. Keep them fresh in your mind. Remember to communicate to your team. Going the Journey alone is never easy. It is valuable to develop relationships that offer beneficial and constructive feedback, support, and encouragement.

Continue to be aware of your self-talk. When you hear yourself slipping into a judgmental frame of mind, make the shift to being a learner. We have learned how negative self-talk and unworkable beliefs limit our ability to see what's possible. Be vigilant about your language, whether it is with others or yourself.

Use your MAP to continue to set your sights on new horizons. Set SMART goals and make the commitment. I also like to recall *Desiderata*: "...beyond a wholesome discipline, be gentle with yourself." The ability to reflect and be appreciative of who and where you are currently is a gift. It supports your self-regard and maintains a positive mindset for continued perseverance on your journey.

Self-actualization, in emotionally intelligent language, is asking whether you are working at or toward your potential. You can only know this if you can take an accurate picture of your current reality. If you are highly stressed or just striving out of anxiety, your reality will be blurred. Always remember to reflect at the end of your day to ensure a continued alignment of values, purpose, and behavior. Remember, happiness is being satisfied with your day-to-day life. Happiness is a sustainable sense of well-being and peace of mind. Optimism is believing you can continue to design the future you want. Balancing the two is a necessary skill.

So, you have completed the CORE Journey you set out on many weeks ago. This isn't the end. This is your beginning. Now you have the power to create whatever life you want to live from this day forth. The ongoing Journey will still require work from your CORE. To tackle the challenges and reach new heights will take courage, openness, reflection, and energy. Congratulations. You know them all. They are yours. They will continue to evolve uniquely mirroring your evolution.

Throughout the CORE Journey we have used the mountain as a metaphor. We used Cairns as our milestones to guide us along the way. Sometimes the path was clear. And at times the path was unclear and required that you push yourself beyond your comfort zone into unfamiliar territory. We used summit goals to encourage reaching beyond what you thought was possible. We asked the question, "What is your mountain?" What is your challenge, your struggle, your dream, and your purpose?

Now as you stand at the summit and gaze out across the vista, you can rest assured that you have accomplished something that not many people achieve. Most people are satisfied with security, mediocrity and are accepting of what life has been offering them. For them, to dream or strive for a "mountaintop" is a scary proposition. If it were easy, everyone would be doing it. You have engaged in the extraordinary.

To look within and challenge yourself to be extraordinary took courage. Like the quote by Younghusband, *Mount Everest—The Reconnaissance* said at the beginning, "to make the effort, to struggle through the change, is like climbing a mountain. And when you do, the mountain, the journey, will lavish you with gifts that you never dreamed of…the mountains reserve their choicest gifts for those who stand upon their lofty summits." You now stand on your summit and I can only imagine the gifts you have realized on your path.

"Part of the blessing and challenge of being human is that we must discover our own God-given nature. This is not some noble, abstract quest but an inner necessity. For only by living in our own element can we thrive without anxiety. And since human beings are the only life form that can drown and still go to work, the only species that can fall from the sky and still fold laundry, it is imperative that we find that vital element that brings us alive...the true vitality that waits beneath all occupations for us to tap into, if we can discover what we love. If you feel energy and excitement and a sense that life is happening for the first time, you are probably near your God-given nature. Joy in what we do is not an added feature; it is a sign of deep health."

—Mark Nepo, *Book of Awakening: Having the Life You Want By Being Present to the Life You Have*

I hope through my words and stories that you don't feel that I have arrived and no longer journey to my own summit. I have traveled many paths and I'm still climbing with new summits in view. I offer the Journey with confidence because we are all on our own mountain, and sometimes, as your coach, I can view your mountain and see things you are unaware of—possible crevices, impending avalanches, an alternative path, or different ways you could use your poles and organize your pack. So I offered practices and challenges to help you realize your summit with the least amount of pain and struggle. And, always remember, as we climb and practice, we're all getting better and better. Appreciate and celebrate your journey and thank you for choosing and continuing to stay the course to your summit.

This is the culmination of the CORE Journey. Jack Kornfield, the Buddhist psychologist, wrote, "We are the beauty we have been seeking all our lives. We are consciousness knowing itself. Empty and spacious, compassionate and joyful, our peace and equanimity begin to transform the world around us." Through engaging in the CORE Journey, you have rediscovered your freedom and joy and true nature. Do not forget the light you carry within. Trust yourself. Trust life. Extend your peace and your love.

"There is a vitality, a life force, an energy, a quickening that is translated through you into action, and because there is only one of you in all of time, this expression is unique. And if you block it, it will never exist though any to determine how good it is nor how valuable nor how it compares with other expressions. It is your business to keep it yours clearly and directly, to keep the channel open."

—Martha Graham, quoted by Agnes DeMille, *Martha: The Life and Work of Martha Graham*

Oscar Wilde said it another way, "Be yourself; everyone else is already taken." Your charge in learning and engaging the CORE Journey is to make it your own and be yourself. I've included practices that I feel might expand your vision, offer a different way of seeing and provide a more expansive view of who you really are. Some of the practices may not have resonated completely with you. So as you continue to practice, use your creativity. Feel free to tailor and refine the tools and practices to fit your personal style. If you feel so inclined, email me and let me know how your journey is continuing to evolve.

Continue to engage the energy to grow. Have the courage to look within and be present to your source, to who you are being for yourself and others. Greet the day with openness to the idea that you hold the key to your life's design and the inner knowing that you can successfully cope with challenges when presented. Reflect at the end of the day. Align actions with your values, purpose and vision; then your day is well spent and you can enjoy peace of mind. Engage positive energy in your endeavors, yourself, others, and your environment. Engage mindful living.

I close with a heartfelt and gracious "thank you!!"

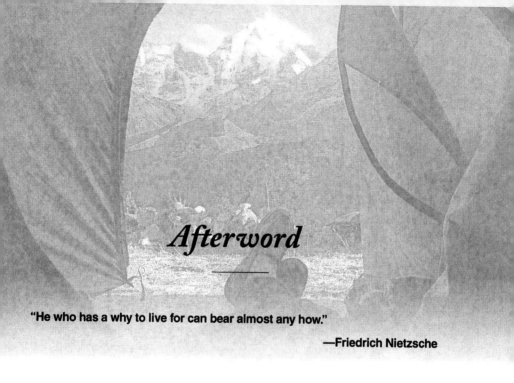

Afterword

"He who has a why to live for can bear almost any how."

—Friedrich Nietzsche

It's been five years since I stood on the summit of Kilimanjaro. In November of last year (2012), I took on another challenge and journeyed to Nepal, where I made the trek to Everest Base Camp and Kala Patar, an 18,300-foot mountain with stunning views of Everest and the surrounding ice fields. These two excursions bookmark parallel experiences, both examples of the strength of the human spirit—when people are willing to look inward and draw on their internal power in order to live with intention and purpose. When people have a strong "why," or purpose, for what they're doing, many times they can accomplish more than they thought possible.

Trekking in the Himalayas around 12-13,000 feet, I experienced altitude sickness, just like I had on Kilimanjaro. I was transported out of my comfort zone not only physically, but also mentally and emotionally. I really felt like I was not going to make it. Three of the trekkers were helicoptered out on the fourth day due to illness, and for a brief moment I considered going with them. I felt that bad. But I remembered having similar feelings on Kilimanjaro, which I was able to overcome. So I decided to persevere, work through the discomfort and push on to accomplish what I had come there to do—reach Everest Base Camp and summit Kala Patar.

As I slowly made my way along the trail, I had plenty of time to contemplate. What came to me was exactly what I've been saying to my clients for years and have hoped to convey in this book. It's not the "what" that motivated me. It was the "why." I felt exhausted, like I had no energy to move my legs at all, much less traverse extremely steep terrain. Deciding to persevere through that malaise meant that I had to call on a different energy for the strength to go on. It really wasn't physical energy, but an emotional and spiritual energy that kept me going. It wasn't about "what" I was doing that gave me energy. It was "why" I was doing it. "What" is about facts and figures, i.e., I was hiking in the Himalayas to experience the highest mountains in the world and reach a destination that few realize. The "why" is much deeper. It is at a level where words don't suffice. That's why it's hard to explain. It has to do with purpose and values. "Why" we do things is the inner motivator that can't be taken away. What we do and how we do it will bring us results, but in challenging circumstances, why we're doing it is what pushes us to greater heights.

When the four trekkers who were very sick had decided to go home and I thought about going home as well, I looked out at those beautiful mountains and thought "It's okay, I've seen them. They are amazing, so I can be done." Then it hit me. Seeing those mountains only skimmed the surface of what I was doing. The "why" came from much deeper. I wanted a challenge—to feel alive; to experience something out of the ordinary. It would've been much easier to stay in my beautiful backyard with all the creature comforts of home. And it would have been easier to just go home when I felt so miserable. I had insurance. The helicopter would've been covered due to illness. But, that wasn't the point.

I remembered people asking me why I wanted to go to Kili, and they did the same with Nepal. I could never come up with a significant answer that conveyed how I felt and why I was going. Now I understand much more. Again, it was never about the "what" I was doing. It was the "why" that was ineffable. I still can't put it into words that really express my thoughts and feelings. It's because the "why," which comes from the limbic, or emotional, center of the brain, doesn't deal in words. The frontal cortex, our rational brain, deals in words and is the "what" and "how." The "why" is more closely related to a feeling. And, emotions are what truly move us. You've probably had the experience when shopping for something and the salesperson gave you all the facts, figures and benefits of an item, but you still didn't buy it because "It just didn't feel right." Well, I had all the facts and figures. I had thought of the benefits. I still felt awful. And I was a bit homesick. The helicopter would be there in the morning take people back to Katmandu. It was covered by insurance. I'd seen the Himalayas. Why not go home? Because something about that decision just didn't feel right. When I decided to go on, I felt a weight lift. And it felt right even though I still felt ill.

I know I'm going on and on, but it's moving when an experience mirrors exactly what you believe. And this was one of those times where an actual event mirrored not only what I know to be true, but what I've been teaching and coaching for years. The two experiences, Kili and Mount Everest, both incidences of an inner motivating force driving performance, led me to write an Afterword. I've studied human performance and motivation for many years. I know and understand how intrinsic motivation, your inner drive, contributes to excellence and high-level performance, both through my own experience as an athlete and through coaching. My adventures on two continents among the highest mountains in the world reinforced my belief that through looking inside with courage and an open mind, we can continue to learn and grow and reach heights we didn't think possible. Drawing on that innermost space offers us the opportunity to take responsibility for our future.

Purpose has been an on-going thread in the CORE Journey and probably by now has become the foundation for decision-making and many of your actions. Maybe by engaging your purpose, what you might call your "why", you've had the experience that you can thrive regardless of external factors because your purpose is much larger than circumstance and has an impact beyond yourself. I have used the mountain experience as a metaphor throughout the CORE Journey, so by now you know that I'm not saying that you should take up hiking or that you need to travel to the Himalayas in order to thrive. And, I am not saying that my "why" was to reach Everest Base Camp or the summit of Kala Patar. Those were goals. And, yes, my intrinsic motivation contributed to my reaching those goals. But there was something with a much stronger energy; my "why". The "why" that I refer to is my desire to thrive. Participating in the wilderness experience provides me with a sense of thriving. My "why", or purpose, is to help people unleash their power to thrive. Each one of you will define what it means to thrive for yourself. Your "why" will be unique to you. Your "why" becomes a much larger goal. In the emotional assessment that I use, the SEI, it is called a Noble Goal. A Noble Goal extends beyond you. It emanates from the inside out. Your Noble Goal integrates your life-your decisions-the choices you make every moment of the day. It's what gets you out of bed in the morning. It is the arrow on your compass pointing north, proving guidance and direction.

It is your purpose. And, to engage your purpose is a conscious choice we can make.

My experiences strengthened a "knowing" that if we choose intentionally to tap into our deepest convictions, our purpose, we will thrive. I know what contributes to my experience of thriving. I know what my purpose is-my Noble Goal. How can I hope that I can help my clients to thrive if I don't tap into my own purpose and "walk my talk"? I guess that's the primary reason I chose to write this Afterward. I wanted to convey that I am on a CORE Journey right there with you. I'm still growing and experiencing and integrating the learning. For me, the experience in the Himalayas reinforced the power of living with purpose. Yes, I had a goal-to reach the summit. More importantly, I had a purpose. I want to coach from experience not just from book learning or research. When I looked inside and asked "Dee, if you go home, what will that say about your purpose?" "Will going home give you an experience of thriving?" Sometimes pursuing your purpose is not comfortable. Like we've said so many times, it takes courage. I learned that again. I came away with a deeper knowing that I can now share with my clients and with you. When you are clear about your purpose-your "why", you will reach great heights.

I believe that within every person exists an inner yearning to feel alive, to experience wonder, to thrive. That conviction translates into my "why"— to unleash people's power to thrive. A major thread throughout the CORE Journey is to clarify and engage your purpose and core values—your "why." The power of that coherence has never been more real for me. Knowing your purpose is a powerful "why." I hope living with purpose became real for you on your CORE Journey and continues to unfold and be a powerful force in your life.

The remaining trekkers reached Everest Base Camp. Only five of us made the climb to Kala Patar. At the summit, I felt exhilarated and so thankful that I had decided not to helicopter out, but to press on. It was truly a reminder of how fierce a person's "why," or purpose, can be. It is what gives us a feeling of aliveness, of thriving, of touching an immeasurable inner space that holds boundless strength. We all have our own way of recognizing that abundant space within us. One of the ways I touch that infinite space is being in nature. For others, it can be art, music, teaching, dance, cooking, athletics, pursuing knowledge and technology—whatever engages our passion, creativity and purpose for living enables us to flourish. Anytime we tap into our intrinsic "why"—whether it's to motivate ourselves toward an accomplishment, to overcome barriers, or to enroll others to realize their potential—part of us flourishes, as well.

My experiences on Kilimanjaro and in the Himalayas confirmed for me that people prosper when they not only know the "what" and "how" of their life, but also have a strong sense of "why." It provides a sense of self-direction mastery, allowing them to be able to do things that maybe even they thought were beyond the scope of possibility. Those that have clarified their purpose have a tremendous advantage in daily living and, in particular, when the going gets tough. At those times, they can draw on that clarity of "why" for strength and stamina. Sometimes that requires a shift in perspective—not only of the external environment, but more importantly of our internal attitude. That change can be quite challenging, and it usually takes us out of our comfort zone. For me, the mountains provide a challenge and an opportunity to shift perspective, to tap into that infinite space within, to push beyond perceived limitations.

The mountain experience continues to be a perfect metaphor for life and the obstacles and storms we all face in our daily living. I don't know what your challenges are, but I know that, in one way or another, we all get tested. When you make an intentional choice for mastery and purpose and make a deliberate decision to navigate a transformation that offers opportunities to access your infinite space, you will add value to your life. You will unleash your power to thrive. And, I encourage you to share your experience, especially with those who don't feel like they have a choice, those who feel powerless. You never know when you might touch something in others that helps them recognize their internal power to choose, to motivate, to thrive.

I believe that the more people there are who recognize their internal power, the more people who intentionally choose to act based on their core values and purpose, that the world will be a place where more people will thrive. I believe that the pursuit of your purpose-a positive energy that extends beyond yourself-will contribute to a more peaceful world. Thank you for pursuing your CORE Journey—for clarifying your internal power—for clarifying your "why." I hope you realized your goals and aspirations and experienced that boundless strength within. I hope you engage your purpose-your Noble Goal throughout your day. Continue to use the CORE Journey as a reminder of your inner power and as a tool to help you navigate challenges and changes as they arise. Use it as a guide, a touchstone, as you continue to pursue self-direction, mastery and purpose. When you do, I know you will continue to thrive. I applaud your courage, open-mindedness and energy. Enjoy learning and growing on your CORE Journey. Keep going no matter what obstacles present themselves. As Shawn Colvin says in one of her songs, "Steady On."

Warm Regards,
Dianna

Recommended Resources

A s an adjunct to the many assets that I used as resources for this book, I'm including this section to provide additional resources that have been very helpful in my own exploration and growth. I've included some books from my bibliography, with a broader explanation about the content. I also mention websites that provide valuable information and tools. There's no way this can be an exhaustive list. My library covers one whole wall in my study with floor-to-ceiling bookshelves overflowing with some of my "best friends." I will keep this list to a minimum as best I can and try to give you a foundation from which you can further explore if you so desire. These are valuable tools that hold a wealth of information. I hope you enjoy where these resources take you and I hope they provide the knowledge and understanding you want in order to create and self-determine your best life.

Adams, Marilee. (2004). *Change Your Questions, Change Your Life: 7 Powerful Tools for Life and Work.* San Francisco: Berrett-Koehler Publishers, Inc.

This book offers a new perspective on how to look at situations. Adams distinguishes between "walking" the judging path, versus the learning path, as a way to enhance our communication and our relationships. Told through a story, the author offers some powerful tools that can be implemented for fast results in both your personal and professional life. In situations where we find ourselves trying to find the right answers, Marilee Adams shows that asking the right questions is far more important if we want to enhance our relationships. Her learner/judger model helps to illustrate how we can move through preconceived notions and assumptions for more effective communication. The methodology is easy to grasp and apply. Her Choice Map, which you can download from her website, is a helpful visual tool.

www.inquiryinstitute.com

Bradbury, Travis & Jean Greaves. (2009). *Emotional Intelligence 2.0.* San Diego: Talent Smart.

This book provides access to an online assessment of your Emotional Intelligence. Based on your results, the assessment presents the key areas of your EI to work on to increase your emotional intelligence: self-awareness, self-regulation, social awareness and relationship management. The book includes strategies that are practical and helpful to enhance the specific area of EI you choose to focus on. I use this assessment tool with my clients.

Bowden, Jonny. (2007). *The 150 Healthiest Foods on Earth: The Surprising, Unbiased Truth about What You Should Eat and Why.* Massachusetts: Fair Winds.

This book is a delight to read, fun to look at, entertaining and solidly backed by the science behind food. It is organized into chapters by food groups: Vegetables; Grains; Beans and Legumes; Fruits; Nuts, Seeds, and Nut Butters; Soy Foods; Dairy; Meat, Poultry and Eggs; Fish and Seafood; Specialty Foods; Beverages; Herbs, Spices and Condiments; Oils, and Sweeteners. In each chapter, Bowden provides an explanation as to why each food is a winner, what nutrients are in each food and why they are good for you, and who will benefit, as well as those at risk for potential negative interactions with particular foods.

Bowden does not rate individual foods, but does give certain foods that he considers exceptional in terms of nutritional value a star. He also gives a thorough explanation of the key factors the reader should be aware of when reading the book, which include omega-3 fats, fiber, antioxidants, and glycemic index. He discusses the ongoing debate about cholesterol and organic foods.

The book is full of additional gems of information including:

- "Ask the experts" top-10 food lists from various authorities, designating the cream of the crop

- A glossary that defines nutrients, hormones, diseases, etc.

- Mini-lessons on hot topics such as the glycemic index, distinctions among fats, and eating organic foods, and

- Interpretation of foods from homeopathic, Ayurvedic, and yoga nutritional therapy perspectives.

"If you are what you eat and you don't know what you're eating, do you know who you are?" This book will help you understand what you're eating, its effect on your body due to the specific properties of each food, why you should eat certain foods and not others, and the benefits of making what you put in your body really count toward health and well-being. Even though it is based on science, this book is enjoyable. It also includes a CD with excerpts from "23 Ways to Improve Your Life!" www.jonnybowden.com

Cain, Susan. (2012). *Quiet: The Power of Introverts in a World that Can't Stop Talking.* New York: Crown Publishing.

This is a book about introverts and their contributions and accomplishments in a world that primarily values extroversion. I found the history of introversion and the shift to valuing extroversion quite interesting. Many of my clients and friends who are introverts highly recommend it. A book that helps close the communication gap and shows how we all bring unique contributions to the world is worth a read.

Cameron, Julia. (1992). *The Artist's Way: A Spiritual Path to Higher Creativity.* New York: Tarcher/Putnam.

This book is about how to let the artist emerge in our lives and bring freedom to the innate creative spirit in all of us. There are many useful exercises in the 229 pages based on the principle that the artist must have faith to be creative. Cameron encourages all of us to engage creativity. The practices I found helpful are Morning Pages and The Artist's Date. You can customize any of the exercises to fit your work or play as well as your time commitment. Try not to be put off by the cutsey puns and hokey metaphors. If you do the exercises, I think you'll find it works and can help you unleash your creative side.

Chopra, Deepak. (1994). *Ageless Body, Timeless Mind: The Quantum Alternative to Growing Old.* Three Rivers Press.

In this book, Chopra offers an alternative perspective on aging based on quantum physics and the science of longevity. It combines philosophy, biology, and modern health research in an attempt to help us develop a new way of approaching the aging process differently then in the past. It's an interesting read. If you're familiar with Deepak's other works, you'll recognize his inspirational conviction that we can and should broaden our belief of what is possible within the worldly framework if we adopt a spiritual perspective.

Crowley, Chris & Henry S. Lodge. (2004). *Younger Next Year: Live Strong, Fit, and Sexy-Until you're 80 and Beyond.* New York: Workman Publishing Company, Inc.

This is a book about functional longevity. The authors provide guidelines for how to live as if you were 50, maybe even younger, for the rest of your life. It's based on the life of 70-year-old Crowley's impressive journey to be more fit, strong, and balanced in his daily activities as well as his hobbies. He says at 70 he skis better then when he was 50. It is written with a male audience in mind and at times seems a bit trite. But overall, it is a very informative and amusing book and I would recommend it to anyone looking for a book on staying, not only functional but also vital as you age.

Damasio, Antonio. (1999). *The Feeling of What Happens: Body and Emotion in the Making of Consciousness.* New York: A Harvest Book, Harcourt, Inc.

Damasio examines current neurological knowledge of human consciousness to answer some of the most complex questions asked by poets, philosophers and artists. How is it that we know what we know? Who is the knower? Where does our sense of self come from? This book presents the science and art of how feeling and emotion lend themselves to a new understanding of the conscious mind. This book isn't an easy read, but it is a beautiful rendition of what happens in our mind as we come to know our world and ourselves.

Deci, Edward and Richard Ryan. (1996). *Why We Do What We Do: Understanding Self-Motivation.* New York: Penguin Group, Inc.

Edward Deci and Richard Ryan are the creators of self-determination theory (SDT). Their book summarizes their findings in the psychology of self-determination and self-motivation. It is a provocative look into how people can become more engaged and successful in the pursuit of their goals and ambitions. The website provides an excellent background into the theory and how it relates to accomplishing goals. www.psych.rochester.edu/SDT/theory.html

Drucker, Peter. (1966). *The Effective Executive*. New York: Harper & Row Publishers.

This is a landmark book that develops the specific practices of the business executive that lead to effectiveness. Peter Drucker is known as the "father of management" and has written over 60 books. He is a solid read for anyone in a leadership position. His ideas are still relevant.

Flaherty, James. (1999). *Coaching: Evoking Excellence in Others*. Boston: Butterworth & Heinemann.

Flaherty takes some probing questions from philosophy and creates a practical use for them by applying them to coaching. He believes that coaching is not about telling people what to do; it's about inviting people to examine what they are doing in light of their intentions. He writes that coaches must know themselves before they can know others. This book looks just as much at the growth of the coach as it does at the development of the client. Flaherty says they go hand in hand. This book is much like a textbook and in that light can be a heavy read. My copy is dog-eared, highlighted, and written in because it has so much to offer. If you lead people and will enjoy seeing modern philosophers' concepts and ideas turned into assessment models and practical tools, this is a must read.

Ford, Debbie. (2010). *The Dark Side of the Light Chasers: Reclaiming yoru power, creativity, brilliance, and dreams*. New York: Riverhead Books.

This book is about working with, rather than ignoring, our shadow side for wholeness and transformation. It is based on a course she developed about embracing the shadow and offers a step-by-step guide to live more fully and authentically. I offer this book to my clients as a way to relinquish judgment towards ourselves and instead using our shadow side as rich learning ground for wholeness.

Fredrickson, Barbara L. (2013). *Love 2.0: How Our Supreme Emotion Affects Everything We Feel, Do, and Become*. New York: Hudson Street Press.

In this book, Fredrickson redefines love and provides an entirely new way of understanding and appreciating it. Like her first book, this book is based on her research from her own lab which demonstrates that our capacity for experiencing love can be measured. More then happiness and optimism, love holds the key to improving our mental and physical health. If you're open-minded, this is a worthwhile read that will expand your mastery and assimilation of this deep-seated emotion.

Fredrickson, Barbara L. (2009). *Positivity: Groundbreaking Research Reveals How to Embrace the Hidden Strength of Positive Emotions, Overcome Negativity, and Thrive.* New York: Crown Publishing Group.

This is an easy book to read, describing the research that supports the premise that positive emotions can make life easier in the good times as well as the bad. It is rich with the science of how and why experiencing positive emotions contributes to health and wellbeing. Fredrickson provides practical, easy tools based on research to help increase your positivity. www.unc.edu/peplab/barb_fredrickson_page.html

Freedman, Joshua. (2007, 2012). *At The Heart of Leadership: How to Get Results with Emotional Intelligence.* Six Seconds Publishing.

I've read many books on emotional intelligence and this is among the best for offering ways to use and apply emotional intelligence. It provides a compelling and simple model for learning critical leadership skills for more creativity, richer relationships, and more joy in your work. Joshua is co- founder of Six Seconds, an organization supporting people to create positive change. I highly recommend this book and the Six Seconds model and organization for training in emotional intelligence.

Haidt, Jonathan. (2006). *The Happiness Hypothesis: Finding Modern Truth in Ancient Wisdom.* New York: Perseus Books Group.

Social psychologist Haidt presents 10 "great ideas" from the world's greatest civilizations as a foundation for exploring the concepts of happiness, growth and development, and the question that haunts many people: "What is the meaning of life?" It is an engaging, readable book, balancing ancient wisdom and modern science. His website gives people ideas for how to use his book as well as other topics of interest in the same arena. www.happinesshypothesis.com/beyond.html

Jendrick, Nathan. (2011) *Gym-Free and Ripped: Weight-Free Workouts That Build and Sculpt.* New York: Penguin Group.

This book is for people needing exercises and routines without having to belong to a gym or buy workout equipment. The exercises, organized into workouts, provide gym-equivalent methods for strengthening and toning your muscles. I've gotten many ideas from this book and refer to it often to increase my repertoire of exercises. With the addition of workout bands, I've found the exercises very helpful in my quest for in increased strength, firmer tone, and better flexibility.

Kabat-Zinn, Jon. (1994). *Wherever You Go, There You Are: Mindfulness Meditation in Everyday Life.* New York: Hyperion.

This book relates very much to the work done on the CORE Journey. It is about an inward journey to quiet your internal environment so you can experience the present moment with calmness. It is a book that can be explored over and over. It can help you enhance your clarity and happiness by establishing new habits of being. It is about how mediation and building the skill of mindfulness can change your life for the better. Kabat-Zinn's book is basic enough for beginners and holds plenty of substance for experienced meditators. I highly recommend "Wherever You Go..."

Keirsey, David and Marilyn Bates. (1984). *Please Understand Me: Character & Temperament Types.* California: B & D Books.

This book starts with a questionnaire that you take to determine your temperament type. It is based on the Myers-Briggs Typology. Keirsey explains the different temperaments, which provide a way to understand people by differentiating their character traits. It is an eye-opener for most people, especially those who wonder why they feel so different and why everyone isn't like them. It's a great way to realize and understand differences in a whole new light.

Kornfield, Jack. (2009). *The Wise Heart: A Guide to the Universal Teachings of Buddhist Psychology.* New York: Bantam Books.

Author, psychologist, and pioneering Buddhist teacher Kornfield offers a systematic and well-organized approach to Buddhist psychology for a wide audience. In his accessible writing style, Kornfield offers his unique experience and perspective on how to apply Buddhist principles for a happier, more fulfilling life. Each chapter presents a principle, followed by a story reliant on the principle's everyday applicability, and ends with a meaningful and useful practice to apply to our own lives. It is a beautiful book filled with wisdom, warmth and insights.

Loehr, Jim & Tony Schwartz. (2003). *The Power of Full Engagement.* New York: The Free Press.

The primary message of this book is that the potential to change your life comes from realizing that managing energy, not time, is the key to high performance and personal renewal. I highly recommend this book to anyone who wants to improve the productivity and effectiveness, as well as the overall quality of his or her professional and personal lives. It is a book I use in my classes and with individual clients. Loehr presents the science behind his ideas, describes how he has used his system with clients, and includes strategies to incorporate the information into your own life. www.hpinstitute.com

Lynn, Adele B. (2005). *The EQ Difference: A Powerful Plan for Putting Emotional Intelligence to Work.* New York: AMACON.

The EQ Difference provides a platform for developing emotional intelligence. It is pragmatic and full of real-life examples to help you understand the importance of EI for your success as a leader in any field and in your own life. Adele presents a self-coaching model that helps people develop self-awareness and self-regulation skills to enhance and engage emotional intelligence in even the most challenging situations. Adele offers an action plan with exercises, practical information, and examples that can be implemented immediately in relationships at work and at home.

Pearman, Roger R. & Sarah C. Albritton. (1997). *I'm Not Crazy, I'm Just Not You.* California: Davies-Black Publishing.

This book builds on the Myers-Briggs Type Indicator, presenting an in-depth study of type. The authors present information on the strengths and weaknesses of each of the 16 personality types, explore type dynamics, discuss valuing differences, and provide extensive descriptions of each personality type. The book focuses on how to understand our own motivations and those of others so we can better understand and appreciate others and ourselves. It is an excellent resource for leaders who have taken the MBTI and want to use it to build trust and support in a work environment. It's a good read to further understanding and appreciation of the power and depth of the Myers-Briggs Type Indicator and how it can positively affect relationships at home and at work.

Rath, Tom. (2007). *Strengths Finder 2.0.* New York: Gallup Press.

This is the book I use with my clients to help them discover and develop their natural talents. It includes an access code for the online assessment. It is a good beginning to explore your strengths and ways to engage them more often at work and at home. www.strengthsfinder.com

Ruiz, Miguel. (2001). *The Four Agreements: A Practical Guide to Personal Freedom.* California: Amber-Allen Publishing, Inc.

This is a simple little book with profound wisdom. If we could embrace and engage each of the four life commitments, we would be much closer to a life of autonomy, mastery and purpose. Ruiz teaches how to move beyond the personal limitations we place on ourselves by the story we tell, to a freer, happier existence and deeper understanding of our true selves. www.miguelruiz.com

Seligman, Martin. (2012). *Flourish: A Visionary New Understanding of Happiness and Wellbeing.* Free Press.

Martin Seligman wrote *Authentic Happiness and Learned Optimism: How to Change Your Mind and Your Life.* Flourish was written some 10 years after those books and shows Seligman's own transformation in his thinking about happiness and wellbeing. His arguments are solid and backed by research. If you are interested in exploring the theory of human flourishing and how to create wellbeing in your life, this book will be a valuable addition to your library. The website also provides tools and assessments. www.authentichappiness.com

Talbot, Michael. (1991). *The Holographic Universe: A Remarkable New Theory of Reality That Explains the Paranormal Abilities of the Mind, the Latest Frontiers of Physics and the Unsolved Riddles of Brain and Body.* New York: HarperCollins Publishers, Inc.

Michael Talbot's book continues to be a landmark work whose conclusions hold true with the advancement of quantum physics, string theory and cosmology. It is a very provocative book and will challenge most people's belief system. His style is clear and lucid and highly engaging. The book explores the nature of consciousness and reality, and includes chapters on paranormal phenomena. Talbot presents a wealth of scientific research from scientists David Bohm, Fred Alan Wolfe, Larry Dossey, Stanislav Grof, Paul Davies, and many more. If you are interested in exploring a new way to view life and the universe based primarily on quantum physics and spirituality, this is a fascinating book.

Tolle, Eckhart. (2005). *A New Earth: Awakening to Your Life's Purpose.* New York: Penguin Group.

If you are familiar with Tolle's first book *The Power of Now*, you will enjoy this book. The New Earth delves deeper into the concept that transcending our ego is the key to personal happiness and fulfillment. Tolle describes how our involvement with the ego creates the dysfunction that causes anger, jealousy, and suffering. He shows readers how to move beyond ego-based actions to purpose-based living by awakening to a new state of consciousness for a fulfilling existence.

Weil, Andrew, MD. (2005). *Healthy Aging: A Lifelong Guide to Your Well-Being.* New York: Anchor Books, Random House.

Dr. Weil shows a host of things we can do to keep our bodies and minds healthy and vital through all phases of our lives. The book is informative, practical and inspirational. Some of the details included in the book are: learning to eat right, understanding the latest research on aging, separating myth from fact in herbs, hormones and anti-aging "medicines", exercise, breathing and stress management techniques, and healthy lifestyle choices. Weil's book promotes healthy and functional longevity.

Zander, Rosamund and Benjamin. (2002). *The Art of Possibility: Transforming Professional and Personal Life.* New York: Penguin Putnam, Inc.

The Zanders present a philosophy and strategy for seeing and engaging in our world from a perspective of possibility rather than scarcity and limitation. I have shared this book with many people in my classes and my private practice. At first, many have thought it would be "fluff." After reading it, though, they acknowledge that The Art of Possibility is a powerful little book filled with inspirational practices and personal stories that can transform your life. It's a worthwhile read that at the very least will be uplifting and pleasurable, and, if you do the practices, has the possibility to make positive changes in your life.

Zukav, Gary. (1990). *The Seat of the Soul.* New York: Fireside, Simon & Schuster, Inc.

In an interview with Gary Zukav, he states that he wrote *Seat of the Soul* as a way to open people's hearts. The book begins as an exploration of our evolution from a five-sensory experience of the world to multi-sensory human beings, moving beyond the limitations of the five senses toward a different experience of who we are and how we effect our lives. Zukav's writing touches the soul. It is well worth one read, and you will probably read it again and again. It is one of those books that with each reading comes a more in depth understanding of its content. It is a book I would invite everyone with an open heart and mind to read.

Six Seconds
www.6seconds.org

Six Seconds is a non-profit, global organization providing training, certification, and coaching to support people in creating positive change. The Six Seconds model offers an actionable method for understanding and applying emotional intelligence in your personal and profession life. The six seconds model uses rigorous science and a proven framework for individual and organizational transformation.

I am certified in the SEI, six seconds assessment for emotional intelligence and I find it a practical as well as inspiration tool for integrating emotional intelligence into your life. It provides insight and tools to develop one's EI and use it to create positive change both personally and professionally. It is the assessment I use with my clients and in my classes.

Peak Performance
www.peakperformancenyc.com

The Wright Fit, Inc.
www.thewrightfit.com

"Nestled in a 10,000 square foot sun-drenched loft high above the streets of Manhattan, Peak Performance takes fitness back to basics, but with a unique twist. Incorporating the most innovative tools and equipment in the industry, Peak Performance offers clients a truly authentic environment."

My brother, Jay Wright, is a recognized expert in the health, fitness and wellness industry and has been featured as one of the nations top fitness trainers on NBC's Your Total Health and the Today Show, CBS's The Early Show, and several leading magazines including Self, Shape, Allure, and Muscle and Fitness. He co-founded Peak and his leadership in training and working with clients propelled Peak to be chosen one of the top 10 gyms in America by Men's Health magazine in September 2009. Jay is also the Founder of The Wright Fit, Inc., a leading design and management company in the health, fitness and wellness industry. Some of his clients include Hillary Swank, Ethan Hawk, Chris Drury, Josh Charles and Mariska Hargitay.

It may seem strange that I would include my brother in the Resource Section, but I truly respect his depth of scientific knowledge relating to fitness, nutrition, and wellness, as well as his ability to transfer his understanding to his clients so they can achieve their goals. He displays a genuine empathy and care for his clients' goals and aspirations and helps guide them to levels beyond their own expectations. I feel comfortable in recommending Jay to anyone interested in pursuing a whole-person, balanced approach to health and wellbeing.

The Wright Coach
www.thewrightcoach.com
dianna@thewrightcoach.com

This is my site. I am a certified Health and LIfestyle Counselor. As our nation confronts obesity in teens and adults, as well as work/life balance issues, I feel health and wellbeing coaching is an important way to contribute to helping people engage mastery and purpose in their lives. We are inundated on a daily basis with the latest information on healthy eating, nutrition, exercise and weight control. People can benefit from an expert to assist in understanding what will work best for them and how they can begin to create a life of functional longevity, balance and optimal wellbeing. It is not just about living longer, but "living long and prospering." Functional longevity is about taking control of our nutrition, fitness and wellness options to ensure our body and mind serve us at optimal levels as we grow in to our wise years. Check out my website for information on my coaching services in the areas of health and lifestyle for optimal well-being.

Clarification of Terms

Cairns   Stacks of rocks in the wilderness that mark the path where it is difficult to see or follow, such as over granite.

Coaching   Coaching is a dynamic conversation and partnership to expand awareness and learning for the purpose of creating strategies and taking value-based actions to achieve personal and professional goals and aspirations. A coach provides a non-judgmental, safe space where the client can address questions that may broaden their perspective and add to their choices while helping them see clearly where they are in the on-going journey of creating a fulfilling life. They are a professional sounding board to help clients set goals and make decisions, and then hold them accountable so they can honor their commitment to self-determination, mastery and purpose.

Coherence   The concept of coherence is used to help understand how the experience of different emotions causes physiological changes. The dictionary defines coherences as "the quality of being logically integrated, consistent, and intelligible." We have talked about the experience of love and compassion as coherent states and anger, anxiety, or irritability as examples of incoherence. Our goal in the CORE Journey has been to learn how to bring our heart and mind into coherence by way of imaging the heart zone filled with love, compassion or appreciation. Research has shown that different emotions lead to measurably different degrees of coherence in the oscillatory rhythms generated in the body. Being able to create coherence within our bodies enables us to function out of wholeness and connectivity. It generates the ability for flexible and relaxed states of being lending themselves to wellness.

Cortisol	A hormone produced by the adrenal gland in response to stress, acting to restore homeostasis. Its primary function is to increase blood sugar, suppress the immune system, and aid in fat, protein, and carbohydrate metabolism. Although it is a natural physiological response to stress, prolonged cortisol secretion due to chronic stress can result in significant physiological changes that can be detrimental to the body.
Creativity	Bringing something into existence that did not exist before. In the CORE Journey, creativity refers to self-determination, mastery and purpose in the service of designing a life that is rich and fulfilling.
Energy Management	Throughout the book we have referred to energy management as fundamental to optimal performance. Performance, well-being and fulfillment are grounded in the skillful management of the body's energy systems. It is the management of energy resources as we expend, renew and revitalize each system.
Engaging Mindful Living	Engaging Mindful Living is to be physically energized, emotionally connected, mentally focused and spiritually aligned with values and a purpose that transcends one's immediate self-interest.
Flow	As defined by Csikszentmihalyi, it is the mental state that arises when one is fully immersed in an activity with energized focus and complete involvement. Other terms that are similar are in the moment, in the zone, wired in, in the groove and present. This full engagement is fundamental in harnessing emotions in the service of optimal performance and learning.
Fulfillment	I've included fulfillment in this section not to define it for people. People need to define fulfillment in terms of what it means for their life-an inside job-rather than defined by outside forces. I offer it here to clarify why I see the word as powerful and positive.
Limbic System	The limbic system is the set of brain structures located at the base of the brain, which includes the amygdale and the hippocampus. These structures support a variety of functions such as behavior, emotion, and long-term memory. The amygdale and hippocampus house all our memories and their related feelings and are important in the management of behavior. In order to ensure that our actions are aligned with our values and purpose, we have to be aware of what we are feeling and how our emotions are prioritizing our thoughts. If we are not aware of these things, we could easily get hi-jacked and say or do things we might later regret.

Mindful Action Plan (MAP)-	A guide designed by the client and composed of goals and action steps that will help them reach their summit vision.
Mindfulness	A calm awareness without judgment or criticism-a simple witnessing of what's happening in our body including feeling states, thoughts, sensations, memories and consciousness itself. Engaging mindful living generates the ability to consciously align actions with values and purpose.
Neurotransmitters	Chemicals in the body that transmit signals from a neuron to a target cell across a synapse.
Norepinephrine	A stress hormone that affects parts of the brain such as the amygdala. It underlies the flight-or-fight response, increasing heart rate, triggering release of glucose from energy stores, and increasing blood flow to the large muscles.
Plasticity	Neuroplasticity is the ability of the brain to reorganize and rewire neural pathways based on new experiences, awareness and intention.

Bibliography

Antonio, Jose, Douglas Kalman, Jeffrey Stout, Mike Greenwood, Darryn Willoughby, Gregory Haff. *Essentials of Sports Nutrition and Supplements.* Humana Press, 2008.

Bayda, Ezra. *Zen Heart.* Boston: Shambala, 2009.

Bohm, David. *Wholeness and the Implicate Order.* New York: Routledge, 1995.

Bowden, Jonny. *The 150 Healthiest Foods on Earth.* Massachusetts: Fair Winds, 2007.

Buckingham, Marcus, and Donald O. Clifton. *Now, Discover Your Strengths.* New York: Simon & Schuster, 2001.

Csikszentmihalyi, Mihaly. *Flow.* New York: HarperPerennial, 1990.

Collins, Jim C. *Good to Great.* New York: HarperBusiness, 2001.

Campbell, Joseph. With Bill Moyers. *The Power of Myth.* New York: Anchor Books, 1988.

   The Hero with a Thousand Faces. Princeton: Princeton University Press, 1968.

Campbell, Phil. *Ready, Set, Go!* Pristine Publishers Inc. USA. 2001.

Das, Surya Lama. *Awakening the Buddha Within.* New York: Broadway Books, 1997.

Damasio, Antonio. *The Feeling of What Happens.* Florida: Harcourt, 1999.

Frankl, Viktor E. *Man's Search for Meaning.* New York: Washington Square Press, 1985.

Fritz, Robert. *The Path of Least Resistance.* New York: Fawcett, 1984.

   Creating. New York: Fawcett, 1991.

Gawain, Shakti. *Creative Visualization.* California: Whatever Publishing, Inc, 1978.

Goldstein, Joseph, and Jack Kornfield. *Seeking the Heart of Wisdom.* Boston: Shambala, 1987.

Goleman, Daniel. *Emotional Intelligence.* New York: Bantam, 1995.

   Working with Emotional Intelligence. New York: Bantam, 1998.

   And Richard Boyatzis and Annie McKee. *Primal Leadership.* Boston: Harvard Business School Press, 2002.

Haidt Jonathan. *The Happiness Hypothesis.* New York: Perseus, 2006.

Kabat-Zinn, Jon. *Full Catastrophe Living.* New York: Bantam, 1990.

   Wherever You Go, There You Are: Mindfulness Meditation in Every day Life. (New York: Hyperion, 1994).

Kotter, John P. *Leading Change.* Boston: Harvard Business School Press, 1996.

   And Deloitte Consulting, LLC. *The Heart of Change.* Boston: Harvard Business School Press, 2002.

Leonard, George. *Mastery.* New York: Penguin, 1991.

Loehr, James and Tony Schwartz. *The Power of Full Engagement.* New York: Simon & Schuster, 2003.

Loehr, James. *The Power of Story: Rewriting Your Destiny in Business and in Life*. Free Press: New York, 2007.

Maslow, Abraham. *Toward a Psychology of Being*. Princeton, N.J., Van Nostrand, 1962.

McEnroe, John. *You Cannot Be Serious*. New York: Putnam, 2002.

Meyer, G. (Writer), & Anderson, B. (Director). (1993). *Bart's Inner Child* [Television series episode]. In J. Brooks (Producer), The Simpsons. Los Angeles: Fox Broadcasting Company.

Pert, Candace B. *Molecules of Emotion*. New York: Scribner, 1997.

Pink, Daniel H. *Drive*. New York: Penguin, 2009.

Rath, Tom. *Strengths Finder 2.0*. New York: Gallop Press, 2007.

Rosenthal, Joshua. *Integrative Nutrition: Feed Your Hunger for Health & Happiness*. Integrative Nutrition Publishing: New York, 2008.

Seligman, Martin E. P. *Learned Optimism*. New York: Knopf, 1990.

Seligman, Martin E. P. *Flourish: A New Understanding of Happiness and Wellbeing*. Free Press: New York, 2012.

Wilbur, Ken. *A Brief History of Everything*. Boston: Shambala, 1996.

Verstegen, Mark and Pete Williams. *CORE Performance*. California: Rodale, 2004.

Zander, Benjamin and Rosamund Zander. *The Art of Possibility*. New York: Penguin, 2000.

Zohar, Danah and Ian Marshall. *Spiritual Intelligence*. New York: Bloomsbury, 2000.

CPSIA information can be obtained at www.ICGtesting.com
Printed in the USA
LVOW06s0242191013

357530LV00005B/39/P